16. NOV 00.

Inside THE TOUR DE FRANCE

David Walsh

PHOTOGRAPHS BY
Billy Stickland

STANLEY PAUL • LONDON

First published 1994

1 3 5 7 9 10 8 6 4 2

First published in the United Kingdom in 1994 by
Stanley Paul & Co Ltd
Random House, 20 Vauxhall Bridge Road, London SW1V 2SA

Random House Australia (Pty) Limited
20 Alfred Street, Milsons Point, Sydney,
New South Wales 2061, Australia

Random House New Zealand Limited
18 Poland Road, Glenfield, Auckland 10,
New Zealand

Random House South Africa (Pty) Limited
PO Box 337, Bergvlei, South Africa

Random House UK Limited Reg. No. 954009

A CIP catalogue record for this book
is available from the British Library

ISBN 0 09 178536 7

Printed and bound in Great Britain by Richard Clay Ltd, Bungay, Suffolk

Editor: Evelyn Bracken

Designer: Paul Wood

CONTENTS

For Kate, John, Simon, Daniel, Emily, Conor and Mary.

The 'how long more before' questions are over.

Acknowledgements

Somewhere in the north of France on a balmy evening in late June, 1993, Billy Stickland, Paul Kimmage and I walked a country road. Knowing our volatile natures, we agreed that a video about the making of the book might be better than the book itself. We may have been right. Billy's photographs adorn the book. Paul, the former pro, provided direction. I thank them for their friendship.

I thank also Marion Paull of Stanley Paul for making me an offer I could have refused. But she's such a nice woman . . . . My bosses at *The Sunday Independent* might have preferred it if I had refused but they were too decent to say. Adhamhnan O'Sullivan, the sports editor, continues to be the most understanding man I know.

Thanks are due to Michael Maher and Fuji for supplying Billy with rolls and rolls of film and to Lisa Pereira for help with a passage from Bernard Hinault's book, *Le Peloton des souvenirs*. I am grateful to John Wilcockson for his many helpful suggestions.

On the Tour I was indebted to the 13 subjects of this book; for agreeing to be interviewed and for being enthusiastic. I hope I have done them justice. Especially Neil Stephens and Stephen Roche. Neil told his own story and later was the bridge between Miguel Indurain's Spanish and the author's English. Stephen told his and then interpreted and translated Claudio Chiappucci's Italian. I depended on my editor Evelyn Bracken. Her patience, encouragement and red pen played a central part in the writing of *Inside the Tour de France*. It was fun.

Selected Bibliography

My Nineteenth Tour de France J.B. Wadley (J.B. Wadley, Kew, 1974)

Tour de France Robin Magowan (Stanley Paul, 1979)

Le peloton des souvenirs Bernard Hinault (Laffont, 1988)

The Game Ken Dryden (Macmillan, 1983)

A Rough Ride Paul Kimmage (Stanley Paul, 1990)

Tour de France: *Three Weeks to Glory* Samuel Abt (Bicycle Books, 1991)

Champion Samuel Abt (Biycle Books, 1993)

PROLOGUE

Pau – 22 July, 1993

Rider 107 freewheels across the line, slows and then slumps over his bike, 32 minutes after the first arrivals. Dog-tired. He is Danny Nelissen, a Dutch rider with the TVM team. Marc André, his *soigneur*, is there with a hat and damp cloth. He puts the hat on Nelissen's head and wipes the sweat from his face. That morning Nelissen was tall and good-looking, now his eyes are lifeless, the expression on his face vacant. Spattered on his right leg are traces of dried vomit. Five journalists stand in a semi-circle by his head, placing microphones and tape recorders close to his mouth.

'How was it, Danny?'

He looks up for the first time, fixes on the questioner and his eyes ask 'Are you happy doing this?' The interview ends before it begins. God knows what Nelissen has been through, how he has punished himself to remain in the Tour. Today the riders have been over the Tourmalet and Aubisque passes. Only Nelissen knows what it has taken him to get here. No, he couldn't muster the enthusiasm to tell 'how it was'.

The little scene in Pau did, however, highlight what attracts us to the Tour de France: the race goes beyond the humdrum world of the everyday and gives us a deeper, more memorable experience. In this three-week and 4000-kilometre race, we see man's limitations and his potential. We see also what happens when the boundaries are reached.

It was before dawn almost 80 years ago as the leaders approached the summit of the Aubisque on the race's first encounter with a Pyrenean pass. They had ridden the bumpiest of dirt roads in darkness. At the top, organizers waited to time and record the names of those who made it. Octave Lapize, one of the leaders, seeing the officials screamed 'Murderers!'

Danny Nelissen knew what to expect on the Tourmalet and Aubisque and wasn't blaming anyone. He needed a shower, food and rest. Tomorrow would be better. His routine acceptance of the extraordinary identifies the draw of this sports event. It also arouses our curiosity about Nelissen and his peers: who are they, where do they come from, what motivates them, what is it like inside *their* world?

Questions which lie at the heart of this book.

To better understand what is attempted, consider the Tour as a pilgrimage and this a book of tales told along the way. As in all storytelling, we learn as much about the teller as his subject. When they tell of their Tour de France, they reveal themselves.

The Tour, said the French racer Pascal Chanteur, is joy, suffering and disappointment. And the rider's greatest disappointment is to have his name listed amongst those forced to abandon. 'When you abandon,' said Bernard Hinault, 'the festival continues without you. You are physically weak and you feel rejected. This feeling of exclusion hurts far more than the physical pain.'

Lance Armstrong, a 21-year-old Texan, comes to the Tour not knowing what to expect. He has never ridden this race, not even anything like it. Damn it, he is only just getting to know Europe and here he is mixed up in one of the weirdest sports events on the calendar. Funnier still is the expectation that Armstrong can take something away from the race. Of all the neophytes, he is the one with a future.

But this sucker isn't fazed. Not Lance, the kid brought up to meet life head-on. Linda, his mother, is the dominant influence in his life and he doesn't want anyone thinking Linda raised a quitter. To tell the truth, he is looking forward to it, expects to find out things about himself and discover if, one day, he can win this race. 'In every Tour,' the French journalist Pierre Chany wrote, 'we see the winners of future Tours.'

Bernard Hinault knows exactly what to expect. A five-times winner of the race, Hinault retired in 1986 and is now part of the Tour's organization. During his time as the sport's best, Hinault was hard and unforgiving. He ruled with a touch of tyranny and even if it intimidated his rivals, it fascinated those who watched. Maybe there was more awe than admiration, more respect than affection but there was no indifference. Hinault had presence.

In his final season he tried to win the Tour for a record sixth time but lost to team-mate and one-time friend Greg LeMond. It was a spiteful Tour which destroyed the Hinault/LeMond friendship and bristled with hostility. Hinault says the record never interested him, not even remotely. He claims he didn't want to win that Tour, rather he wanted LeMond to be a worthy successor.

Now retired, he is an affable, charming man. He comes to the Tour, he says, to share his passion with those he meets. And if, through his experience as a racer, he can make it a better Tour for the riders, that would please him greatly.

Nothing pleases Jean-Paul Van Poppel as much as winning sprints. He used to be the fastest but, at 30, he is beginning to lose it. Forgive him if he doesn't go along with that because the sprinter can never lose faith in himself. But Van Poppel is intelligent and has seen the tell-tale signs of decline. He must be cleverer now to beat the younger ones. Van Poppel also knows unless he wins a stage of this Tour, the slide will continue.

He is apprehensive. Having sprinted well in the Vuelta a España, where he won two stages, he crashed near the end and missed four weeks' Tour preparation. It preys on his mind, makes him think he has lost sharpness. Besides, things are not right in his Festina team. Results have been disappointing and the team's *directeur sportif*, Dutchman Jan Gisbers, was fired a month before the race. Gisbers' sacking and the appointment of Frenchman Bruno Roussel shifted the balance of the team from Dutch to French. Van Poppel is Dutch and not optimistic about Roussel's chances of revitalizing the team.

There was a time, says Stephen Roche, when he got hung up about problems in the team. He complained, but nothing much changed except the colour of his hair. It turned grey before its time. So he minded his own business and things improved. Now the man who won the Giro d'Italia, Tour de France and World Championship inside three miraculous months merely wants to leave with dignity. Back in glorious '87, it was hard to see the music die: Roche had class, charisma, success and wealth. He was husband of the beautiful Lydia, father to Nicolas and Christel.

After '87, the descent began. Kick-started by injury, it accelerated on the weakness of Roche's impatience. Frustrated, he blamed his team, quarrelled with his friends and, in the end, realized that the wound could only be healed from within.

Signs that Roche had survived the black years came in last year's Tour when he won spectacularly at La Bourboule. Satisfying as that victory was, Roche could not delude himself. If he stayed around long enough the injuries would recur and the bad days return. This, he says, will be his last season and his final Tour de France. It is his chance to leave the sport through the right door.

Harry Van den Bremt remembers Roche's year. A journalist with the Belgian newspaper *Het Nieuwsblad*, Harry was reporting his twentieth consecutive Tour when Roche won. He didn't go quite as well as Roche that year, falling off a kerb early in the first week and fracturing his ankle. He worked on, hobbling from the car to the press centre, filed his report and then surrendered to the pain. A younger man replaced him and Harry thought it time for him to ease out of the Tour. Since '87 he has worked on the race from *Het Nieuwsblad*'s office in Brussels.

Harry hasn't seen it all, but he has witnessed more than most. He was there when 50 journalists followed the Tour and present through the extraordinary growth of the 70s and 80s. He has no hankering for the old days of unreliable telephones and pre-computerized journalism. But, from the old reporter, there is one lament: the media presence on the race has now grown so big that most journalists must watch the race from afar or, even worse, from the inside of the press room.

His return to the Tour this year is fortuitous. One of *Het Nieuwsblad*'s younger Tour reporters moved from the sports department and Harry was offered the chance to follow the race again. An offer he couldn't refuse.

Sean Yates is laid-back, takes life in his long, easy stride. People see it as a weakness; not enough drive, not enough meanness; not enough this, not enough that. But the ambitious came and went, Yates stayed. Now he is 12 years in the *peloton* and counting. Through the early years he suffered through poor health and his easy approach. Friends worried he would lose his place in the team, big Sean said if that happened he would return to England and do some gardening. But Yates had too much talent for that. His health improved, then his results; teams sought him, his salary increased and his reputation grew. The one thing which didn't change was Yates himself.

He began as an *équipier* (team-rider) and felt no inclination to aim higher. It suited him to help others because the *équipier's* role was less pressurized. Some said he was afraid of responsibility; Roger, his dad, thought he knew what he was doing. Better to serve well than to lead badly. Whatever his reasons, Yates carries on one of the sport's great traditions: the devoted team-mate.

Vincent Lavenu's devotion is to the bike. His life has followed a bicycle path. As a young boy in the Alpine town of Briançon, he was taken by his father to see the Tour de France. Monsieur Lavenu would soon leave home, never to return, but the effect of that Tour experience remained with his son. At first he simply wanted to race, then he wanted to compete against the best; and each achievement conceived another. Modestly talented, Lavenu struggled at every stage. Others said he was mad but they didn't realize what it meant to him.

When he could race no longer, Lavenu set about starting his own team. It was his most ambitious project but he did it. Now his team, in its second year, is about to make its Tour debut.

Vincent is, of course, its *directeur sportif.* Chazal, a small and relatively low-budget team, will not worry the bigger squads in this Tour but its presence is good for the race as it accommodates the small- to medium-level sponsor. It also offers an opportunity to the less gifted rider.

Lavenu relates easily to the less talented for, as a racer, he moved in those circles. Now his team is well organized and spirited. 'It is a team with soul,' says Lavenu. Chazal, the team, is the achievement of his life. 'We do things well,' he says, 'when we have a feel for them.'

Claudio Chiappucci has a feel for climbing mountains. In the hills around his home town, Uboldo in northern Italy, young Claudio cycled with his pals until the road steepened. Then he left them. As a prelude to the rest of his life that was about right, for Chiappucci has spent his career trying to distance himself from his rivals. He did so, spectacularly, on the Sestrière stage of the 1992 Tour, leading from the start and outclimbing every adversary including Miguel Indurain.

Second in the Tour of '90, third in '91 and second again in '92; Claudio attacks first and works out tactics later. A style more appreciated by fans than by fellow riders but Chiappucci cannot do it differently. Without his free spirit, the Tour would be simpler to predict and easier to ride.

No matter who makes the tempo on the hills in this Tour, Neil Stephens is not going to find it easy. An *équipier* with the Once team, the Australian lost two months' preparation because of a hernia operation. 'Ride yourself in,' says his *directeur sportif* Manolo Saiz, 'you'll be strong in the final week.' Stephens appreciates Manolo's confidence but it doesn't stop him worrying.

Stephens takes a realistic line. He was never going to be a star, nor is he one. When he left Canberra, 10 years ago, he hoped to make a career in European cycling but wasn't sure if he had the talent. The first four years reinforced his pessimism and almost destroyed his ambition. But, being an Aussie, he found it hard to quit. There have been surprising twists: Stephens' assimilation of European culture has been remarkable. He lives in the Basque country of Spain, has a Basque girl-friend and speaks Spanish with a Basque accent.

Nicolas Terrados is a tall, well-built Spaniard. What you might expect an ex-pro basketball player to be. But the game merely paid for Terrados' medical studies. Now the doctor epitomizes the great change which has swept through cycling. Where once riders were treated by untrained *soigneurs*, they are now cared for by qualified doctors. Terrados works with the Once team. While on Tour he will use the mobile laboratory, built into one of Once's team buses, to monitor the riders' health. Terrados must work within the confines of the sport's stringent anti-dope laws but there are considerations beyond the black and white of the banned substances' list.

What, for example, should the doctor do if there is a performance-enhancing product which does not contravene the sport's laws? Should we expect him to be governed by the morality of fair play?

Did you say fair play? What's fair about asking Edwig Van Hooydonck to race the Tour de France? Standing 6' 4" flame-haired and light-skinned, Van Hooydonck would never choose to take his bike to the mountains on a hot July afternoon. Especially to a 20-kilometre Alpine climb, but WordPerfect, his team, needs good riders in the Tour. He is a very good rider. 'Very good,' he says, 'but not great,' reflecting a deep-rooted modesty. Twice winner of the Tour of Flanders, he is one of the best in the sport's one-day classics.

That isn't a surprise, because Van Hooydonck is Flemish and, in his part of Belgium, the classics of the spring define status and, occasionally, greatness. Edwig is part of this tradition and hard in the Flemish way. He listens to the weather forecast in the days before a Tour of Flanders or a Paris–Roubaix, half hoping for bad weather. The harder it is, the better he likes it.

But this Tour de France? It's not meant for big Flemings.

Neither is it meant for the wives of the men who ride it. Brigitte Rominger knows she will spend some time on the Tour but wants it to be a short visit. Rachel, her daughter, is now five and doesn't find the Tour much fun and Brigitte doesn't like being away from her. If things work out as Mum hopes, she will visit her husband Tony on the Tour's first rest day in Grenoble and then return to her daughter. But Brigitte can't be certain. She and Tony have been together since they were teenagers and he doesn't like being away. On a long Tour, he can cope for two weeks but in the final week he needs to see her.

Brigitte flew from their home in Monte Carlo to be with him for the final week of the Vuelta a España in 1991 and again in 1992. She hated all the attention the first time and even though she avoided that the second year, too much time was spent waiting around and too little time with Tony. Now she suggests following this race on television, settling for telephone calls every day and taking Rachel to Paris for the end of the Tour. Tony says that's fine. It's a deal.

When Miguel Indurain races the Tour, his needs are basic: a clean yellow jersey every day, *por favor*. Winner of the Tour in '91 and '92, Indurain is the master of the bigger stage races. Such is his even temperament, his robust good health and his talent, it is hard to see him being beaten in the forseeable future. Four or five consecutive Tour victories lie within his scope, although Indurain would laugh at the suggestion. 'Tranquilo, tranquilo,' he might say, asking us to calm down and take one Tour at a time.

He would protest his limitations and emphasize the folly of looking beyond the next race. But his actions speak louder than words and going into this Tour, he stands apart from his rivals. His dominance is generating restlessness. That Spanish guy, he lacks charisma, doesn't excite passions, he's too bloody regular. Laments which reflect the angst of those who prefer their Tours packed with suspense. What they are saying is 'Give us a conflict, make it harder for Indurain.' The vague dissatisfaction adds to the challenge which awaits the champion.

So far, he has done well with challenges.

THE NEOPHYTE'S TALE
In the Wake of Neil
LANCE ARMSTRONG

1. Lance Armstrong
2. Awaiting the obligatory Tour medical at Le Puy du Fou, Armstrong was unusually cool for a neophyte
3. The shades protect Armstrong from the sun and they offer a little distance. John Wilcockson, editor of the US magazine *Velo News*, is in the foreground of the right lens, trying to get a little closer
4. The moment before he acclaims his stage win at Verdun, Armstrong's face is full of the winner's aggression

On the fifth night, the Tour de France stopped at the town of Avranches. The following morning Lance Armstrong pedalled through the tented village which offered breakfast to the race's 3800 entourage. As he weaved through the forest of bodies, Armstrong was stopped by an Italian journalist from *La Gazzetta della Sport* .

The journalist explained how his newspaper asked a different rider to predict the winner of each day's race and today they wanted Armstrong to nominate the likely winner. Aware of his responsibilities as a professional racer, Armstrong listened courteously.

As the journalist explained, two glamorous French women walked past. Both tall, in their early 20s and, at nine o'clock in the morning, unmissable. They caught Armstrong's attention. 'Bonjour' he said, wanting them to stop, but they pretended not to hear. He tried to take in what the newspaperman was saying but it was difficult. His eyes followed the women as they disappeared into the crowd.

'Wow,' said Armstrong and then, remembering the question, he continued, 'Sciandri, my teammate, is my choice for today. He should like the finish and I will do what I can to help him.' Writing down Armstrong's prediction, the journalist thanked him and moved on. Armstrong scanned the crowd for the two passers-by. As his eyes darted in vain, his hopes fell and he settled for gallant admiration: 'They were something, weren't they?'

At that moment, he stood over his bike as the kid he was. Twenty-one years of age, youngest rider in the race, a neophyte in his first Tour de France. But also the young American in Europe, wanting to succeed but not prepared to suspend other longings. At once strong, capable and vulnerable. An ambitious, intelligent, interesting kid. But, a kid nevertheless.

This race, he liked it better each day. First day was the worst but it had got better. Now he was beginning to think that maybe, just maybe, he could do something. Win a stage, leave a mark, let people know he had been here. Who knows? He wasn't giving up. As he talked about the possibilities, the two young women returned. They had a pen and some paper and they asked for his autograph. Armstrong was thrilled, flattered by their interest.

He signed with enthusiasm. They thanked him warmly, he tried to detain them but, in a wonderfully French way, they left him yearning.

When he is out with Linda, which is as often as both can manage, she introduces him with a flourish. 'Ah this is my baby, this is my son.' It cannot be, they say. 'Really, really, this is my son.' Can't be, they insist. He has been witness to this little skirmish over his status so many times. Eventually the doubters are convinced but they cannot let go. 'You two don't want to know what we were thinking.' Lance laughs at that, people seeing him and his Mom as boyfriend and girlfriend. He knows she's 39 but she doesn't look it and she's got a cute figure, 5' 3" and 100 lb. An incredible little lady, he says.

Linda was 17 when pregnant with Lance. People then were unsympathetic to teenage motherhood and Plano, Texas, would have reflected the conservatism of the time. Linda and Lance's father married, an alliance which did not last. About his father, Lance is emotionless. 'I never met him. Ah, I guess I met him but I was a one-year-old at that point. That's when he left.'

A couple of years later Linda remarried and Lance was legally adopted by his stepfather, a man he never liked. Linda and her second husband stayed together for 12 years before the relationship ended. It was a tough time for mother and son, the difficulties ending with the break-up of the marriage. Lance's memories are without bitterness; whatever resentment existed at the time has been obliterated by the intervening years.

'We grew up middle-class but you know we weren't a very happy middle-class family. My stepfather had a job that was okay I guess and he made enough money to classify us as middle-class but aside from that he wasn't a very good guy. We had food on the table, shelter and stuff but I don't think Mom or I were very happy with that.

'When I was very young I got along with him all right. You don't know how to dislike somebody at that age but I tell you the first day I learned how to dislike somebody, I disliked him. I took on his name because he adopted me so that's where I get the name Armstrong. I don't care to carry it on but it's now at the point where it would be kind of hard to change it.'

Linda's memories of her son's arrival are joyous. Although she was young and on her own, she wanted the baby. She expected a girl and had picked a name. When they told her it was a boy, she drew from her instinct and came up with Lance. Maybe that was instinctive vision for there is a slang expression in French cycling: *Je lance le sprint* (I begin the sprint).

Lance was Linda's baby and that was how Mom wanted it. She would take control. Tend it, feed it, protect it, rear it. When it was necessary to have two jobs to make ends meet, Linda got two jobs. When Lance looked for his mother, she was always there.

'My life revolved around my son. It might have been difficult but because I didn't know anything else I didn't see it as such. To me, this was just the most wonderful thing. Having a baby at 17 was unheard of back then but that didn't bother me. I had so much fun with Lance. When he was doing his swimming, we were both up at 5 a.m. I would prepare a good breakfast and he would always be cranky. And just when he was at his most cranky I would say "Okay Lance, make this the first day of the rest of your life." Because this is what I said every morning, we would both laugh. We have our children such a short time and when he left to live in Austin a few years ago it was like my right hand was cut off. I wasn't ready for that.'

Lance's youth came in two parts: his life before the separation of his mother and stepfather and his life afterwards. The former was trying when not downright unhappy, the latter a wonderful union of mother and son. Because he has a natural capacity to see life's funny side, he laughs now. But it is humour in hindsight.

'When you're growing up, you're 14, 15 or 16 and you're in High School or whatever, your friends' parents are getting divorced and the kids are falling apart. They start crying, they get upset, they gotta have counsellors and they gotta have this, that and the other. I'm looking around, seeing all of this, and my stepfather has left. And I had a party, you know, because it's such a load off my back. I got confused because I thought "Well, man what is wrong with you? This tears kids up and yet we're kicking this guy out and you're ecstatic."

'For a while I thought maybe something's wrong with me but then I just realized how happy we both were. Actually my Mom wasn't that happy because it is just like any relationship, you're miserable being in it but you don't want to end it. And so she broke it and then she was lonely and nobody's happy when they're lonely. But I tell you she was a helluva lot better off than being miserable. And that's true for everybody. I don't care what the situation is, it's always better to be lonely because you can always find somebody else and she has.'

Describing Greg LeMond as a typical American, a friend once joked that he was conceived in rock 'n' roll and delivered in a pick-up. An image which does convey something of LeMond's natural innocence. Lance Armstrong is a different kind of American. He lived just five kilometres from the ranch at Southfork, home to the TV soap opera *Dallas*. As a boy he rode by the place almost every day, knew it to be an ordinary house, nothing like as shown on TV. Big steel sides, pretty cheesy. Now it is a tourist attraction, friends from his boyhood work there as guides and ranch hands. And Lance, you see, could have walked straight off the *Dallas* set.

He grew up 'like any kid'. Played the sports, went on vacations, hung out with neighbourhood friends, jumped in creeks, got dirty, got in trouble, skipped school. At football, baseball and basketball he was average or slightly below. Swimming was his first serious sport. Two work-outs each day from the age of 11. One and a half hours in the morning, two hours after school. Ten thousand metres each day and Linda always cajoling and always there.

Because he could swim well, he was attracted to the triathlon. He was 13 when he attempted his first: a 200-metre swim, 10 kilometres on the bike and a two-kilometre run. He won regional races in Dallas and Houston and finished second in the nationals at Orlando. In the triathlon, he was good. Because he was good, he liked it.

'I'd done all these sports all my life and I was never any good and then I came across the triathlon and I said "Hey man!" It wasn't the attention I got, it wasn't the trophies. I just liked the reward of winning and the reward of being the best. This was something I never had before.'

Encouraged, Lance tried harder. He knew he could make some money doing triathlons, maybe even earn a living. This opportunity came at a time when decisions were being made. 'I was sort of at a point where I could have gone either way. You know kids reach a stage where they either become a hoodlum with drugs or crime, or they get into sport or they get into school or they get into religion.'

Triathlons began with the swim, where he was certain to do well. He was also a strong cyclist and, at school, he did track and cross-country and so, at the age of 15, he became a professional triathlete. His big test came in a triathlon in Dallas as it pitched him against the best guys. Two thousand competed, of whom the top 100 were professionals.

He finished the swim joint second with Mark Allen, a famous triathlete. Allen looked at the teenager alongside and his expression said 'Who the hell are you?' At the end of the bike leg, Armstrong sprinted to get ahead of Allen and so begin the final running leg alone in second place. From there he fell back, dropping to sixth at the finish. 'I didn't care about sixth place, I did the swim with those guys, I did the bike and I just thought it was unbelievable. I got my picture taken with Mark Allen afterwards. And everybody was saying "Who ARE you? What do you think you're doing?" That was pretty cool.'

Although Lance was young and boyish, there was a toughness which belied his youth. The kind of toughness you see in kids that are about seven years old at birth. Nothing excited him as the big challenge did. Hardly had the Dallas triathlon ended but he was looking towards the National Championships. As he was a professional, he sought sponsorship but, an unknown, he couldn't raise a cent.

He didn't let that bother him for, at the time, life was good. His stepfather had left and Lance was setting out on a pro triathlon career. Without a sponsor, he went down to a local shop in Plano and had 'I LOVE MY MOM' printed on his tank-top. Nothing could have been more appropriate for Linda was his greatest sponsor. He finished a creditable eighth in the nationals and Mom thought the top 'a cool thing'.

Armstrong progressed as a triathlete. Sometimes he could make a thousand dollars at the weekends, he compared that to what his friends earned in Burger King and reckoned he was doing okay. These were also happy days with Linda. She was his driver, his motivator, his companion and when he needed to have a sponsor's logo stitched onto his tank-top, she was his seamstress. If the going got tough, Linda offered the advice which had governed her life. 'If you give up, you give in.'

The move from the triathlon to cycling was gradual. It began with Armstrong entering bike races to help his triathlon preparation and grew from there. But it grew fast. At the age of 17, he was a member of the US cycling team which competed in the World Junior Road Race Championship on the famous Krylatskoe circuit in Moscow. A teenage phenomenon: phenomenally strong and, in matters cycling, phenomenally ignorant. A weakness which cost him that Moscow race.

'At that time I knew nothing about cycling. I started the race in my skinsuit, like a one-piece. I had no food, no water, no nothing. I said (to the team manager) I don't need this, I don't need that, I don't want a jersey. I want my aerodynamic skinsuit. I'm going off in front, okay. I want to be aerodynamic. So I go off in front, all day long, all day. Didn't eat a thing, didn't drink a thing and on the last lap, WOW, did I hit the wall. Man, was I wasted!'

But he learned. Soon he knew he could earn a living on the American circuit, where amateurs and professionals race together. He remained amateur until the Barcelona Olympics in July 1992. By then Armstrong's name meant something in bike racing and he was one of the favourites for the 1992 Olympic road race. But on a hot, clammy day he failed to get near a medal.

Barcelona was his last stop on the amateur route. Immediately after the Olympics, Lance Armstrong became a professional with the Motorola team. Jim Ochowicz, manager of Motorola, recognized his potential and, months before the Olympics, he reached an agreement with the rider. A couple of weeks after Barcelona, Armstrong rode the San Sebastian classic. One of the tougher classics, this was too much, too soon. He finished last. 'That was hard for a proud Texan like me,' he says. But the memory of that first professional race is the resilience shown by the then 20-year-old. He was not going well but he refused to stop. The public humiliation of finishing last was, for him, easier than the private pain of surrender.

'If you give up,' Linda had said, 'you give in.'

Slow down. You're talking too fast.

But Lance, the newest kid in the Tour, has to travel so far, so quickly. There isn't time. Measured reflections are not his style. Considered opinions, he doesn't have. This racer, so full of life, sees no danger. On this wonderfully sunny French evening, 10 miles south of Grenoble, Lance has taken off. Through the highs and lows of his career and his constant yearning to be somebody.

Maybe it is this mid-Tour resting place, Chateau de La Commanderie. Much more chateau than hotel, old and quiet in a serene way. Chairs around the pool, chairs facing the lawns, big trees, no rush. A nice home on the night before the race goes to the mountains. All the guests are silently encouraged to relax. Andy Hampsten, leader of the Motorola team, sits and chats with visitors. Another rider, Sean Yates, jokes with a photographer friend. A Colombian journalist gently prods his young compatriot, Alvaro Mejia. Lance Armstrong needs no prodding.

He has come to the part of the story where his first Tour begins. He is here to learn, basically. Jim Ochowicz looked at him and saw the hardness which the Tour demands. This neophyte could take it. And Lance understands why they have sent him. To see everything that's going on, to get a feel for the race, the atmosphere, the hype. The Tour is a Show and the rider has to learn to see only the race. It takes time. Do it this year and get a start on the guys who stay away.

But Lance has to be more than a learner. He is the boy who says 'Why can't I try that?' He wants to be in there, mixing with the big boys. As a participant in the Tour, he must compete. Three days earlier there had been a race from Peronne to Châlons-sur-Marne and a breakaway group of seven riders. Three riders from his Motorola team infiltrated the breakaway party, giving the team a strong numerical advantage over the other four riders. The odds favoured victory for one of Motorola's three; Mejia, Sciandri or Anderson.

When it became certain that the breakaways would not be caught, Lance Armstrong was happy. Back in the pack, he high-fived his mates. Other riders wondered what they were about, Lance and his friends laughed. At the finish he heard the team got second, not first. He couldn't believe it. Three guys in a group of seven and second place. He was furious.

His team lost when he thought it should have won. 'I mean when I am in there, I don't know if it's . . . physically I'm not any more gifted than anybody else but it's just this desire, just this rage. I'm on the bike and I go into a rage, when I just shriek for about five seconds. I shake like mad and my eyes kinda bulge out. I swear, I sweat a little more and the heart rate goes like 200 a minute.

'And it's funny, every time I do that I think about my mother. I really do because if she was there, she didn't raise a quitter and I would never, I'd never quit. I'd never, just never. And that's heart man, that's not physical, that's not legs, that's not lungs. That's heart. That's soul. That's just guts.'

Popeye telling what happens when he takes his spinach.

Frankie Andreu it was who helped plant the seed. Frankie's a Motorola team man, from Detroit, likes to play big brother. Midway through the first week he said 'Lance, I got a stage for you.'

'The one into Verdun?'

'That one's for you.'

'I know it. I know it,' said Armstrong.

Riders on the Tour de France are ambivalent about the official race manual. Some call it 'the race bible', for they know the detailed information about each day's race must be assimilated. But too much time over the manual can lower the spirit in a wasted body. For a rider uncertain about his chances of surviving the next day, next week's mountain stages are not relevant. The same principle is applied when they arrive, weary, at the first slopes of a big mountain pass. Few wish to look to the very top, for that too clearly foretells the pain.

Lance Armstrong tried to confine himself to a brief look at the next day's stage in the manual. But he didn't always stick to that and in his glancing assessment of the various stages, Verdun stood out. There was a short, steepish hill 16 kilometres before the finish and it would fragment the pack. The sprinters would be left behind and those with the power to accelerate on the hill would have a chance of winning the stage. Armstrong privately listed himself a contender.

Then when Frankie Andreu came with his discovery, expectant bells began to ring. That hill would suit Armstrong and, after that, there was just a long descent to the finish in Verdun. Made for a man with strength on the climb and a reasonable sprint at the end. Armstrong's hunger to win this stage was sharpened by Motorola's loss of the previous day's race to Châlons-sur-Marne.

One hundred and eighty riders began this, the 80th Tour de France. Five, maybe six riders set out with a realistic chance of winning the Tour. Every other racer began with the hope of picking up one of the 20 stages. For the majority of the 20 teams in the race, one stage victory would be sufficient. 'We came into the Tour,' said Belgian rider Edwig Van Hooydonck, 'hoping we could get one stage win.' An aspiration which Van Hooydonck's heavily backed WordPerfect team did not realize. But stage wins do not come easily. Three riders would win eight stages on this Tour, leaving 12 stages between 177 racers.

And yet this young American believed he had a chance as the riders rolled out of Châlons-sur-Marne on the ninth day of the race. His plan for the day was straightforward: he hoped that when the race approached the hill before the finish, the Côte de Douaumont, he would be in a position to win. Because quite a few of the stronger men also saw an opportunity in that hill, they too wanted the race to stay together. This wasn't a day for adventurous breakaways.

Of course in a race like the Tour de France there is always somebody willing to take on the pack. On the day to Verdun it was coincidental that the adventurer was the Tour's other Lance, Pascal Lance, a French rider from Lorraine. Before his own people and over roads he trained on, Pascal had to try. Sixty kilometres from the finish he broke clear, building a lead of one minute, 25 seconds.

When Pascal arrived at the foot of the Côte de Douaumont, tiredness destroyed his pedalling rhythm. The effort which gained the advantage cost him his chance of sustaining it. Behind him Claudio Chiappucci accelerated at the bottom of the two-kilometre hill, reminding everybody that the climbs were his terrain. Miguel Indurain rode close behind Chiappucci, as did Gianni Bugno. Tony Rominger joined the front line by surging forward from a position in the middle of the *peloton*. Soon the faltering Pascal was reeled in by the accelerating pack and Chiappucci's effort became a downright attack.

French rider Laurent Brochard countered, as did Lance Armstrong, both getting into the Italian's slipstream and then momentarily slowing to draw breath. But Brochard accelerated again, surging past Chiappucci and into the lead. Determined to cover every move, Armstrong followed Brochard and was himself followed by the Italian, Davide Cassani. Behind them, the pack splintered into countless pieces. Every rider struggled to stay close to the wheel in front of him: the long snake which began this short climb now resembled a disjoined bunch of wriggling worms.

It was, of course, the strongest who got to the front. Indurain was there, Stephen Roche, Bugno, Zenon Jaskula and Rominger. And it was Rominger who made the next move. As Armstrong closed down on Brochard and tried to recover his strength, Rominger flew past. The summit was now in sight and Armstrong went after his Swiss rival. His strength was formidable.

At the top of the Côte de Douaumont, Rominger was first, then Cassani, Indurain, Bugno and Chiappucci. Armstrong crossed close behind but he was suffering.

'I was starting to kinda hurt a little and I thought, shit I'm a little bit wasted. I needed to sit down and recover a bit. Just spin it out and I could see guys coming by me because I'm kinda soft-pedalling and I think shit, it's still all together. I figured it hadn't snapped. It's strung out and it's going to come back together. It's going to be this big full sprint which I have no interest in. And guys are coming by me and I said "One more look around, just to see." I looked around and there was like three more guys to come by and then there was nobody. I said "shit, this is it."

'I had to sprint like mad to get on to the guy who just came by me and then I turned around, we had a gap, there was like 40 guys and I thought maybe . . . . But Museeuw was there and some other fast guys and 40 guys is not exactly my speciality because that's still a pretty big sprint. And then three guys got out; Perini, Roche and Arnould. I saw them get away but at that time I was still cooked so I was on the back. I kept telling myself "Recover, recover, recover, see them up there, damn, this is the move. I got to make it, I got to go now."'

Giancarlo Perini, Dominique Arnould and Roche were 100 yards clear. Behind, Armstrong rode at the front of the pursuit but was struggling to recover from the climb. He felt panic, fearing the race was being decided without him. But, at that instant, Armstrong's will overcame his tiredness. He counterattacked in pursuit of the three breakaways; Raul Alcala and Ronan Pensec followed his move and soon there were six riders at the front, 200 yards ahead of those who chased.

Emotions swirled, panic was replaced by relief and then an overwhelming need to win. 'We all just started working, perfect rhythm. Just six guys buzzing along together and nobody playing games, nobody sitting on. I told myself ". . . . I didn't say I'm going to win this sprint. I said there's no way I'm gonna lose this sprint."

Sharing the pacemaking, the six went about 400 yards clear of their pursuit. They were helped by the descending road to Verdun. Roche, Perini, Pensec and Alcala might have believed they had an outside chance of winning the stage but they were motivated more by the certainty of a top six finish. Arnould, a stage winner in the previous year's Tour, was an obvious contender for victory, as was Armstrong.

Riding the final kilometres, Armstrong assessed his five rivals. Roche, who didn't have a sprint, would attack early. Perini wasn't fast enough, neither was Pensec, Alcala had a bit of a sprint but, no, he wasn't quick enough. Arnould was the one who stood as a threat. As the six prepared themselves for the final sprint, Armstrong positioned himself directly behind his French rival so he would know what he was up to.

Arnould feared Armstrong and didn't want him in his slip-stream. He slowed, feigned an attack to get his young rival to pass him. But Armstrong was nerveless. Refusing to move, he spoke to his rival. 'Hey man, you're on a French team, you're a French rider, this is the Tour de France, you're the one who can't afford to mess this up.' Arnould might not have understood the words but the message was clear. The terms would be Armstrong's.

Roche, predictably, surged from far out. Pensec followed, Arnould accelerated from fourth position, Armstrong moving at the same time. As the speed went up, the six moved from the left side of the road to the right. Pensec went past Roche, Arnould tried to overtake but couldn't. Armstrong was in a tight position, boxed in by Arnould and Roche. But as Arnould attempted to close on Pensec he moved slightly to his left, leaving a narrow corridor for Armstrong.

Arnould on his left, the crash barriers on his right, Armstrong moved up to Pensec. The French rider sensed his presence and veered towards the barriers, narrowing the corridor. Armstrong's mind raced as fast as his legs. 'Pensec was coming to the right and I was thinking he can't. They have this new rule, "the Abdu Rule", you have to hold your line in the last 200 metres. I remember looking at him coming towards me, thinking "he can't come over."

'We were right at the 150 sign so he can't come over, that's against the rules but he kept moving towards me and I didn't know what I was gonna do. I decided to just yell as loud as possible and maybe freak him out a little. I mean no matter how bad an ass you are, you are still going to get a little hesitant when somebody screams. And so he hesitated and that was my gap. Right there, that's all I had.'

Armstrong went past Pensec so fast that, at the line, he was two bike lengths clear. More than enough for him to raise both arms in celebration.

It was a success which touched a number of chords. Armstrong was the youngest rider in the race, he was American and he had ridden heroically. Most of all, he represented cycling's future. Poor form and ill-health persuaded his compatriot Greg LeMond to stay away and he was missed. But, now, there was another American. Not a LeMond, maybe not a rider rounded enough to win a Tour de France but still a rising star.

That was apparent in his uninhibited racing style and in his casual confidence off the bike. He breezed through the winner's duties, unfazed by the success and the questions which followed. One journalist asked if he was the second LeMond? 'I am the first Lance Armstrong,' he answered with certainty. To the assertion that this had to be his greatest victory, he replied the US Professional Championship win meant more. Asked if he was married or had children, he said he was not married and didn't think he had children.

At a distance the honesty could have been mistaken for arrogance but it was not that. With Armstrong there is no false modesty, no playing down of his qualities but neither is there conceit. After the sprint he thought aloud about Pensec's attempt to discourage him in the sprint. He couldn't complain, he said, because if the positions had been reversed he would have done the same.

Yet to see only the straight-talker is to miss the wide-eyed boy in his first Tour. The smiling debutant who turned heads at the compulsory medical examination in Le Puy du Fou two days before the start of the race. So comfortable with the attention that the older, more experienced riders thought this kid will come to no good. When a photographer asked Andy Hampsten and Armstrong to pose for a photograph it was the older team-mate who demurred and the kid who smiled and said 'Let's do it now and get it over.' As the photographers zoomed in, his face radiated happiness.

Used to the less expressive men of European cycling, Armstrong struck us as naive. We, who expected newcomers to arrive in awe of the Tour, said he would soon learn. He didn't seem to understand how difficult this race was, didn't realize that public smiles came only in victory.

What we did not see was the naturally articulate and confident American who considered only the opportunities. Trying to tell us he was an ambitious cyclist and there was nowhere else he would rather be.

An American in Europe. More than that, a very American kid in a very European sport. Happily unaware of the traditions of this 90-year-old race, he could travel lightly. All the people and all this fuss, it gave him a buzz.

Once, just once, Lance Armstrong didn't have an answer. It might have been 30 minutes after the victory into Verdun and the Italian journalist delivered his question with charming clarity. 'On 21 July, 1969 Neil Armstrong became the first man to land on the moon. How high can this Armstrong go?' Lance in the wake of Neil. For once the American was silent. The expression on his face said he was a cyclist, a good one but still a cyclist.

Next question.

For a rider, the Tour is a journey. Physically and psychologically: the peaks and valleys of the route mirrored in the physical and emotional responses of the racer. One day he feels up, the next day down. Nobody enjoys a smooth ride . . . .

The 1993 Tour began with a 6.8-km individual time trial at Le Puy du Fou, a cultural theme park located in the Vendée region. For the privilege of hosting the first three days of the Tour, private business and municipal authorities paid 5.5 million French francs (almost £700,000 or $1 m). It was an imaginative starting point, certain to interest the 1000-plus army of media people. From the racer's point of view, Le Puy du Fou was just another prologue course, a little longer and a little more difficult than average.

Lance Armstrong felt good about his participation. As a neophyte he did not have to produce results. If he saw an opportunity he could go for it. And Lance, being Lance, saw an opportunity in the prologue. He accepted he could not win it, for Indurain, Alex Zülle, Tony Rominger and Gianni Bugno were the specialists but he could gain from the Tour's first race.

If he finished high up, he would be in a position to try for the yellow jersey by getting into a breakaway in the first week. Armstrong also knew a strong performance in the prologue would lift his spirits.

But this was the Tour de France, a race where ambitions are like babies: easy to conceive but difficult to deliver.

On the evening of the prologue, Armstrong's Motorola team lodged at Les Jardins de l'Atlantique hotel in Bourgenay on the west coast. Earlier in the day Lance had taken his first Tour lesson. Desperately wanting a good time, he completed the 6.8-km prologue in eight minutes, 59 seconds. That left him 81st: far removed from the yellow jersey, and very depressed.

He started so fast that when he arrived at the foot of the Côte du Fosse, four kilometres into the test, he had nothing left. On the hill he deteriorated. Before the top, there was no rhythm in his pedalling and he felt helpless. His time was 47 seconds slower than the winning performance of Indurain, meaning Armstrong lost seven seconds per kilometre to the champion. For a young rider with hopes of one day winning the Tour, this was discouraging.

That evening Armstrong came from the hotel restaurant with Jim Ochowicz at his side. The Motorola manager said the rider was down and couldn't talk for very long. Armstrong was very low. 'Starting well is a big priority of mine. Today was awful.' What troubled him most was his failure to ride intelligently. 'I rode the stupidest race. I gave it everything and then hit the bottom of that hill. Boy, I tell you, it was a helluva lot harder and a helluva lot longer than I expected.'

Immediately after the prologue, Armstrong's humour was foul. His team-mates told unsuspecting enquirers that 'Lance wasn't very happy'. Motorola's team doctor, Massimo Testa, saw the danger and reminded the rider he had come to learn. 'If you're going to get upset and pissed off over that, then you're going to become more tired and you're not going to be able to stay in this race. So there's no sense in wasting energy over something that has happened.'

It was now 9.30 in the evening at Les Jardins de l'Atlantique. Five hours after the prologue. Darkness had fallen. Lance Armstrong sat on the terrace of the hotel's bar. He was coming round, but slowly. He couldn't feign good humour, couldn't speak hopefully about what lay before him. He wanted to call his coach Chris Carmichael in America and he needed to talk to Linda. After that he would sleep.

Lance's first taste of the Tour had not been what he expected. He would go from here older, wiser.

What most hurts the rider during the long tour is the constant chipping away at his strength. Per Pedersen, a Dane with the Amaya team, believes there is a pattern. 'First week you feel good, the second week you lose strength. Third week, fucked.'

Rising at 6.30 in the morning, halfway through the Tour and feeling wasted, what human thinks beyond immediate survival?

Later in the morning three or four riders sit over a coffee at the tented village: one will be coughing, another complaining of a stomach bug, another with cold sores. The symptoms of the rundown.

'It is a problem,' says Nicolas Terrados, doctor with the Once team. 'At the hotel the beef we eat is slightly gone off, just a day or two. You or I don't notice it and it does not do us any harm but the next morning three or four of the cyclists are off-colour. Because their systems are drained, they are vulnerable to the slightest threat. Then, because they are racing they cannot recover. Given one day's rest, they would be fine. But, in the Tour, they are forced to abandon.'

Lance Armstrong complains about his upper body. Too bulked out. The small incredible hulk, he says. It is the swimmer's physique, developed through the years when rising at 5.30 a.m to go to the pool. Since concentrating on cycling, his upper body has been toned down. But he is still enormously strong. It is how he is seen within the Motorola team. Alain Bondue, a former pro from northern France and now working with the team, passes and greets him.

'Hi there, strong-man.'

Others achieve through the suppleness of their pedalling, others through their ability on the steepest climbs and others make it because of their rapid finish. But Armstrong's greatest quality is his endurance. He can survive when the pace is at its fiercest and he recovers quickly from violent effort. Then, when the race nears its climax, he finds something extra. Hennie Kuiper, the assistant manager of the Motorola team, likens Armstrong to the great Dutch rider of the last generation, Jan Raas. An apt comparison because Raas, too, depended upon his strength.

Yet without mental toughness, physical strength is a blunt weapon. Maybe it was his life without a father and Linda's need for him to mature quickly; whatever the reasons, Lance Armstrong soon learned to stand up for himself . . . .

Drawing you closer, he says he must keep his voice down because Motorola team members are not permitted to discuss the million dollar question while the Tour is on. It caused friction and Jim Ochowicz outlawed the subject while the Tour lasted.

It all began in February of 1993 when Lance heard there was a one million dollar bonus for the rider who could win three nominated races on the American circuit. Prize money in professional cycling is generally derisory as riders' salaries are paid by their sponsors. Although the million dollars offer received a lot of publicity, those within the sport would have viewed it as a piece of gimmickry. Against the possibility of one rider actually winning all three races, the promoters took out an insurance policy with Lloyds of London.

When Armstrong won the first, interest grew. Here was a rider strong enough to give this a shot. He did not intend to ride the second race, a five-day stage race in West Virginia, but tempted by the million he changed his plans. With considerable help from his Motorola team, he won the West Virginia race and then it was down to the US Professional Championship. Should he win that, the million was his.

He did. It was then that the difficult questions had to be addressed. Payment of the million could be accepted in 20 annual instalments of $50,000 or Armstrong could take $600,000 straight-up. He did not deliberate too much on this one. He read the newspapers, Lloyds were going through a bad time, posting significant losses and Lance believed he couldn't trust them. Not for 20 years. He would take the $600,000 straight-up, thank you very much.

Then came the really tricky part. Armstrong was unsure how the money should be split with his team-mates. Motorola's policy was to put all the winnings into a kitty and divide equally at the end of the season. It is how most professional squads operate and it ensures that riders who work for the team but don't often win are fairly rewarded. But, as prize money is small, the share for each rider is not that significant. Armstrong considered putting $600,000 into the kitty in the normal way but came to the conclusion that it was a once-off and should be treated as such.

Everybody in the team was conscious of the $600,000 and wanted to know how it was going to be split. Armstrong asked the team's most senior riders, Englishman Sean Yates and the Australian Phil Anderson to adjudicate. Neither was sure how it should be done, others offered opinions and it became a contentious question. At one of the meetings where it was clear there was going to be no agreement, Armstrong ended the arguments:

'I said, "Heh, it's my money. I'm gonna do it. Leave it to me. I'm gonna be the bad guy here. I'll take care of it."'

Armstrong's mind is clear on what should happen. He figured the five-day stage race in West Virginia was the key event. West Virginia is a beautiful state but not much into bike racing. 'Here,' he says indicating the Tour de France, 'you have a million people along the roadside. There you had maybe five. No, not even that. Winning that race was hard. There were a lot of times when my team-mates were on the front, buzzing along, controlling the race for me.

'At the same time we had a team riding the Tour of Italy, nine guys there. So my attitude is that this is a unique situation and it's going to be handled uniquely. The guys who were in West Virginia and had the pressure of having to help me and all the attention that went with that, they deserve more money. There's no way that some guy who was halfway round the world should get the same cut. No way. I am not saying "Heh, I want $599,000 and everybody else can do whatever they want." I don't want a dime more than the guys who rode in West Virginia. But this money is different and that's my attitude.'

It was not certain that Armstrong would have his way on the division of $600,000, neither was it sure his reasoning was fair. Questions to be debated. But, beyond argument, was the inner strength which enabled him to make a decision. 'I am gonna be the bad guy here,' he said, 'I'll take care of it.'

This was Lance Armstrong, 21 years of age, riding in his first professional team. Standing up for himself.

Before the Tour ended in Paris, 44 riders were lost along the way. Some too sick to continue, others too tired, others crashing out, a few eliminated because they couldn't cross the mountains quickly enough. Lance Armstrong left the race voluntarily. His departure reflected the modern view that young, talented riders should not be pushed too far.

He made his departure on the morning of the 14th day, the same day that Miguel Indurain celebrated his 29th birthday. Next day the newspapers showed Indurain, clad in the yellow jersey, sitting before a hefty birthday cake. About Armstrong's exit, there was one short paragraph. It said his leaving of the race conformed with Motorola's original intentions: he had come to learn and to leave before the lessons grew too painful.

From the team's point of view, the decision to select Armstrong was fully vindicated. His victory on the Verdun stage was Motorola's greatest success and it played a part in the reversal of the sponsor's decision to discontinue its involvement. Before the Tour it was accepted Motorola would not continue their sponsorship beyond 1993. Midway through the Tour it was announced the sponsor had reversed that decision.

Motorola's change was influenced by the team's performance, which was outstanding; Alvaro Mejia finished fourth overall and Andy Hampsten eighth. It was the only team to place two riders in the top eight. There was also Armstrong's stage win and he offered great hope for the immediate future.

Lance Armstrong left the race with an understanding of what it was about. The day after his stage victory at Verdun he competed in the long individual time trial at Lake Madine. Considered the first great *rendezvous* of the race, this 59km-test showed Armstrong what it was like when the favourites stretched themselves. Before this race, he reckoned he could time trial well.

Hard as he tried, he finished only 27th, conceding six minutes to Indurain. He was staggered by the margin of his loss. Armstrong then rode the two Alpine stages before abandoning his first Tour. Through the Alps he rode solidly, that is he pushed himself hard without ever going into what an old pro once called 'the red zone'. On the first mountain stage he finished 21 minutes behind Rominger and Indurain, on the second day he was 28 minutes behind the same two riders.

The two Alpine stages showed him how punishing the race could be. At the end of the first day to Serre Chevalier, he had ridden for six hours over three mountain passes. Nothing extraordinary about the bare statistics but, at the end, he was extraordinarily tired. Back at his hotel, he went through the recovery rituals: shower, massage, food and sleep. Next morning he felt no better. What was lost had not been replaced.

On the second day in the Alps the Tour raced over the Col de la Bonette-Restefond which, at 2802 m, is the highest mountain pass in Europe. He hurt more than he had the previous day. At the end, he felt more wasted than ever and he knew he should stop. That evening he spoke with Ochowicz, Hennie Kuiper and Dr Testa. All agreed he should pack up and head for his European home in Como, Italy.

But even then Armstrong landed on his feet. Friends of his from Texas, JT and Frances Neal, were following the race through the Alps and they offered to drive him down to Como. And so a lonely exit was cushioned by the company of friends. Three weeks would pass before his body recovered from the Tour.

The two days in the mountains completed the neophyte's education. There were things he could do in the Tour de France, things that maybe he couldn't do. His deficit in the time trial worried him for it suggested he might never win cycling's greatest race.

'The time trial, it's the biggest thing on my mind. I know I gotta learn how to do it. At the same time I know I can do it. I lost six minutes. I mean it's as plain as day, I know exactly where I am. I went all out, Indurain went all out. I'm six minutes down. But he's the greatest time-triallist there's ever been. Hinault never killed people, never killed the competition like he does. So maybe it's not rational to compare yourself to him.'

But Lance does just that.

'If I can get a minute a year, a minute a year isn't that much. I'm 21, he's 29. When you're 30 you're not gonna be nine minutes faster than your are at 21 but maybe in three years I will be three minutes faster. Then you are dealing with something manageable.'

And suddenly Lance is flowing again. Looking to the next Tour and visualizing good times. Considering Indurain and seeing him as beatable. You want to say hold on son, it isn't this simple but you know that against his enthusiasm, your reason counts for nothing.

Blaise Pascal once said it: 'The heart hath reason that the Reason never heard of.'

2

1

THE PATRON'S TALE
Shades of Disguise
BERNARD HINAULT

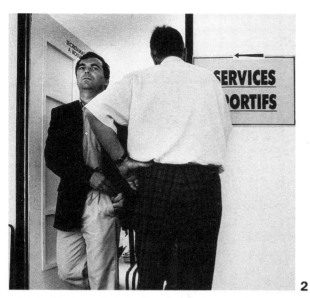

1. Bernard Hinault
2. As a racer, Hinault left the Tour through *la grande porte*. He returned as one might have expected, through the same door
3. Relentlessly affable in his PR role for the Tour, Hinault hoped this would not be mistaken for softness

He is listed in the literature of the Société du Tour de France as a *conseiller technique*. Technical advisor? It is hard to imagine him as that, this old champion. With him it was instinct and passion and pride. He was a Breton and that was used to explain his way. And if he was loved it was for his strong character, his insatiable need to be the boss.

Now he is on the Tour to provide technical advice. Champions age, times change: Bernard Hinault in sunglasses, green blazer, green tie, light green shirt and beige slacks doesn't quite bring *le blaireau* (the badger) to mind.

They called him that when he raced and he liked it. For the name suggested combativity; a quality he admired in himself. He won the Tour de France five times, the Giro d'Italia three times, the Vuelta a España twice, the world pro championship and most of the one-day classics at least once. But the wins tell only part of Hinault's story.

Which is to say that he wasn't just the best rider of his era (1975–86): it was he who gave the era its character and, now, it is common to hear Hinault remembered as the sport's last great *patron* (leader). He spoke for his fellow riders and, on race days, he laid down the unwritten rules. If it was okay by Hinault, it was okay by them. Because of his aggressive and sometimes superior manner, he got more respect than affection.

They tell enthusiastically of a Tour morning when Hinault decided there would be no serious racing. This was appreciated, for most of his rivals were more exhausted than he.

Joel Pelier, an inexperienced French racer, felt strong that day and defied Hinault by breaking away. Everybody waited to see what Hinault would do, expecting he would order his team-mates to pursue and recapture him. But he was going to make an example of Pelier. He accelerated clear of the pack and in minutes was alongside the breakaway, scolding him as a master might an errant pupil. Humiliated, Pelier slowed and Hinault's order was restored.

This was one demonstration of his style but Hinault's presence meant more than the imposition of authority. He could be sensitive and compassionate, as he was at the moment his team-mate Christian Jourdan abandoned the 1984 Tour. Aware he would be leaving his leader with one less *équipier*, Jourdan was distressed. Hinault heard of his team-mate's upset, went to the back of the *peloton* and comforted him. Knowing Hinault understood was all Jourdan needed.

Then there was the hardness so emphatically displayed in the 1980 Liége–Bastogne–Liége classic. An icy wind froze the racers that afternoon in the Ardennes: it rained, it snowed and it was so cold the riders could not bear to continue in their wet clothing. So they received dry replacements from their team cars, only to have to repeat the exercise again and again.

One hundred and seventy started, 20 finished. Hinault wanted to stop but once he thought he could win, he had to continue. His hands suffered the most, especially the right one where he lost the feeling in two fingers. It was three weeks before he regained it. Hinault won the race by nine and a half minutes, not so much out-riding his rivals as overwhelming them.

Bernard Hinault stopped racing in 1986 and every year since he has come back as part of the organization. Jobs for ex-pros have long been part of the Tour's official policy. You see them every year; driving a publicity vehicle, chauffeuring a sponsor, erecting signs. Often the job reflects the old pro's achievements as a racer and, in Hinault's case, this is certainly true. He travels at the head of the race and each night after the stage has an office with his name on the door.

He says he came back to help today's riders and to share the pleasure he had as a racer with those he meets on the Tour. He has had limited success with the former, outstanding success with the latter.

It is true the Tour no longer has its freak show quality where riders were dragged out of bed at five or half-past five to perform twice in one day so that one extra town could be squeezed onto the itinerary. They now get the sleep they need and Hinault helped bring this about. Sleep, he says, is the most important thing.

But he has not been able to right every wrong. As a rider he complained about the chaos at the end of a stage when journalists literally did not give the racers space to breathe. This hasn't changed since Hinault's retirement but his attitude has. 'The riders must understand what puts the bread on their table.'

In his PR role, he is surprisingly effective. Partly because he likes talking and partly because he is a professional. He takes a sponsor in his car one day, a politician the next, then a celebrity and explains the race as it happens. Sponsors, he says, are the people with money and the Tour needs them.

It also needs good publicity and a good image. Hinault projects both. Accessible, courteous and never short on opinions. Each evening he speaks from the press room to a reporter at *L'Equipe* responding to readers' questions. Next day his replies make one column of the newspaper's coverage of the race. Jacques Anquetil, another five-times winner of the Tour, did this column up to his death in 1987 and Hinault maintains the tradition of the past master commentating on the modern race.

An intelligent and witty man, Anquetil was once asked if he agreed that women's desire to ride racing bikes could stem from the pleasant sensations caused by the friction of their bodies on the saddle. Anquetil replied there might be something in this, for he had experienced it once or twice himself.

Not the kind of question that a *L'Equipe* reader would dare put to Hinault. For him, cycling is serious sport and there is only one way to race, aggressively. He rode to win, everybody must. But few racers are blessed with Hinault's talent and it is easy to imagine today's generation of racers turning a deaf ear to his advice.

Early in the race Roger Tubaut, a *L'Equipe* reader from Paris, wondered what was to be become of the poor French riders who had not won the Tour since Hinault did in 1985. Accepting that no French rider was good enough, Hinault said they must attack every day and try to win stages.

Pierre Richard asked what the French-based Gan team should do without its injured and out-of-form leader, Greg LeMond. Hinault said the absence of the leader freed the others to attack, to pursue their own ambitions: they should see the loss of their leader as an opportunity. For that was his way: adversity merely added to the challenge.

On the day the Tour ended another *L'Equipe* reader, Daniel Gay, suggested to Hinault that he should become the *directeur sportif* of a French team.

'No,' said Hinault, 'I have chosen another way of life [business] and I have no wish to change. I am also convinced I would demand too much of the riders, that I would make their life hell.' Those who rode with Hinault, who knew the power of what his team-mate Bernard Vallet once called 'his destructive rage', would agree.

It is hard to reconcile the old Hinault, *le blaireau*, with the smooth PR man. But the old champion has changed, not just in the lengthening of his forehead but in the softening of his expression. He smiles more now even if the expression is a mixture of warmth and hardness, a fighter's smile. More indicative of the change is his relentless affability. When he raced, his body-language intimidated and invisible guard dogs frightened people away. They have disappeared.

The change, he says, is natural. Without the worry of competition it is easier to be *plus* cool. It bothers him that people might mistake the affability for softness. 'I still have the old hunger to succeed, not in racing but in business now. We launched our company (suppliers to the confectionery industry) in May last year and today we are number one in Brittany. I think you are born to win and when you have that in the blood . . . .'

Mornings or evenings, cloudy days or sunny; Hinault wears sunglasses. They kill the glare and protect him from the public. He can mingle and joke and chat and touch but, behind the shades, he keeps something back.

It is the morning of the race from Tarbes to Pau; he moves through the crowd performing as he has for the previous two weeks. If he is tired of the performance, it doesn't show.

Not far away another celebrity mixes with mortals. Alain Prost, the Formula One champion, walks like the Pied Piper except that the children who follow carry cameras. It is inevitable that Prost and Hinault cross paths and 15 minutes before the start, they do.

Hinault sees it coming and a couple of seconds before the moment of contact he takes off his sunglasses and puts them into his jacket. It is as if he is saying that amongst champions, there are no barriers and he has no wish to hide anything from Prost. For the photographers it is a shot; two French champions together at the Tour de France. They pose enthusiastically and Hinault is obviously pleased to meet Prost. While they speak, he is smiling, warm and charming.

Prost is friendly if not as animated by the meeting as Hinault. He is the current champion; Hinault, the former champion. Soon the motor racer is called from another direction and is gone. Hinault reaches into his inside pocket and retrieves his shades.

With them back in place, he too moves on.

Bernard Hinault shows so much, no more. An open book, yes, but one that has been carefully edited. He is comfortable telling that his two sons prefer motocross and tennis to cycling but when asked if his retirement allowed him more time at home he is slightly less so. 'I am so busy with my business interests that I feel I am away as often as before.'

He collaborated with Paul Rembert in 1988 to write the story of his life, *Le Peloton des souvenirs*. It is a work devoted to his career and one which studiously avoids his personal life. With one notable exception.

Sitting starkly between his abandonment (through injury) of the 1980 Tour and his world championship victory later that season is an account of two strange visitors to his Quessoy home in Brittany. First he tells of a young Dutch woman who came to his door.

As she spoke a little English, Martine Hinault tried to figure out what she was saying but could not fully understand. Eventually Martine left to put clothes in the washing machine. Her husband takes up the story.

'The Dutch woman suddenly told me she wanted to make love with me. Just like that, bluntly, she told me that's what she wanted. I immediately called Martine to tell her. The girl was annoyed at my frankness and started swearing at me in Dutch. I don't speak Dutch, but I have cycled with Dutch cyclists enough to understand what she was saying to me. Without further ado I kicked her out. She rang the doorbell again to ask us how to get back to Holland without going through Paris. She left just as she had arrived: on foot and carrying nothing but a plastic bag.'

Hinault's second visitor was less easily dismissed. He was sitting outside the family's front door as they arrived home late one evening. The man waited until they were inside before ringing the doorbell, he wanted to talk with Hinault. As it was eleven o'clock at night, Hinault suggested it would be better to wait until morning.

At six o'clock next morning little Mickael Hinault noticed the stranger and his bag at the front door. However, when his dad got up, only the bag remained. Some time later Hinault saw the stranger at the bottom of the field adjoining the house. He was well-dressed; shirt, tie, blazer and neatly cut hair. Before Hinault could say anything, he told him 'I have a gun, I want to kill myself.'

'Are you mad or what?' asked Hinault. 'Do you have a bullet in it, is it loaded?'

'No, no.'

'What kind of gun is it?'

'A point-22 long rifle.'

'You're kidding. You won't kill yourself with that. If you put it to your head you're only going to wound yourself, that's all you're going to do.'

When the stranger opened the case, Hinault noticed two boxes of bullets.

'Why do you want to kill yourself?' he asked.

'Because I am fed up with life, what else can I do?'

Hinault talked with him, found out he was from Paris and had spent some time in hospital. Not knowing what to do, Hinault persuaded him to leave the gun behind. This he did. He left, like the Dutch woman, on foot. That afternoon Martine saw him in the town but then they never saw him again. Hinault wondered if he could have done more.

'Maybe it would have been enough to find him a job so that he could snap out of his melancholy. When you're a cyclist, always going somewhere, up mountains and valleys, you don't have much time to look after others. You're caught up in a whirlwind and to try and save people who are adrift like that, you have to have time.'

Without the amorous Dutch woman and the suicidal Parisien, readers of *Le Peloton des souvenirs* would never have been taken inside *chez* Hinault.

Amongst their peers, great sportsmen are not remembered for their results. It is their style which distinguishes them. Hinault's was belligerently confident but there was also leadership, and loyalty to his fellow professionals.

The latter quality was apparent from his first Tour in 1978 and the discontent which produced a riders' strike. The riders had good reason: they arrived at the summit of Saint-Lary-Soulan in the Pyrenees at five o'clock in the afternoon, took a cable car from the mountain down to the town of Soulan and only then began the drive to hotels in Tarbes.

Because of traffic congestion some did not reach their hotels until eleven at night. After eating and massage, they got to bed around one o'clock which, if they went to sleep immediately, meant they had four hours' rest before breakfast call at five. The following day's race was broken into two legs; a morning race from Tarbes to Valence d'Agen (84 km) and an afternoon stage from Valence d'Agen to Toulouse (96 km).

Not the kind of day to be tackled on four hours, sleep – the *peloton* was in rebellious mood. During the morning stage, riders pretended to sleep under trees, faked crashes and did everything except race. Almost two hours late into Valence they dismounted their bikes 100 yards from the finish and walked across the line.

Somebody had to lead the rebels. Hinault might have been just 23 and in his first Tour but he was French champion and, even then, the star. He stood in the front line of strikers and when Valence's deputy mayor Monsieur Baylet vented his anger, it was Hinault who replied.

He wanted to explain why they protested but M. Baylet wouldn't listen. 'Mr Mayor,' raged Hinault, 'when somebody speaks to you, you should close your mouth until he has spoken, then you can reply.' That was Monsieur Hinault.

Bernard Vallet tells of one moment which epitomized Hinault's style. It was on an August afternoon in 1980 when Hinault won the world championship at Sallanches in the Alps. As the French team left the hotel Hinault said '*A la guerre comme à la guerre, ce soir on a le maillot.*' (Come on, we'll make the best of things, this evening we will have the jersey.)

Like everybody else in that team, Vallet's role was to help Hinault. When he had given as much as he could, Vallet dropped out. Before stopping he wished Hinault good luck but was simply told 'Go back to the hotel and put the champagne on ice.' That evening they toasted Hinault, the new world champion.

Then there was the 1985 Tour and Steve Bauer's wonder at the same aggressive self-belief. On the morning of the long individual time trial from Sarrebourg to Strasbourg he and Hinault loosened their legs on a training ride over the course. On a longish hill, over halfway along the route, Hinault told Bauer this was where he would overtake Kelly (Sean Kelly, the Irish rider who would start two minutes before him). And he did.

Hinault retired from racing on the day of his 32nd birthday. Years previously he decided this was the day to stop and there was no suggestion he would do otherwise. It mattered not a whit to him that, at 32, he was still the best and cycling's salary explosion had just happened.

'I looked at Eddy Merckx and Jacques Anquetil, I saw the way they had finished their last two seasons and it wasn't very good. I decided it was better to stop before [the decline], to get out at the summit. Also, to re-enter normal life you need a lot of spirit, you need to want to win again, to transform the energy and vitality you had on the bike into normal living, you cannot afford to be physically or mentally tired.'

It is in a sports hall at Vannes, converted for the Tour into a press room, that Hinault sits to talk. To get to his seat a four-foot railing has to be scaled. He quickens his step as he approaches it, places his right hand on the upper bar and bounds clean over the barrier.

He looks in good shape. Thirty-eight years old and there is no trace of middle age, no obvious concession to six years of retirement. After stopping he cut down on his food, especially the carbo-hydrates, and took up motocross and jogging. He will jog every morning on the Tour. The energy and vitality he brought to racing *is* being transformed into normal living.

He talks about his business interests in Brittany and his ambition to do as well in this as he did in his sporting career. The same old Hinault?

'Oh yes,' he says. 'If I was to take out the bike, I'd be fighting again.'

He expects it now: the preoccupation with his last Tour, 1986. He won in '78, '79, '81, '82 and '85 and is constantly asked about '86 when he finished second to his team-mate Greg LeMond. This replaying of '86 doesn't bother him.

'Without wanting to sound big-headed or to shout that I was the strongest . . . if I wanted to win in '86, I would have won in '86, I was still the boss (*c'est moi le patron encore*).'

But *le blaireau* always wanted to win?

'I had given my word to Greg LeMond, I told him he would win because we were in the same team and I had won the year before. I told him he was going to win.'

The ambition to become the only rider in history to win six Tours de France meant nothing?

'I never raced to break records, I raced to enjoy myself.'

So, the hunger to win six, it wasn't there?

'No, but I was pulling the strings, it was a little bit my win as well.'

Hinault's assessment of his performance has not changed since 1986 and he delivers it with the same force now as he did then. Further questioning is discouraged. Yet it is difficult to believe that he was not trying to win that year and if he wasn't trying, somebody should have told LeMond, who almost lost it worrying about Hinault's challenge.

Part of the reason why this race is so constantly resurrected is because it dismantled the barriers and showed a vulnerable Hinault, offering insights into the darker, more interesting corners of his character. It also glorified him in the eyes of his public. They saw him attack recklessly when he felt good and then refuse to give up when beaten.

Neither did the public disapprove when he mercilessly taunted LeMond, for they could empathize with his combativity. What badger easily forsakes his territory? 'This Tour was fantastic, and we owe it all to Hinault,' wrote Anquetil at the time. 'Even if he didn't win, it was his greatest Tour de France.'

The '86 Tour began at the end of the '85 race when Hinault said he would help LeMond win the next. LeMond believed Hinault's pledge as, in '85, he sacrificed his chance to help him win. As they were friends at the time, LeMond had no reason to question Hinault's sincerity.

Doubts about the informal agreement surfaced after the long individual time trial of the '86 Tour. Hinault won it. Did this not indicate he was strongest in the race? The mountains would tell. Hinault attacked with Pedro Delgado early on the first mountain stage and they finished well clear of their rivals. Hinault led the race by over four minutes, and that evening in the Pyrenees, LeMond admitted he was riding for second place.

Hinault's lead was unassailable. He could sit behind his rivals and defend his position, a tactic he had long mastered. But the very next morning, he attacked again. Taking a five-minute lead on the fragmented pack, he stretched his advantage to over nine minutes on LeMond. But then on the final climb to Superbagnères, Hinault ran out of gas.

Overtaken by a group which included LeMond, he lost a further four minutes on the last hill. At the end of the day he barely held onto his yellow jersey. LeMond was very much back in the race.

The most plausible explanation for Hinault's second attack is that he did not believe his four-minute lead was enough: that for all his aggression and assertiveness, he felt he might wilt in the Alps. Why else would he gamble everything in a high-risk attack? *Le blaireau* wished to kill off his prey at a time when everybody believed LeMond was already finished.

Hinault paid for that second Pyrenean attack, as LeMond was stronger in the first Alpine stage and took over the race lead. The rivalry which simmered beneath the surface was apparent to all but, on the next day's stage to Alpe d'Huez, Hinault and LeMond crossed the finish line hand-in-hand. First and second and the rest well behind.

That was it, the battle was over. For when they held hands it seemed Hinault had, at last, passed the torch to his successor. But the next morning he bewildered (and delighted) journalists by announcing the race wasn't over. He had been stronger on the Alpe and would continue to challenge his team-mate until the time trial at Saint-Etienne four days before the end. Vulnerable to Hinault's psychological games, LeMond was reduced to a nervous wreck.

With most of the La Vie Claire team supporting Hinault, LeMond felt betrayed. On the brink of becoming the first American to win the Tour de France, he spent the last week looking over his shoulder. When he crashed in the Saint-Etienne time trial, LeMond didn't dismiss the suggestion (made by a member of his family) that his bike had been sabotaged. Daft as the accusation was, it did show how Hinault had unbalanced his rival.

LeMond made it to Paris in the yellow jersey but the journey was far from comfortable.

Now Hinault says he was never trying to win that Tour. His strategy through the first part of the race and on the two Pyrenean stages was to draw the sting from LeMond's rivals and make it easier for his team-mate to win. His little games over the last week were no more than a ruse to test LeMond, to ensure he was a worthy winner.

He wished merely to pull the strings, to be the race-maker, to leave everybody believing he was still in control.

Steve Bauer rode in the La Vie Claire team that year and watched as the dual developed. He scoffs at the idea that Hinault wasn't trying to win. 'I don't think I could agree with that.' Bauer trained with LeMond and although he wanted his fellow North American to win, that couldn't diminish his admiration for Hinault's performance.

'Bernard enjoyed hurting people, riding them into the ground. As a *patron* he was much more impressive than, say, Indurain. This was because of his character. Within the team he was easy to like, he always wanted to talk and he created a good ambience.'

Why did a man as shrewd as Hinault risk and then lose everything by attacking on the second Pyrenean stage? 'That was his all-or-nothing day. He wins the Tour here or he doesn't. I thought it was a tremendously gutsy move, a lot of teams weren't in good shape and if there is a weakness, Hinault will find it.'

Bauer recalls the last week of that Tour with a mixture of amusement and amazement. While Hinault was telling the world he was stronger than LeMond on Alpe d'Huez, LeMond was privately assuring Bauer he was the stronger. 'Greg said he stayed with Hinault on the Alpe because he feared that, alone in the lead, some French fan would take a swing at him.'

At different times in that Tour Bauer rode for both. Towards the end the in-fighting descended into farce. On the final Alpine stage to Saint-Etienne, LeMond was ahead in a break; behind, Hinault was chasing him, further behind Bauer and Niki Ruttimann were vigorously chasing Hinault. All were members of the La Vie Claire team.

Although Bauer believes Hinault tried to win that Tour, he says he was a man of his word and the assurance he gave to LeMond was one he intended to honour. 'But when it came to it, Hinault could only race one way, that was to win. He was an honourable man, he just committed himself to something he couldn't do.'

LeMond's belief that Hinault betrayed him is difficult to gainsay. But from that Tour Hinault's popularity soared, both within and beyond his native country. People liked the way he attacked and enjoyed his defiance. One TV commentator, began a post-Tour interview with LeMond thus: *'La victoire pour Greg, la gloire pour Bernard?'* and thousands of armchair viewers would have agreed.

Seven years on what is so remarkable is Hinault's insistence that he wasn't trying to win the race. Implausible as this is, he believes it. Why should he mind talking about '86? LeMond won the race 'but that's because I let him, I pulled the strings. *C'est moi le patron encore* (I was still the boss). '

After Hinault retired, LeMond became the star but never filled the void. Indurain came and eased into LeMond's position. He is a leader but not in the style of *le blaireau*, a point which Hinault is quick to make. 'I like him [Indurain] a lot but then I like all the riders. If he lacks anything it is a bit of panache, he needs to put his foot down a bit more, remind people he is the boss.'

He doesn't consider Indurain unbeatable in this Tour, but then he rejects the very notion of invincibility. How can Indurain be beaten? The former champion says if he were riding he would watch Indurain every day to see where he positions himself in the pack. If he's at the back, he would attack; if he looked tired, he would try to exploit that. He would search until he found a weakness.

In this Tour, he says, the challengers need to coalesce. Tony Rominger, Gianni Bugno, Claudio Chiappucci and Alex Zülle must ride in a way that maximizes the chance of beating the champion. Nobody disputes Hinault's judgement but Indurain's rivals take no notice. When the race reaches the mountains, they go their separate ways and the challenge to Indurain comes from just Rominger, who is the worst placed of his rivals.

Next morning the smooth PR man has vanished from his space in *L'Equipe*. In his place *le blaireau* snarls. He had followed the race through the Alps to Serre Chevalier and was contemptuous of the challengers' tactics.

The Once team of Zülle and Breukink helped Indurain's Banesto team to stabilize the race at a time when a breakaway group of 19 threatened destabilization. Then, when the leaders tackled the Col du Telegraphe, Rominger's acceleration hurt everybody except Indurain.

Hinault's anger could not be contained. 'Indurain is not unbeatable but he needn't worry if people continue to ride as they did yesterday. Everybody facilitated him. I couldn't understand Once's decision to ride in the [Maurienne] Valley, they didn't have anything to defend. The Amaya team was no better. Then there was Rominger, who did exactly the wrong thing. Indurain was on holidays yesterday.

'He was the boss but it was easy, given the attitude of the others. I don't understand their behaviour. Indurain rode at his own tempo without anyone attacking him. His principal rivals must use other means of finding out if he is really the boss.'

There was much truth in Hinault's analysis. Neil Stephens, an *équipier* with Once, was one of those involved in the pursuit of the breakaways in the Maurienne Valley and he wondered what his team was thinking. It is also true that Rominger's aim on the climbs of the Telegraphe and Galibier had been to remove the obstacles which blocked his route to the podium. He got rid of Bugno, Chiappucci, Zülle and Stephen Roche. It would have been good to distance Indurain as well but Rominger did not believe that to be possible.

As for the failure of French riders, Hinault offered a straightforward explanation. 'They are too well paid for the results they get. The system must be changed so that they are paid on performance – when you win, you get well paid – then we'll see some results.'

But it was Indurain's easy ride which most bothered Hinault. Maybe his sensitivity to the mistakes of the challengers was understandable. For years he had been in Indurain's position, casting a shadow which intimidated, subtly encouraging his rivals to believe they were racing for second place and then watching as they unwittingly submitted.

It troubled Hinault to see his successor grow and dominate in the way he had dominated. Like he had watched somebody leave the tracks he had left, only fresher and more visible.

On the morning of the seventh stage, he is at the start in Peronne. Sifting through the early risers at the tented village; he stops to chat with journalists and signs an autograph for a man who says it's for his little boy. Smiling as he writes, he enjoys the man's compliments, likes the recognition. It is clear he enjoys his work on the Tour.

For a moment he is on his own. No autographs, nobody asking about Indurain's form, no old fogey wanting to reminisce about the '78 Tour. And Hinault is uncomfortable. His eyes scan the crowd for a familiar face but there is nobody.

Why doesn't he just walk the 10 yards, sit at one of the tables, pick up a newspaper and immerse himself? That's what others do in the same circumstances.

But Hinault needs to find someone. His eyes continue the search, eventually he turns and right behind there is a young woman sweeping paper coffee cups off a table. He walks over to her, puts his arm around her, showers her with smiles and asks if all goes well.

It is half past ten in the morning. The woman doesn't know to what she owes this warm greeting but doesn't complain. It is not every day she gets to rub shoulders with a legend. But then it is not every day on the Tour de France that Bernard Hinault is lost for company.

THE SPRINTER'S TALE
The Morale of the Story

JEAN-PAUL VAN POPPEL

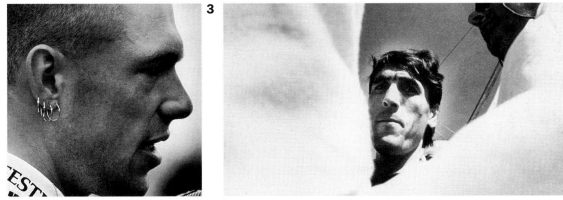

1. Jean-Paul Van Poppel
2. At the end of the day the journalist asks the question and the answer is in Jean-Paul Van Poppel's expression
3. The shaven hair and earrings distinguished Gert Jakobs, as did his loyalty to team-mate Jean-Paul Van Poppel
4. Djamolidin Abdujaparov was the best sprinter on the 1993 Tour, respected if not liked by Jean-Paul Van Poppel

Gert Jakobs worried about his friend. Jean-Paul wasn't himself, the team hadn't done enough for him, his morale was low. And in the Tour de France it is hard to get anywhere without good morale. It boosts the spirit, cajoles it into ignoring the demands of a tortured body. Without morale, the Tour is impossible.

He and Jean-Paul had been friends for 10 years; together as teenagers on Dutch amateur teams and then as pros for SuperConfex, PDM and now Festina. Within the team, they are a partnership; two Dutchmen who sit together at the table, share rooms and jokes and are loyal to each other.

Within the race they remain a team, for Jakobs is Jean-Paul Van Poppel's *fidèle équipier*. His devotion is both personal and professional; his job is to mind Jean-Paul and so he is paid to help one of his close friends. He takes satisfaction from Jean-Paul's successful career, knowing he has helped shape it.

Jean-Paul Van Poppel's strength is finishing speed and it has made him one of the best sprinters of his generation. Jakobs admires his friend's attitude, recognizes 'a winner's mentality' and even enjoys the furious silence in the hotel room on the evenings after Jean-Paul has lost. Like a latter day Sancho Panza, not speaking until his master's rage has passed.

Jakobs guides Jean-Paul through a race, shelters him from the wind, tells him it'll get better when it's bad, gives him a wheel when he punctures but, for Jakobs, the race ends at the 500-metre sign. He takes Jean-Paul to that mark but in the heaving, reckless surge of the final sprint, his friend is on his own.

They are equal in the mountains. Every time the road rises they both think only of survival. In the Tour de France it is not easy; without fight, it is impossible. And that's it: Jakobs thinks the fight has been knocked out of his friend in this Tour. No morale.

It angers him because Jean-Paul is good and, given support, he can win flat stages. Since his first Tour in 1987 Jean-Paul had won eight stages, all in mass sprints. But Bruno Roussel, Festina's *directeur sportif*, decided the team should concentrate on his French riders Pascal Lino and Richard Virenque and their pursuit of the yellow jersey. Gert Jakobs doesn't think either is good enough and, within the team, his opinion is no secret.

Jean-Paul Van Poppel agrees with his friend but it is not his way to strike the board and damn the boss. His disapproval is expressed in diminished enthusiasm. Or, as the riders themselves say, no morale.

It is the morning of the eleventh day of the race and the first journey through the mountains. Soon after the riders leave Villard-de-Lans Jean-Philippe Dojwa has a problem with his bike. As it is being seen to, Dojwa loses contact with the *peloton*. His Festina team-mates Jean-Paul Van Poppel and Gert Jakobs wait and pace him back to the pack. They usher him into the big group at the foot of the Col du Glandon, the first of the day's three Alpine passes.

Dojwa, a promising climber, immediately moves ahead as Van Poppel and Jakobs settle into a rhythm which will pain them for the following hour. Although close friends they don't always ride the mountains side by side. Sometimes Jakobs finds himself going well in the early part of the climb and he will move ahead, knowing Van Poppel will catch up later.

It is different this morning. Van Poppel starts well enough and it is Jakobs who falls behind. But that changes when Jakobs finds his climbing rhythm and begins to overtake some fellow strugglers. Soon he catches Van Poppel, they ride together for a little bit and even though Jakobs is stronger, he wants his friend to stay with him.

'Come on Poppel, let's go, go, go.'

'No Jakobs, you ride at your tempo.'

Jakobs sees Jelle Nijdam alongside Van Poppel and tries to convince himself his friend will be okay. All three rode together in the SuperConfex team of 1988, Nijdam now rides for the rival WordPerfect team, but in the Alps these cyclists have no rivals except the mountains themselves.

Maybe it is the sight of Nijdam and Van Poppel together but Jakobs thinks back to the time they were at SuperConfex. What a team! Then they weren't permitted to leave Jean-Paul behind and if they did, Jan Raas, the *directeur sportif,* ordered them to wait.

He especially remembers the climb of the Glandon in the '88 Tour, on the way to the summit finish at Alpe d'Huez. It was at the height of SuperConfex's success and Jakobs rode the Glandon with his team-mate Gerrit Solleveld. Although exhausted, he and Solleveld were part of a big group and were confident they would make it to the finish inside the time limit.

About halfway up the 21-kilometre climb, Raas drove alongside and ordered both him and Solleveld to ride back down the mountain to help the weakening Van Poppel. He laughs now even if he was not amused then. 'Jan,' he said to Raas, 'you must be mad, I am dead, totally dead. I can't do it, this is incredible.' Raas repeated the order. 'You have got to do it.'

Never in his career before or since has Jakobs been asked to turn back down a mountain in search of a team-mate. He and Solleveld free-wheeled downhill, hoping to discover Van Poppel around every corner. They rode for almost three kilometres before they found him.

Seeing Van Poppel, Jakobs' annoyance dissipated. They went to either side of him and talked and pushed their team-mate up the mountain. Inspired by their generosity, Van Poppel fought harder and once they reached the summit of the Glandon his speed on the descent and in the valley was important. Alpe d'Huez was hellish but the three helped each other and all were inside the time limit.

Jean-Paul rewarded his team-mates by later winning in Bordeaux and on the Champs Elysées. What Jakobs liked about SuperConfex was the sincerity of the team spirit. They may have grumbled when Raas ordered them back but, once they agreed, they felt good about it. Jean-Paul was their friend and SuperConfex was their team.

But that was a long time ago and Festina is not SuperConfex. Now alone on the Glandon, Jakobs has doubts about his team-mate. Anxious, he asks Thierry Marie, a Festina rider who has come alongside, 'Have you seen Poppel?'

'No, I haven't.'

On some corners of the Glandon Jakobs takes long backwards glances but he cannot pick out Jean-Paul. He knows his friend is having a bad day and hopes that wherever he is, he can get to the finish at Serre Chevalier inside the time limit.

But further down the mountain Jean-Paul Van Poppel is riding the last kilometres of his Tour de

France. He struggles to the summit, losing time with each pedal-stroke and somewhere along the way he decides he will go no further than the feeding station in the valley.

He stops alongside a Festina team car, has his Tour numbers (47) ripped off his jersey by a *commissaire* and is out of the race. He travels back to the hotel in a car driven by Gaby Albelda, a Festina *soigneur*. Not much is said.

It is Van Poppel's third elimination in seven Tours but this is different from the others. He doesn't feel the awful sense of loss experienced in '89 and '91. Then he couldn't bear to be at home while the Tour continued. Now he is strangely indifferent and he cannot fathom it.

From the beginning of the day he feared he wouldn't make it. He told himself he was fine but, inside, he wasn't. Something in his head told him to watch out, to prepare for the worst. Once he makes the decision to quit he is relieved, glad to be going home but he cannot believe he is leaving without tears.

Pressed, Van Poppel attributes much to a crash late in the Tour of Spain which cost him four weeks of preparation. But his easy acceptance of elimination showed his low morale and suggested he was a casualty in a team which was not working. Van Poppel disagrees, he says he was getting along fine with Bruno Roussel and his Festina team-mates.

Gert Jakobs doesn't see it like that. He believes the team broke Jean-Paul's morale and that when he reached the mountains, he didn't have the will to fight.

For all their fearlessness, sprinters are a delicate breed. Each year they come to the Tour to show their speed and in search of the pack sprints which can make their day. At the peak of form they effuse an aura of invincibility, suggesting no bicycle rider ever pedalled as fast.

Mario Cipollini left such an impression at the end of the first stage, gliding through the forest of lurching, swaying bodies to win at Les Sables d'Olonne. 'Super Mario' said the newspaper headlines and the Italian didn't discourage those who hailed him as cycling's champion sprinter.

But that was merely the first sprint. Next day at Vannes Cipollini was beaten by Wilfried Nelissen and Djamolidin Abdujaparov, and at Dinard on the third day he was again beaten by Abdujaparov and Nelissen. Within three days Cipollini's status changed from being the best sprinter to being one of the best.

After winning the mass charge at Dinard, Abdujaparov stated the obvious, 'One day you win, the next day you lose. Nobody can pretend to be the best.'

To win, sprinters must have everything: physical condition, confidence, luck, aggression and committed team support. An elusive combination, attainable but not sustainable.

The Tour's mountain stages cause them particular stress for their bigger bodies weigh them down on the climbs. Of the first six finishers in the pack sprint at Dinard, only Abdujaparov would make it to the Tour finish on the Champs Elysées. The other five would be eliminated in the mountains.

Just as the sprinter's vulnerability is reflected through the course of one race, so too it is mirrored in the roller-coaster route of their careers. Jean-Paul Van Poppel is no different from the rest. He has enjoyed great days and outstanding seasons but these have been outnumbered by the bad days, the miserable seasons.

Born in Tilburg, a Dutch town in the southern province of Brabant, his parents wanted him to become a wholesale supplier to floral shops. He liked cycling and once he discovered he could win sprints, his like became an addiction. The discovery came at 17 when Van Poppel broke away with Hans Baudion, a noted Dutch amateur whom nobody could outsprint. But that day Van Poppel did. From then on, he considered himself a sprinter.

As an amateur international he beat the fastest finishers from eastern Europe, not always but often enough to convince him he should try to be a professional. At the age of 22 he got his chance with the low-budget Scala team. That was 1985 and in his first year he beat some of the best of that era; Sean Kelly, Eddy Planckaert, Paolo Rosola, Eric Vanderaerden, Jef Lieckens and Guido Bontempi. Mostly they were sprints for second, third or fourth place but that didn't matter to Van Poppel.

Neither was it important that he did best in the smaller, less demanding races where his lack of strength wasn't a factor. For the sprinter, speed is the thing. Jean-Paul Van Poppel had it.

Scala merged with Skil in his second pro year, bringing experienced riders Hennie Kuiper and Ferdi Van den Haute into the team. Van Poppel immediately took to Kuiper. They shared rooms and Kuiper tried to school the young sprinter in the ways of the *peloton*. Part of the secret, Kuiper told his pupil, was to be discreet, to blow softly on the trumpet.

'In the room I had such a big mouth. I told Kuiper "I can beat these guys, in the sprint I can do it." He would have a look on his face, "What's this guy talking about?" Then when I won my first big race, a stage in Tirreno–Adriatico, what I remember is Kuiper's surprise. "You have a big mouth," he said, "but you really can sprint."'

Jan Raas offered a place on the SuperConfex team for 1987 and Van Poppel moved to the front line of world cycling. Raas was a part of the success. He sensed Van Poppel's gentle nature and didn't pressurize. Before races the *directeur sportif* didn't make any demands and Van Poppel never felt the team depended upon him.

Thirty or 40 kilometres from the finish of the Troyes stage in the 1987 Tour, Raas told his team to gather at the front and control the race to the end. Van Poppel knew this was for him but, through the final pulsating hour, there wasn't time to worry. He attacked into the final corner, believing there were 200 metres to go. When he looked up, the sign said 350m. He hesitated and his momentary confusion was heightened by the sight of Guido Bontempi flying by.

Realizing his rival had bolted, Van Poppel didn't bother closing the stable door and Jorge Dominguez sprinted past to claim second place. What did it matter, second or third? A lot as it turned out: Bontempi failed to pass the drugs' test and the stage was awarded to the Spaniard.

That evening Van Poppel's wife Leontine was at the team hotel and, furious at himself for losing, he could hardly speak with her. Later in the room he lashed out at the door. At breakfast next morning Raas smiled knowingly.

'I think you understand what happened yesterday,' he said. Later that day the Tour got within 40 kilometres of the finish at Epinay-sous-Senart and Raas again asked the team to control the race for its young sprinter. This time there were no mistakes. Van Poppel won his first stage of the Tour de France.

Catapulted onto the winner's podium, he was dazzled by the attention. 'They pick you up after the finish, take you to television, take you to the radio and they make you crazy. You think what is this? I have just won a race. I didn't say very much and when I look back on the interviews I did then, I see the boy from Brabant, the one who was going to be a farmer or a bike rider. That was what television did, it was not me. I came from a big town in Brabant.'

By now Van Poppel was 23 and exceptionally fast. Further on in the '87 Tour he won his second stage, beating Bontempi at Avignon. For those who saw the dual, it was more than just another sprint victory. Stephen Roche's acceleration through the last two kilometres burned off most of the challengers and created the opening for his team-mate Bontempi who surged with 250 metres to go. It was hard to see anyone overtake him.

But Van Poppel was prepared and he went with the Italian. They raced shoulder to shoulder for 200 metres, neither able to shake off the other, but right at the line Van Poppel inched past his rival. 'It was a beautiful sprint but I was so fucked, I didn't care who won. It was so close, I was lucky. On the podium they were giving me the keys of a Peugeot car which went to every stage winner and suddenly I saw my parents in the crowd.

'That was a nice moment, better than all the crazy stuff. I did not expect to see them and they were happier than I was. My father just about knows the way out of Holland but he came to Avignon.'

Van Poppel's two stage wins helped him take the sprinter's green jersey and left him with a memorable first Tour. His second year with Raas was even better: he won four stages of the Tour de France. At 24 he was fastest in the *peloton* and looked certain to dominate his rivals for the following three or four seasons.

But the sprinter works with fine margins.

Van Poppel changed teams at the end of 1988, leaving SuperConfex for Panasonic, a team managed by Raas' former mentor and then bitter rival Peter Post. Such was the ill-feeling between Post and Raas that one could not bear to see the other win. In forsaking one for the other, Van Poppel created difficulties for himself which would not be easily overcome.

Raas resented him for joining Post's team and planned his tactics to stop his former star winning. This was especially obvious through the first 12 days of the 1989 Tour de France when Raas' team attacked and attacked again, leaving the race without one bunch sprint and Van Poppel without opportunity. He won sprints for third and fourth but they didn't mean a thing.

On the thirteenth day the riders crossed four Pyrenean passes; the Tourmalet, Aspin, Peyresourde and Superbagnères. It was a relatively short mountain stage which, for the non-climbers, was especially dangerous. As the mountains came in rapid succession, those left behind on the first had no opportunity to recover. On such days the race to beat the time limit can be the most difficult race of all. From early in the stage Van Poppel knew it would be a struggle.

He rode through the mountains as fast as he could. On the descents, desperation destroyed his caution. He flew into blind corners and shivered with fear as he suddenly came upon a slick wet road. He was part of a 10 or 12-rider group, travelling at 100km-per-hour. They went quiet, closed their eyes and hoped.

On the final climb of Superbagnères, Van Poppel couldn't stay with the group. One by one the stragglers caught and passed him. It was over. At the finish he was almost 30 minutes behind the day's winner Robert Millar and one second outside the time limit.

Van Poppel had been hampered by official cars on the ascent of Superbagnères and his Panasonic team appealed to have him reinstated. The appeal jury accepted he lost time because of the cars and allowed him two minutes but then they penalized him two minutes, three seconds for taking pushes from the public (three seconds for each of 41 pushes).

Riders are not permitted to accept help from bystanders but it is a tough rule which puts the onus on the exhausted rider to ensure it doesn't happen. Imagine the dilemma for the man utterly without strength: does he fight the good samaritans or does he accept the momentary relief?

Van Poppel may have taken more pain relief than was prudent but the greater mistake was to appeal his elimination. Nothing makes the autocrat bristle as much as someone contesting his judgement and the Tour organization looks harshly on appeals. Before lodging his, Van Poppel's exit from the race was gallant and tantalizing. He had failed by just one second to save himself. At the appeal it was ruled that he had, in effect, been propelled upwards by masses of helping hands. Not quite so gallant.

As the first important failure of his professional career, the exit from the '89 Tour tested Van Poppel's mental strength. He tried to be philosophical, focusing on how lucky he had been through his first three seasons and reminding himself that professional athletes needed their downs. More experience of the latter came in 1990, his second year with Panasonic when he just couldn't win at the Tour.

He was third, fifth, sixth and seventh but through the entire Tour he did not once sprint well. The view at the time was that fatherhood diluted his aggression; he and Leontine had produced their first child, a boy. His own view is that he succumbed to pressure.

'I was nervous because it was the first time I got big money and I felt people were saying, "There's the money, you have to win to earn this." I was convinced I could do it in my first year at Panasonic but things went wrong in the Tour and that meant I had to win in my second year. Every race I told myself, "You have to win, you have to win, you have to win." In this state, you make mistakes.

'It began to eat me. A stupid thing for a rider to allow but it happened. You have to sprint on feeling, not on thinking. You must have faith in yourself but you cannot think about it too much. In the 1990 Tour my legs were the same as before but I couldn't win.'

Towards the end of 1990 the crisis in Van Poppel's professional life deepened. He was promised a two-year extension to his contract by Panasonic but, close to the eleventh hour, they told him he would have to look elsewhere. After two disappointing years, Van Poppel was not top of anybody's list.

Angered by Post's refusal to honour what he believed were verbal assurances, Van Poppel sued his former employers. He went to court and lost. Before the judge he learned the law demanded proof, he could give only his word. He also found that people were reluctant to speak against Post. 'Nobody would say anything, they needed him more than they needed me.'

He was foolish to take on the might of Post and an international corporation. Brilliant at 24 and washed up at 26, Van Poppel crawled to PDM's door and asked for a job. They agreed to take him on, offering a paltry salary but the promise of good bonuses if he won. He was grateful. Post's sacking of him and the unsuccessful law suit left serious questions. PDM gave him the opportunity to reply.

The Vuelta a España was his first serious race of 1991 and he pleased his new team by winning four stages. His renaissance continued on the Tour de France where he won at Argentan. That was in the first week of the race. Four days later he and the entire PDM team were on their way home. As mass exits go, this was the most extraordinary in the history of the Tour de France.

There are no Monday mornings in the Tour, no knocking off on Friday evening and no leisurely Saturdays. On Sunday evening, 14 July, 1991, the Tour set up camp in Rennes; nine days of the race behind them, 14 to go. PDM's nine riders lodged at the Hotel du Cheval d'Or and Jean-Paul Van Poppel had the single room.

Two Dutchmen Erik Breukink and Jos Van Aert always shared, as did the two Irish riders Sean Kelly and Martin Earley and the Germans Falk Boden and Uwe Raab. That left the Dutch rider Nico Verhoeven, Raul Alcala from Mexico and Van Poppel. He preferred not to share with his compatriot Verhoeven. That left Alcala. He liked Alcala but considered him strange. Throughout the Tour Van Poppel got the single room.

It suited him this Sunday evening because his parents Cor and Clazien turned up unexpectedly at the Cheval d'Or and he invited them to his room. He dried himself, changed into shorts and top and put off taking a shower until his parents went.

After they left, PDM's Dr Wim Sanders came to his room to give him an injection. Within professional teams this is not unusual as it is accepted that vitamins and minerals used during the Tour need to be replaced through regular supplements.

In his first year in the *peloton* Van Poppel hated the needles and insisted upon taking his supplements orally; vitamin and iron tablets, glucose drinks. This satisfied his conscience but upset his digestive system. Delicate stomachs run in his family and his couldn't handle the normal load, not to speak of the cyclist's needs. Eventually he agreed with the doctors that he would be better off taking his supplements intravenously. He was surprised at how quickly he got used to the injections.

Van Poppel knows that once a rider admits to taking injections, he leaves himself open to the accusation of drug-taking. For cyclists' age-old desire to hitch their systems to an outside motor has created perceptions which are hard to change and the picture of a rider being injected leads to one conclusion: doping. It is a mistaken view, out of touch with the realities of modern sport but, for the armchair enthusiast, nothing good comes through the tip of a needle.

Van Poppel is against doping and does not take banned substances. In his nine professional seasons he has been drug-tested countless times and passed every examination. One positive test, he says, would cast a shadow over all the wins, all the good times, and he is determined there won't be one.

That is not to say he disagrees with Jacques Anquetil's oft-remembered line that 'nobody rides the Tour de France on mineral water.'

'Our bodies are like a car,' says Van Poppel, 'when you drive a lot and drive very fast, you need more oil than a normal car. A man riding the Tour needs more vitamins than a normal person, he also needs more iron. I think you can ride the Tour de France without vitamin and iron supplements but I don't know for how long.'

 Dr Sanders came and went quickly. The injection took less than a minute. Van Poppel hadn't encountered Dr Sanders before the Tour but he thought him less organized than other doctors. Once or twice while in the doctor's bedroom he noticed his open and untidy suitcase.

But riders must trust the doctor and his presence does ensure the medical treatment is supervised and administered by a professional. That Sunday evening Van Poppel did not know what substance Dr Sanders plunged into his blood system. As long as it helped and didn't produce a positive drugs test, he didn't mind.

A half an hour after the injection Jean-Paul telephoned his wife Leontine, telling her he didn't feel well. He then decided to take his shower but, standing up, felt wobbly. He lay down, waiting for whatever it was to pass. But it wouldn't go away. He abandoned the shower.

Soon a PDM *soigneur* came to the room. Van Poppel asked him to fetch the doctor. When Dr Sanders came Jean-Paul found it difficult to explain the symptoms. His stomach was fine, his temperature was normal, he felt strange rather than sick but so weak that when he left his bed he could hardly stand. His neck muscles could not support his head which drooped towards his chest; his shoulders and back ached.

He took some paracetamol and, feeling slightly better, joined the rest of the team at the evening meal. Food was the furthest thing from his mind and he returned to his bedroom without eating. Wondering what brought on this strange illness, he considered for a second whether it could be related to Dr Sanders' injection but put the idea out of his head. Doctors are supposed to make you feel better.

Once back in bed Van Poppel began to shake violently, like a man with a raging fever. Taking some more paracetamol, he again improved a little but was far from well. He flitted in and out of sleep, awaking at 4.30 to go to the toilet. In the morning the fever was gone and he got up for breakfast.

Maybe he should have stayed where he was but in the Tour de France there is no wife to coax her off-colour partner to lie in, no mother to order that the patient stay put. Van Poppel changed into his cycling gear, packed his belongings and tried not to think of the 202-kilometre race to Quimper in Brittany.

At breakfast he was relieved to hear that every member of the team felt unwell. It wasn't just him. Verhoeven was so sick he could not leave his bed, Raab got to the start but once there realized he couldn't even try to race. He returned to the hotel. Two down, seven to go.

As the *peloton* moved sedately out of Rennes, Van Poppel was able to hang on for an hour. But there was no strength in his legs and he continued to feel strangely unwell. An attack by the Belgian Hendrick Redant after 37 kilometres caused an acceleration which Van Poppel could not go with. He lost his place in the pack, finding himself adrift with his team-mate Earley.

For a while he carried on, in the way that a gazelle struck by a tranquillizing dart fights against inevitable collapse. 'Don't fall, don't stop.' But there was no point and he let Earley go on. Dismounting, someone came to comfort him but all he could say was, 'Please, let me go home.'

Not long afterwards, Earley abandoned and soon Falk Boden was cut adrift by the *peloton*. The German rode to the finish but reached it outside of the time limit. Five down, four to go. Breukink, Alcala, Kelly and Van Aert all made it to Quimper but were on their last legs. Not one of the four was well enough to start the following morning. The PDM Affair was born.

Not that anybody within the team was prepared to discuss it. Journalists arrived in battalions at the Hotel Grifflon in Quimper but the *directeurs sportifs* were unavailable. There was genuine confusion in the team.

Their public suggestion was food poisoning, something in the chicken at the hotel in Rennes. Valerie Rossi, daughter of the *patron* at the Cheval d'Or, was outraged and told *L'Equipe* that Verhoeven was unwell before his team-mates went to eat and, in any case, all of the team officials had eaten the same food, officials who were remarkably well.

'PDM played games afterwards,' says Van Poppel. 'How do you tell the journalists and the outside world that you are giving injections to your riders? I wasn't interested in telling anybody anything. From the moment I felt unwell, I just wanted to get better. Nothing else interested me.'

On the Tuesday morning the Tour de France left Quimper for Saint-Herblain and the PDM team left the Breton town for Holland. Though still weak, the riders were already beginning to feel better. On the team bus, they had the first opportunity to discuss their elimination and soon it was clear they suspected Dr Sanders' injection.

Intralipid, they discovered, was the name of the substance they had been given, a harmless compound which should have left them feeling stronger. The riders reckoned the doctor left the bottle containing the Intralipid in his suitcase when it should have been refrigerated.

Dr Sanders travelled back to Holland by car and along the way stopped at a pharmacy for medications. The bus stopped alongside so the doctor could give these to the riders. By then the anger was considerable. Van Poppel sat alongside Sean Kelly who was particularly upset. As the doctor passed, Kelly challenged him, saying the sickness came from his bottle.

'But the doctor would not agree with us,' says Van Poppel. ' "No, no, no," he said, "it's not Intralipid."

'We said "yeah it is."

' "No, you must look elsewhere."

'And then Kelly said "If it's not Intralipid, you take it. You get the bottle and take it. Take it. If there's no problem with the bottle, you take it and if you're not sick we will know it wasn't Intralipid."

'But he would not take it. We told him we had to have the bottle. "It's gone," he said. Then we were sure it was Intralipid.'

Three weeks after the mass elimination a Dr Schollaert, acting for PDM, wrote to the Tour organization explaining what had happened to its riders. Concerned about the damage to the race's image, the Tour organization issued a statement. The important paragraph read:

'The probability of a bacterial infection is confirmed. On the causes of this infection Dr Schollaert believes, given the symptoms and the absence of diarrhoea, that an infected product Intralipid was responsible. As the product was not conserved at the proper temperature we are no longer in any doubt as to the reasons for the infection.'

Inside a week Dr Sanders disappeared from the team without accepting responsibility. Van Poppel never saw him again. Eventually the PDM bosses spoke publicly about the controversy, admitting that while they were sorry for the riders, sales of their products were boosted by the worldwide interest in the story.

Van Poppel is now 29, at an age when sprinters begin to lose it. Amongst his peers he is not the man he was six years ago, still fast but not the fastest. He holds to the belief that when things are right, he can beat any rival. Two months earlier he had twice beaten Abdujaparov in the Vuelta a España but the Vuelta is not the Tour and, in this race, he has struggled.

From a good position, he couldn't make it in the Tour's first big sprint. That was Les Sables d'Olonne, next day at Vannes he was unlucky because paper, carried on a swirling wind, jammed itself into his *derailleur*. On the third day's pack sprint, he had the position but not the legs.

Not once did Festina help to control the race, revealing its lack of faith in Van Poppel. Even more illuminating was Van Poppel's acceptance of the team's strategy: he did not seem to want Festina to work for him, an indication perhaps that he, too, had doubts.

But he doesn't concede. 'I think I'm the very best but I'm so scared not to have a good position when the sprint starts. It makes me nervous in bed the evening before but when I'm in a good position, I will have my old legs back. I know I can beat them all but this is something you must have, this belief. When you don't have it, you've only got a half chance.'

But the years have taken their toll. There was a time when Jean-Paul Van Poppel *was* the best. Summer days when the weather was dry and the stakes high: Tour de France days. On such days he sprinted without fear.

'When it's dry, I do stupid things and the others say, "How can you do that?" Afterwards I think, "How did you put your bike through that small gap?" I take a lot of risks but I don't think of it like that. I am like the drunk, you do things but you don't think too much. But when it's raining, I'm sober. I see things too clear. That's my problem, I see I have a bad position and I think I can't win. In my head I'm not with the race.'

Van Poppel sees Cipollini, Abdujaparov and Nelissen being feted as the sprinters of this Tour and it irks him.

He has always wanted a link with his rivals, something which acknowledged that the enemies of the final kilometre were a brotherhood who shared the same risks. If they accepted this, empathy would come easily. Van Poppel liked to talk with his rivals; a *ça va* or *va bene* in the morning, a *well done* in the evening.

Like the prize fighters who, bruised and bloodied, wish only to embrace each other, Van Poppel wished to touch his opponents, a pat on the shoulder or a handshake.

But with Cipollini, Abdujaparov and Nelissen, Van Poppel doesn't have that closeness. He saw Nelissen being interviewed on television after his victory at Vannes and heard the first-timer's incredulity, amazed that he, Wilfried Nelissen, should have the yellow jersey in the Tour de France. Van Poppel wanted to shout, 'Hey, man, it's a jersey. It's not God.'

Abdu, as he calls Abdujaparov, is difficult. They fought dangerously inside the final 200 metres on the second leg of the Vuelta a España. Abdu deliberately bumped him, he pushed back, antics which were played out at a speed of 60km-per-hour and which would be replayed 25 times on Eurosport television. Van Poppel won and was allowed to keep his victory. Abdu finished second and was relegated to last. The sprint caused such a furore that out of it came the 'Abdu Rule' forbidding riders from straying off a straight line inside the last 200 metres.

But he was not upset at Abdujaparov. The victory was his and the publicity was good. His refusal to be intimidated by Abdu didn't harm his image. Later in the Vuelta he played psychological games with his opponent. 'I was in his wheel sometimes and I let him know I was there. I gave a shout, I yelled and I saw him look and it made him nervous.

'He's thinking about me, what I'm doing there. "Is he going to surprise me?" Because of this he goes too early or he goes too late, but he doesn't make a good sprint. It is mental war.' In his prime, Van Poppel beat many of the older sprinters. They tried to scare him with their toughness and when he beat them they said he was lucky. Now he is the older one: doing to Abdu precisely what was done to him.

Van Poppel reckons Abdujaparov is the fastest of the current generation and respects him as a bicycle racer. He has less regard for him as a person as he does not see much beyond the sprinter. He respects Cipollini as an outstanding rider, one capable of winning more than sprints. Once he liked the man and enjoyed his babbling conversation. Success brought change, Cipollini became a star and Van Poppel's attempts to fraternize were rebuked.

But it is Cipollini, Nelissen and Abdujaparov who perform in this Tour, Van Poppel who fails. Maybe this colours his view.

A couple of days after Van Poppel's departure, Gert Jakobs was first to the table for a team meal. Without his friend, Jakobs was lost and rode only to reach Paris. But, to do that, he had to be positive and make a better attempt to get on with his French team-mates. So he showed early for the team meal.

He sat and waited. The first to arrive chose to sit at the other end of the table, as far away from Jakobs as he could be. Then a second came and eventually all took seats far away from Jakobs. He felt this was ridiculous but didn't know what to do about it. Of his French team-mates he liked only Thierry Marie but their indifference to him still hurt.

At last Ramon Gonzalez Arrieta, the only Spaniard in the team, joined Jakobs. He told Gonzalez Arrieta how he had been slighted. The Spaniard was not sympathetic. 'You're now feeling what I felt for the first 10 days of the race. You had Van Poppel, the French were always together and nobody ever spoke to me.'

Jakobs was touched. 'I didn't realize that Arrieta was being left on his own, so I felt a little bit of a shit. For the rest of the Tour we shared rooms and even though he didn't speak Dutch and I couldn't speak Spanish, he tried to speak English and we had a very nice time. Arrieta also rode much better because he had somebody to talk with.

'I think you must always respect people. There are big riders and not so big riders but you must respect everybody. That's what they told me in my home when I was a little boy.'

Jakobs' relations with his French team-mates Lino, Virenque, Dojwa and the French-speaking Belgian Michel Vermote didn't improve. He made no attempt to speak French and, consequently, they did not involve him in their conversation. On the evening Pascal Lino achieved Festina's only success in the race, a stage victory at Perpignan, Dutch television asked Jakobs how he felt about his team-mate's win.

'This win,' he said, 'will make a big head even bigger.'

The disharmony in the Festina team would have been hard for Miguel Rodriguez to accept. A Spanish industrialist, Rodriguez invested in cycling as a means of promoting the worldwide sales of his company's Festina watches. His decision stemmed, in part, from his own love for the sport.

From a relatively humble starting point, the Festina team expanded significantly in 1992, an investment that was rewarded when Sean Kelly won the Milan to San Remo classic race. Rodriguez travelled with the team to the Tour of Colombia in South America at the end of that season and discussed with Kelly his plans for 1993. A veteran of the *peloton*, Kelly angled to have the team scaled down from the 1992 level of 24 riders to 18. 'I told Miguel Rodriguez that an 18-man team was plenty, any more than that was uncontrollable.'

'Okay, you're right,' replied Rodriguez.

Rodriguez hired two *directeurs sportifs*, Dutchman Jan Gisbers and Bruno Roussel. Miguel Moreno was already employed by Festina to manage the team in Spain. Gisbers brought with him a group of riders from the old Dutch-based PDM team; Steven Rooks, Van Aert, Van Poppel and Jakobs. Roussel persuaded Rodriguez to take on a number of French riders he had worked with at his old team, RMO. Lino, Virenque, Dojwa, Vermote and Marie came with Roussel.

Festina began the season with 29 riders, 11 more than the number agreed by Rodriguez and Kelly and, as Kelly predicted, it was soon uncontrollable. The squad had the capacity to campaign in three different countries simultaneously but it did not do so successfully.

'You had three *directeurs sportifs* from three different countries and you could say with totally different ideas,' says Kelly. 'You throw riders from 10 different countries into that and you are going to have problems. A big majority of the French riders are very hard to work with. Outside of France they think everything is *merde*, Belgium is *merde* because there's too much wind, too much rain, too many cobblestones. Spain is *merde* because they race too hard.

'We had 29 riders but when we tried to put out three teams we weakened all of them. The organizers of each race want a name so we had to put some top riders in each race. That way we diluted the force of each team.'

Cracks appeared in the organization. Jan Gisbers was the chief *directeur sportif* but he lost face with his riders when equipment for the bikes did not arrive on time. He said he ordered it but the order had not been processed. It didn't matter where the system broke down, the riders expected the *directeur sportif* to ensure it worked.

A widespread criticism of Gisbers was that he was too easy on the riders. Even the riders themselves admitted there was truth in this and it didn't help Gisbers that his assistant Roussel was not supportive.

Kelly could see the cracks widen. 'Gisbers was a good man with riders but he needed good organization behind him. He didn't get this and Roussel was there, looking to become the number one.' Before the Tour de France, Gisbers was sacked and Roussel became the team's chief *directeur sportif.*

Roussel's promotion was reflected in the largely French composition of the Festina team for the Tour. Kelly, an old head who might have brought a little peace to a troubled team, was left at home. Lino's stage win at Perpignan was a negligible return on Festina's estimated $15m investment and before the year's end Miguel Rodriguez zapped to another channel when cycling came on television.

Rodriguez may not have seen one of Gert Jakobs' last interviews for Dutch television. The interviewer wondered did Jakobs have any message for his friend Van Poppel who was at home. 'Jean-Paul,' said Jakobs, 'you made the right decision.'

Jean-Paul Van Poppel would have smiled at Jakobs' frankness, not sure his friend was wrong.

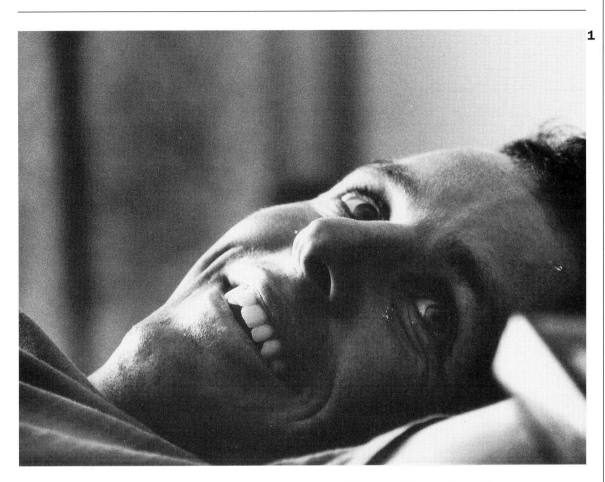

THE WINNER'S TALE
A Graceful Exit
STEPHEN ROCHE

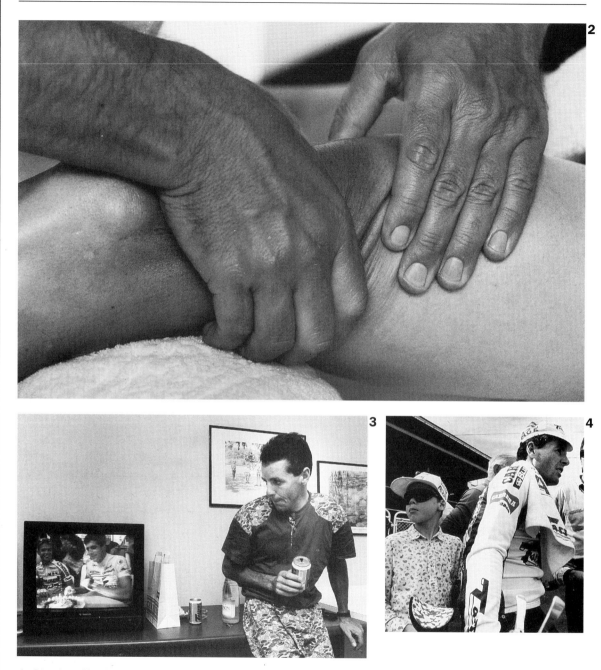

1. Stephen Roche
2. At the end of the day the rehabilitation of Roche's body begins with a massage: his troublesome left knee receives special treatment
3. Watched by an old champion, the new champion Miguel Indurain receives a cake on his twenty-ninth birthday
4. Towards the end of his career, Roche divided his time more equally between family and cycling. His son Nicolas shows up on the Tour and stays close to dad

Imagine him 40 years from now. He is 73; arthritis in his knee, mild discomfort in his back. He sits in his chair, his grandson close by. There is nobody else around and the boy wants to talk about grandad's cycling.

'What was it like to win the Giro, the Tour and the World Championship in one year? You must have been something? They say Italians spat at you during the Giro, that you collapsed at the end of a stage in the Tour? Did the Irish prime minister really come to Paris to congratulate you? Back in Dublin did a quarter of a million people welcome you home?'

'Yes, all of those things happened. I can show you the pink jersey I won in Italy, the yellow I got here in France and the rainbow jersey of world champion. They were what I wanted.'

'Really grandad?'

'No, I suppose they weren't.'

'Didn't they make you happy?'

'Ah,' the old man will say, 'that's a long story.'

Stephen Roche used to tell about his first day in Paris. A delayed flight, nobody to meet him at the airport, a difficult journey into the centre of Paris and gnawing hunger. Choosing the restaurant was straightforward, choosing from the French menu wasn't. He went for something he thought was an omelette.

Before that day he had never eaten pasta, didn't know green pasta existed. But it arrived, a plate full of it and the sight destroyed his hunger. He would have left it but not wishing to offend, worked his way through it. That was Stephen, anxious to please, eager to get on.

He was also innocent and charming and full of enthusiasm. France excited him. One evening, five months after his arrival, he rode a race at Longjumeau on the south side of Paris. Before the start his new friends at the ACBB amateur team were raving about this stunning-looking girl. She was Thierry Arnaud's sister.

Thierry raced and although he sometimes won, he was better known as Lydia's brother. Roche heard the boys' talk and guessed from what they said that this girl would be at the race. The Longjumeau event was over a short circuit which had to be covered many times. It gave the admirers a chance to pick out Lydia and, seeing her, Roche threw his hat into the ring. He made his first play by winning the Longjumeau race. Two years later he and Lydia Arnaud would marry.

His charisma worked in less likely places. François Hervo, the butcher in Boulogne, saw Roche coming and lowered his prices. François invited him to the back of his shop for coffee and Stephen always washed his cup before leaving. Poor Irish boy thought François, so far from home. But poor Irish boys grow up, especially when they ride the bike well. Roche was one of the best of his generation.

His career would have a natural rhythm, determined by his talent and his physical frailty. One year up, the next year down, then up again, then down again. He would say he was a better fighter than he was a winner, suggesting it was his yearning for recognition which most motivated him. That may be but it is equally true his thoroughbred physique wasn't made for the constant pounding of professional cycling.

Through his good seasons he developed the knee problem or the back problem which caused the bad ones. He performed in the odd years; '81, '83, '85 and '87. But when he was down he showed a different kind of strength, refusing to doubt his ability, believing he was just one knee operation away from being the best.

Roche was a first-year pro when he won Paris–Nice in 1981 and to others that was sensational. To him, it was a mere first step. He left other markers; the performance which claimed a bronze medal at the World Championships in Altenrhein in 1983 and his third place in the 1985 Tour de France.

On that Tour he won the 52-kilometre stage to the summit of the Col d'Aubisque, a remarkable performance in its own right. But he is remembered for the one-piece skinsuit he wore with his race number stitched into the fabric. This is what riders use in time trials better to resist the wind but the race to the Aubisque was no time trial.

Other racers saw Roche at the start that morning and wondered what he was doing. This isn't a time trial, their eyes said. You want to bet? He enjoyed their anxiety. This was Roche; showy, confident, even a little outrageous but with the talent to get away with it. That morning he broke away from the pack early on the climb of the Aubisque and they never saw him again. For him this *was* a time trial.

Then there was 1987. His year. Brilliant. Through the tours of Romandie, Italy and France: each time, the winner. At the end of all this, he went to Villach in Austria to make his compatriot Sean Kelly a world champion but, near the end, Kelly lost his place and Roche had to win himself. Only Eddy Merckx had won the Giro d'Italia, Tour de France and the World Championship in the same year. Roche was The Class of '87.

A year later he was down, forced off his bike by a third operation on his left knee. It was the beginning of four depressing years which caused upheaval in his professional life and turmoil in his private life.

At first Roche thought the problems could be eased by re-arranging the props: he changed teams as a hypochondriac might change doctors. After achieving so much with Carrera in 1987 he moved to Fagor, spent two seasons with them before leaving for Histor, a year with them was followed by a year with Tonton Tapis. He went from one bad experience to another, never sure that the worst was over.

The lowest point of all came on the second day of the 1991 Tour de France when he turned up late for the team time trial and the Tonton Tapis squad started without him. He rode off in pursuit but, into the wind on his own, he didn't have a chance. Outside of the day's time limit, Roche was eliminated from the Tour.

He was late, he said, because an eleventh hour visit to the toilet caused him to lose track of time. At best, Roche's mistake was unprofessional. Not many took that relatively charitable view, preferring to believe that Roche had deliberately ridden himself out of the Tour. Unfair as he swore it was, that remained the majority view.

Eventually he realized things could not be made better simply by changing teams. He looked at himself and, for the first time, understood why things were going wrong. On the way to the top he had been guided only by his need to get there. Much was neglected, especially his own development as a person. When he stood before a mirror, the reflection did not please him.

Yet the honesty of that admission could not assuage the hurt caused by the questioning of his character. Neither could it stop him from noticing that when he fell, there weren't many reaching to pick him up.

The Carrera team list hangs in the foyer of the Hotel Campanile at Cholet in western France. Nine riders divided into four twin rooms and one single. Stephen Roche occupies the single. He considers it one of the perks of seniority, likes to have this privacy on his last Tour de France.

Throughout the race he will joke with his team-mates that if they are going to abandon they should do so in pairs, so he gets to keep his single room. How changed he is from the young Roche who once insisted that a good team ambience depended upon riders constantly changing room-mates.

On the road he likes to talk with Tony Rominger for he sees in him the maturity he once lacked. Rominger says he will leave cycling as soon as he earns enough money. You're right, he tells Roche, now is the time to be getting out of the sport; everything is going crazy, faster and more ruthless racing, pressure from the sponsors, hassle from the organizers, young guys who have no respect, the old decency disappearing.

They joke about organizing a conference for ex-pros in Geneva at which a new cycling constitution will be drawn up. There will be no feeding stations except when the race is longer than 300 kilometres, riders will not be allowed to wear their capes in the rain and there will be no prize money on days when the speed is less than 43km per hour. It is their view of where the sport is going.

Yet there is no bitterness in Roche, just the foolish laments of an old pro saddened by the imminence of his retirement. Foolish because this old pro wants to leave. Roche also wants to enjoy his last Tour and savour the good moments. One which cheered him came on the 11th stage to the Alpine ski-station at Isola 2000. It was at the end of a long day and a race made brutal by Claudio Chiappucci's mood . . . .

Disappointed that he was left behind the previous day, Chiappucci accelerates on the first mountain, the Col d'Izoard. It is 10.30 in the morning and nobody is prepared for such an early start to serious racing. Chiappucci fires the first shots in a battle which will continue for six hours.

At the back of the pack, they fall like flies. Chiappucci's team-mate Marco Artunghi is one of the first to drop, Rik Van Slycke is another, Wilfried Nelissen, Johan Capiot, Marco Lietti, Jean-Cyril Robin and Bruno Boscardin. For each one, there is the same desperate race to stay within the safety of the *peloton*. They fall two or three lengths behind the last wheel, surge to make up the deficit and grimace through the terrible pain.

But each Chiappucci acceleration causes new gaps to appear and at the back Artunghi, Van Slycke and Nelissen let go of the invisible thread which ties them to the pack. Eventually they look up and there is nothing but an empty road. All will abandon before the finish.

Laurent Fignon arrives at the foot of the final climb to Isola 37 minutes behind the leaders and stops pedalling. 'There was no point in continuing,' said Fignon, aware that he was likely to be outside of that day's time limit. Another six make it to the finish but three or four minutes late. In all, 14 riders are eliminated on this 180-kilometre leg from Serre Chevalier.

Roche rides the final climb in a nice group about 10 minutes behind the leaders. Gianni Bugno is alongside, Roche's team-mate Vladimir Pulnikov is there, also Eric Caritoux, Bruno Cornillet, Thierry Claveyrolat, Alex Zülle, Johan Bruyneel. Riders he knows well, fellows who help each other.

On each of the 31 bends to the summit the organizers have placed the name and year of a previous winner of the Tour. It is a small but moving tribute to the old champions. Because the names are listed in chronological order, the oldest winners on the early slopes, the dedications read like a concise history of the race. From Bartali to Coppi to Bobet, Anquetil, Gaul, Bahamontes, Gimondi, Merckx, Ocana, Thevenet, Van Impe, Hinault, Zoetemelk, Fignon, LeMond . . . . Even though the riders are tired, they cannot help noticing. They play games with the names, for each one is a step closer to the summit. There's Gaul, wish I could climb like him . . . that's Gimondi out of the way . . . ah Thevenet, saw him on television last evening, he won this twice . . . if it's Hinault we must be getting close to the top. Roche knows what is coming and is going to enjoy it. After Hinault it is Zoetemelk, after Zoetemelk comes Fignon, then LeMond and after LeMond it is . . . .

Gianni Bugno sees it first. 'Look Stephen, there it is.' A white board sits at this, the third last bend, same black lettering as all the rest: *Stephen Roche (1987)*. Those close to the sign cheer for him, *allez Stefan, allez, allez*. He feels good.

Twice world champion, Bugno did everything possible to win the Tour but it hadn't happened. Now, riding side by side with a man who had, Gianni is envious. 'Do you know Stephen that out of the 180 riders in this Tour, only two have been world champions, you and I.' Roche hadn't realized it and thinks 'yeah, isn't that something.'

That evening he thought about the ride to Isola. How strange that his name printed on a white board could make him glow with pride, especially when the actual winning of the Tour had not. But he is now six years older and what is the compensation of age if not wisdom?

Thinking of that little sign on the third last bend and the basement garage of his home in Sagy, north of Paris, he reckoned the two would go well together. As the next day's race began from the summit of Isola, he would collect the sign as he descended, slip it into a Carrera team car and take it home from there.

Alas, he was beaten to it. Somebody else, no doubt with another inadequately decorated garage, had got there first.

The memory would have to do.

Stephen Roche has been a professional cyclist for 13 years. This is his final season. The thought of leaving frightens him. They say it is the same for all the old champions who dread the normality of retirement. But greater than the fear of going is the fear of staying too long. He wants to take his bow while the audience still applauds.

He now has the chance. Twelve months earlier he rediscovered his old self and his victory in a

Tour de France stage on a bleak mountain top at La Bourboule rates amongst his best performances. That afternoon a dense fog shrouded the finishing climb. Roche broke away from a pack racing as fast as it could. The odds favoured the pack, conditions made it difficult to see and it was quite a moment when Roche ghosted through the fog, threw his arms in the air and announced his return.

Next morning the French newspapers carried the picture of a triumphant Roche coming out of the mist. Words were not necessary. Since then he has continued to ride well but he knows the time has come to move on. For four years he worked to get back and, having arrived, there is nothing to keep him.

But it isn't easy to leave. Part of the rehabilitation was the return in 1992 to the Carrera team with whom he had enjoyed his supreme season in 1987. It worked better than he dared imagine. Carrera is family now. Four of them sit around the dinner table; the managers, Davide Boifava and Sandro Quintarelli, the team leader Claudio Chiappucci and he, Stephen Roche, an unofficial team captain: an important contributor to tactical discussions and decision-maker at critical moments in races.

Boifava has always understood him, admired his professionalism and appreciated that talented athletes can be very demanding. More than anything Boifava liked Roche and offered the kind of support that is not often seen in professional sport.

At the beginning of the year Roche crashed while out training and, worried about his troublesome knee, he flew to Munich to see his private physician, Dr Muller. Before leaving he telephoned Boifava that things might be going wrong.

Next day Boifava drove from his home at Brescia in northern Italy to Munich, simply to be there when Roche was being examined. They had a cup of tea together, Boifava said Carrera would wait for his knee to recover fully. That kind of faith was what Roche needed and what he felt he deserved. Now he thinks if he stays in cycling, say in public relations or team management, it must be with Carrera.

But they want him to continue racing. Every second evening at the table the talk wends its way into his future. Boifava prods gently, stay one more season, ride just one Tour next year, or the classics, just do the classics. And if you do one big Tour, prepare as you want, go away, bring your wife, it's not a problem anymore.

Then Sandro Quintarelli, louder but no less persuasive. Look at old Perini who won a stage of the Tour of Puglia the other week. He hadn't won a race for 12 years, if he can do this what can Stephen do? Quintarelli, warming to his subject, answers his own question. 'Stephen, on one leg, you'd still be up there next year. You know it. Talk to Davide, tell him what you want, come and ride on your terms, if you want more time at home, take it. Don't come to training camp. It would be a shame to stop.'

Talk like this unsettles Roche because he knows it is true. But there are other truths. A year from now Quintarelli could be the one telling him it is over. What then? He knows he could sit down with Boifava and Quintarelli, work out a new contract, guaranteeing himself something around £200,000 for his final year. He also knows what would come next.

'I'd get up on my bike, I'd go down the road and I'd say "hell, this leg again." Thinking to myself that if it was only right, I could be much better. But the way it is, I'm only going to be just there, no better. I say to myself if you gave it one good winter, doing weights and everything else, maybe that would help but I know it won't. When you do a Tour of Italy, or 20,000 km in the year and there's no improvement in the muscle in your knee, you know then nothing is going to change.'

He will not be persuaded to stay. The Glory of Sport, he has been there, experienced that. It's bullshit, he says. 'When I add it all up there are hundreds of reasons why I should stop and only one reason for carrying on, money. I could earn in one year what it would take six years to earn in a normal job. But that's the only reason I have to continue and it is not enough.'

And a man who says no to £200,000, he must have a story to tell.

Marseilles, almost five o'clock on the 14th day of the Tour de France. It could be any Tour afternoon. The race is over but not the show for it doesn't end until the tall man sings. Daniel Mangeas, the Tour announcer, is the tall man and, for those who stand at the roadside or come to the finish, he is their guide.

Miguel Indurain is walking to the centre of the victory podium, two women wearing *Credit Lyonnais* uniforms wait to help him into another yellow jersey. Mangeas describes a scene replayed countless times and makes it vibrant. 'Miguel Indurain, winner of the Tour de France in 1991 and '92, winner of the Giro d'Italia in 1992 and '93 and now wearer of the yellow jersey in the 1993 Tour de France.'

There is so much enthusiasm in Mangeas' voice that you want to applaud and most do. His reverence is not just for winners but for the Tour participants. Every rider who comes before him is recognized and praised. He has searched through the careers of the lesser known, found their best performances and highlights them to deliver his message: in this race, there are no small riders.

In his mid-40s, Mangeas is pencil thin, his lean body suggests he knows what it is like to pedal a bike. His hair is fashionably long, his expression always open: a modern man who holds to the cycling values of an earlier age.

But people have homes to go to, hotels to find, journeys to make. Most of the racers have left, their hurried departures being the first stage in their preparation for the next day's race. Stephen Roche prefers to avoid that rush. He hangs around, does an interview for Italian television, another for British television, then the Irish newspapers.

Doing in a small way what Mangeas does on a grand scale. Bringing people into the race, telling them what it felt like on the road. And because he is not here to win, he has more time.

Finished with the Irish journalists, he heads towards his bike but is intercepted by a reporter from Radio Monte Carlo. One radio man draws another and soon there is a cluster around Roche. He talks, they nod. He has done this so often, there is now no need for questions and they don't ask any. A young man comes towards him in a wheelchair, Roche bends so they can chat, he takes off his Carrera hat, signs it and leaves it with the disabled fan.

It's true he wants to be remembered for the great cyclist he was. But he also wishes to be remembered for the decent man that he is. Through the bad years he got a name for being a troublemaker. He believes it wasn't deserved and now he works to change perceptions.

A year earlier he won the Tour's Fair Play award and it pleased him no end. This prize goes to the rider judged to be most cooperative with the Tour's entourage and its public. It was recognition which he felt entitled to. Now he is leaving the Tour riding well, still respected and enjoying his last performance.

Call it a graceful exit: it is what he wants most.

As a young turk Roche was the scourge of his team. He was the leader who demanded correctness; jerseys had to be right, bikes had to be perfect and riders had to be on time for the evening meal. The team had to play to his standards. Amongst themselves, his team-mates would have asked who the hell did this guy think he was but they did not often complain publicly.

Through the good years their protests were silenced by his performances. As team leader he was the one bearing the greatest responsibility and if he won, everybody got well paid. Roche won regularly.

His ambition made him restless; it didn't matter where he was, he felt he could do better somewhere else. In a different team, under a new *directeur*, he would prosper. From his first team Peugeot he moved to La Redoute, from there he joined Carrera.

Along the way, he teamed up with Patrick Valcke. A mechanic with Peugeot, Valcke's loyalty was to the team and Roche. As the years passed and the teams changed, Patrick's loyalties remained the same but the order changed. The rider became Patrick's priority. That was how Roche wanted it. For as he progressed towards 1987 Roche narrowed his focus all the time, leaving Patrick to take care of the peripheral things and when success arrived, the mentor was lauded for his part.

Roche left Carrera for Fagor at the end of that year and he made Valcke manager of his new team. It was an appointment he forced upon the sponsor, one they were unhappy about. Injury prevented Roche from competing in 1988 and, without performances from the star, Valcke was vulnerable. Roche defended him but could not keep him in control. Valcke was sacked. That year marked the beginning of Roche's bleak period.

'Everything went great until 1987, then I had my operation (knee) and I just wanted to be as competitive again. I hadn't got the time or the will to look after all the small things which needed looking after and I handed over control to Patrick. I gave him too much power, confided too much in him. I could see only through him at the time. I couldn't see anything else. As far as I was concerned, he never did anything wrong and he never did me any harm. He performed for me. If I asked him to come down from Lille where he lived to help me with a training spin, he was always there.'

Valcke's rise from team mechanic at Peugeot to *directeur sportif* at Fagor was unusual in a sport where serfs remain serfs. Many believed he rose on the strength of Roche's patronage and resented him for that. What they chose not to see was Valcke's unflinching commitment to his job and an honesty which wasn't common in professional cycling. 'With Patrick, you always knew where you stood,' says Paul Kimmage who rode for Fagor in 1989.

But it was an honesty which could be brutal and often rude. It offended many. That might not have mattered if Roche had been fit and riding well but he wasn't and disappointment felt at the rider's injury problems was channelled into anger against the *directeur sportif.* Confrontational by nature, Valcke did not back off. His enemies became Roche's enemies, minor splits became major rifts and Roche soon found himself embroiled in the disputes.

He knows why he invested so much in his one-time friend. 'I can't really blame Patrick. It came down to me, I did it because I wanted to win. So I can say if I hadn't got the ambition, if I hadn't been such an egotist, if the will-to-win hadn't been so powerful, I wouldn't have fallen into this trap. But then without those things, I wouldn't have won what I won. The same quality that helped me to win the Tour got me into trouble.'

The break with Patrick was acrimonious and the bitterness remained for months after the split. Upset at being discarded, Patrick tried to hurt the man to whom he was once devoted. He spoke publicly about what he had done for Roche and how he been let down and the criticism stung Roche who was still struggling to regain fitness.

Without Patrick and without the protection of good results, he was alone and had the time to look at his life. Here he was, a 32-year-old cyclist, former winner of the Giro d'Italia, Tour de France and World Championship. What was it all for?

'I went from 20 to 32 and, mentally, I didn't age a year. It was only when I started having problems with Patrick that I started to mature. You are living in an atmosphere of men and you can become very chauvinistic. Your bike is your wife, your master, it's your best friend and all you want to do is succeed. And you don't think you are getting older and you don't think about what happens at home or with your family or who pays the bills.

'You don't mature because, on the road, life is going at 110 miles an hour and you don't have time to think how the world actually moves. You arrive at the hotel, your bags are taken. You go to the airport ticket desk and you are recognized straightaway. At the customs you are brought through in front of everybody. When you go home and the bins are outside the door, you think they got there by themselves.'

The previous day he telephoned Lydia who ran from the garden to take the call.

'Everything okay?' he asked.

'If you saw me now, you wouldn't recognize me,' she replied.

'Why not?'

'Because I've got big rubber boots on, I have red overalls, I've got a woollen hat, a face mask and I have a jerry can in my hands for spraying the flowers with poison for the solitary worm.'

'Yeah?'

'Yeah, either they die or I'll be dead from this poison.'

He tells this story to bring you into the world he has not known. This, he says in a moment of self-mockery, is a world which isn't turned by pedals. In this world, he discovered his children.

'I didn't realize I had children until I was 32. When I came home they were in bed, when I got up in the morning they were being fed and ready for school. When they came home I was training or away racing. At the weekends they were going to sport and I was off racing. One day last year I woke up and realized that I had two young children, Nicolas and Crystel, who were missing something. Now I regret I was not around for their early years.'

Sometimes he thinks of talking with Lydia about having another child, so he can see the baby grow. But it wouldn't be fair, Lydia has moved onto a different stage of her life and it was nobody else's fault that he missed Nicolas and Crystel as babies. It's a strange thing, he says, this feeling that you've come back from another planet and life has continued in your absence.

He arranges things differently now. On the Sunday before the Tour began he drove to the coast with Lydia and the kids and spent the afternoon at the beach. He says he should have done this kind of thing earlier in his life and saved everybody a lot of misery. Now he can see how tough it was for Lydia. His operations, the public disputes with teams and fellow riders, his contentious elimination from the 1991 Tour, the fall out with Patrick; these consumed him to the exclusion of everything else. He was fortunate, he says, that when he returned, Lydia was still at home.

In dividing himself more equally between home and cycling, he has achieved a balance which brought peace. From this he rebuilt his career, not back to the level of '87 but to a high level nevertheless.

'Winning at La Bourboule last year was better than winning the World Championship, better than the '87 Tour de France. I appreciated it more. Because I was older, more mature, I could savour it. I was disappointed Lydia wasn't there because she had taken a lot over the years but still played a big part in getting me back.

'At the time Lydia and I were still a little angry with each other. I called that evening but she didn't say she had seen it on television and I didn't ask. After the Tour we got together, close again. I asked had she watched the Tour. She said she had. I asked had she seen *the* stage and she said she had.

' "And?" '

' "When you crossed the line and you won I cried. I didn't want to cry but I was happy because of what happened and everything else. I was happy." '

The memories amaze him. He is struck by the kind of competitor he was, as if recalling the actions of somebody he once knew. How could a sensible and sensitive boy like him, the kind who hurts easily, have survived that Giro in 1987. But it was he who defied one of the sport's fundamental principles by attacking when his team-mate Roberto Visentini was leading the race. Inevitably, that turned his Carrera team against him.

Visentini called him Judas and tried to ride him off the road. One evening at dinner other teammates, Bontempi, Cassani, Ghirotto and Leali, told him what they thought and he felt they were only a moment away from punching him. Most Italian newspapers said he had betrayed his own team and he was called a traitor. At the time Roche's justification was straightforward: he was a better rider than Visentini and he wanted to win the Giro.

Having unseated Visentini, Roche felt the anger of the Italian public. Through the last week of the race he was punched on the climbs, spat at, taunted, big banners screamed obscenities and there was the daily need for police protection. He wonders now: was that really me?

At the time he was fiercely ambitious and saw only the prize. When the Giro ended, he thought of nothing only the Tour de France which would begin in less than three weeks. On the very evening he won the Giro, all he wanted was to get back to France.

His friends Bruno and Corinne had followed the last days of the Giro and he offered to drive their Peugeot 104 back to Paris. Three hours after the race ended in St Vincent, Bruno and Corinne rolled down the back seat, fell asleep and let the new cycling champion drive them home. They left at 7.30 in the evening.

Eddy Schepers, the one Carrera rider on his side, drove Roche's car and Patrick Valcke travelled with him. They all arrived back in Roche's house at 4.30 in the morning, went to bed around 6.30 and three hours later Stephen was on his way to the local *boulangerie* for croissants. After breakfast he and Schepers went for a two-hour training spin. Eighteen days to the Tour de France: there was no time for celebration.

Neither was there rest, nor relaxation. Sooner or later, Roche was going to look back and ask what was it all for? A young man in a hurry, he didn't understand much about life. He won a bitterly contested Giro d'Italia and it didn't seem to mean anything. It wasn't that he disliked the view from the summit, but in his haste to move on to the next mountain he had not given himself time to take it in.

Then in the Tour de France he was The Calculator, winning by his cleverness. Every attack was premeditated, every counterattack measured and when the critical moment arrived he saw the way to unseat the then race leader and likely winner, Jean François Bernard. It happened at the small town of Leoncel in the Vercors. Roche knew Leoncel was suitable for an attack and that the strong Systeme-U team planned to breakaway at that point. The approach to Leoncel was fast and wide, narrowing as it reached the town and certain to produce mayhem as the teams' personnel handed food to their riders. Such scheming excited Roche as it brought his sharp mind into play.

Bernard's chances of surviving the Leoncel attack were destroyed by the mechanical trouble which caused him to be at the back of the *peloton* as it raced into the town. By the time he reached the front, his rivals had bolted. Bernard finished four minutes, 15 seconds behind Roche, losing his yellow jersey and all chance of winning the Tour.

Roche's most vivid memory is of the stage, two days later, to La Plagne in the Alps. He set out in second place overall, 25 seconds behind Pedro Delgado, and surprised everybody by attacking in the Maurienne Valley early in the stage. Having taken a one-minute 40 seconds advantage on Delgado, he looked on his way to victory.

But then the pursuit gathered momentum and before the final ascent to La Plagne, Roche was recaptured. He knew Delgado was stronger and accepted he would lose time on the last climb. When Delgado accelerated on the early slopes of La Plagne, he held back, understanding that he might lose all in the frantic effort to stay with the Spaniard.

Official time checks told him Delgado's lead was 40 seconds, then one minute and later one minute and 15. As Delgado already had a 25-second advantage, he now held the Tour in a vicegrip. But Roche conceded nothing, believing that his counterattack would win back time. The important thing was the timing of the counter.

He moved it at the 4km-to-go sign, knowing that the enormity of the crowds meant there were no official time checks through the final four kilometres and in that way he would enjoy the advantage of surprise. Once he went in pursuit of his rival, Roche discovered reserves he did not know he had. The lead of one minute, 15 seconds tumbled to a slim four seconds at the finish. Exhausted, Roche collapsed into semi-consciousness seconds after his arrival at the La Plagne summit. He was taken back to his hotel by ambulance.

Writing in the next morning's *L'Equipe*, the then Tour director Jacques Goddet said 'Roche arrived at the finish line in La Plagne and collapsed, suffering from a total lack of oxygen. He was given oxygen for what seemed a long time. It was a day when he showed he had the heart and character of a true champion: one who succeeds in going beyond himself and so reaches the zenith of sporting performance.'

Now, he finds it hard to credit that he could be so competitive, so desperate to win. 'Janey,' he says using an Irish colloquialism, 'I must have been great.'

But that is hindsight and a more relaxed Roche. At the time he felt nothing. Back in the hotel, there were questions to be answered. In our admiration, we said 'You won the Tour today.' He corrected us, 'No I didn't, I just stopped myself losing it.'

It disappoints him that he was so matter-of-fact. 'I felt nothing. Everything I did, I considered normal. That's the sad thing about it, there was nothing spectacular about it. It was just part of success, part of what I wanted. I worked to be successful, I made the sacrifices and then when I won I couldn't digest it, I couldn't appreciate it. You have to be mature to do that.

'Everybody told me I was mature and I felt I was mature. But what they meant was that I was able to read the races, make the right moves. Give an intelligent answer to a question afterwards. I wasn't mature. I think back now and I wonder how was it possible to have been so naive, so ignorant. But then that's life.'

Once he sat in the waiting room of Dr Muller's surgery in Munich and overheard a Dublin accent. He looked towards the speaker who said 'Ah Stephen, howya doin?'

'Okay,' he replied, not knowing his fellow Dubliner.

'Sorry . . . I'm Larry Mullen . . . drummer with U2.'

'Oh . . . howya Larry.'

That was around the time U2 were on the cover of *Time*. Roche was going places too but read only the cycling magazines. He knew of U2 for theirs was the song the television played when it reviewed his climb to La Plagne.

With Or Without You. Action slowed, shoulders moving to the beat of the music, the neckchain given to him by Lydia bouncing from one side to the other, drops of sweat forming and dropping, pain written all over his face: he thought the words were right for him.

> *'Through the storm we reach the shore,*
> *You give it all but I want more.'*

At the Hotel Van Redon on the outskirts of Marseilles, Roche has a room to himself. Two teammates, Rossi and Artunghi, are out of the Tour leaving seven; three twins and a single. It is a big room; he has showered and changed into Bermuda shorts and top.

Without shoes or socks, his angular body looks longer and thinner than it is – still the thorough-bred's physique. He is on the floor, sitting on a white towel, stretching his legs and upper body, this way and that, holding it until the strain becomes too much. Then another position, holding it at full stretch until he must let go.

He chats at those moments when the pain recedes. 'If I didn't do this . . . everything would seize up . . . I'm not looking for any more Tours after this you know . . . there's talk about riding the Tour of Catalonia but I don't know . . . what I want to do now is . . . I'd like to stop . . . to cross the line on the Champs Elysées and say that's it . . . but the team wants me to ride until the Worlds . . . and they are paying me until the end of the year.'

For seven hours and 50 minutes, he had raced with the pack from Isola to Marseilles. At the finish he spent an hour answering questions. He got to his hotel a little after six o'clock, showered and began this 30 minutes of stretching which will be followed by a 30-minute massage.

His body now takes so much looking after. He tells this with resignation, like a man might speak of his 10-year-old car.

In his book *The Game*, Canadian Ken Dryden told of his life as an ice hockey goalkeeper and how, towards the end of his career, he looked upon his body.

'There is nothing romantic in the way we view our bodies. Used and abused through a grinding season, aesthetic only to those who watch, like a plumber's wrench or a carpenter's hammer they are our instruments pure and simple; a collection of disembodied parts – legs, hands, head – that work well or not so well, that are built up, fuelled, and conditioned, that get broken and cut.

'They are parts we know and understand; parts that wear out – sometimes from injury, sometimes from cumulative injury and age, suffered in private for a while, later as an object of public sympathy/disdain/ridicule ("his legs are gone").'

Roche would understand this; the parts of his body that don't work well, the dud left knee, the wear and tear in his lower back, the signs of ageing obvious to him before they are to anybody else. The lean, perfectly proportioned body is not what he sees. Two days previously his lower back deteriorated to the point where he could not sit comfortably on the bike. With over 2000 kilometres of the Tour in front of him, it wasn't a problem he could ignore.

From the hotel at Serre Chevalier he faxed Dr Muller in Munich. Muller came and brought with him Hans Montag, a chiropractor. They flew to Nice, hired a helicopter to take them to Isola 2000 and last evening they treated their patient. Montag manipulated the lower back, getting deep into the troubled parts and Muller followed this with a series of injections into the affected areas.

Normally it takes a couple of days for Roche to enjoy the benefits of Dr Muller's treatment but today, on the long race to Marseilles, he could feel the improvement. He straightened his back like he had not done for the previous four days.

'The way I felt today, I should be able to get through the Pyrenees. It will start to get bad again next week but the mountains will be behind us then and I should be okay.'

Misha Pivovarov, one of Carrera's masseurs, works silently. Roche lies stomach down, his face pressed against a pillow. As Pivovarov rubs and loosens, Roche tries to calculate what Muller's visit will cost him; two airfares from Munich to Nice, the hire of the helicoptor to Isola, the fees. Won't be much less than £1200 ($2000) but he's not complaining.

Like any 10-year-old car, the older his body gets the more costly it is to run.

By the end of the Tour Roche's wish to leave the sport through *la grande porte* was realized. Of the 136 riders who finished, he was 13th. Even though the experience of 13 years in the *peloton* mellowed him, he could not quite bring himself to take satisfaction from placing 13th. Once a winner . . . .

He left a more worthy souvenir on the last big day in the mountains. The 230-km race from Andorra to Saint-Lary-Soulan crossed four Pyrenean passes before the final and very steep 10-kilometre rise to the finish. About 25 riders were clear of the pack when they began the final climb and Roche was one of the leaders.

Tony Rominger's sudden increase in speed destroyed the unity of the group, Miguel Indurain reacted immediately, Robert Millar countered, followed by Zenon Jaskula as every other rider tried to restrict his loss. Roche could not react to Rominger's violent acceleration but he was not about to give up.

Pushing himself a little harder, he settled into a rhythm which brought him up to the rider in front of him, the Colombian Alvaro Mejia. The Colombian was riding to keep second place overall and soon he and Roche got up to Millar who had failed to catch Rominger and Indurain.

Roche, Millar and Mejia were joined by Mejia's Motorola team-mate Andy Hampsten. Mindful of preserving Mejia's second place overall, Hampsten quickened the pursuit but the Colombian could not keep up and Hampsten had to slow. With five kilometres to go Rominger, Indurain and Jaskula led Roche, Millar, Hampsten and Mejia by almost 40 seconds. On a long straight stretch leading to the 4km-to-go sign Roche counterattacked, accelerating clear of his three companions and reminding us that age may blur but it could not obliterate his quality.

His chase of Rominger, Indurain and Jaskula was courageous, exhilarating and vain. At the red kite indicating the final kilometre, the 40-second advantage was down to 14 but Roche then realized he was not going to make it and settled for fourth. On this day, over this terrain and in this company, fourth was a prize.

Two hundred metres from the line, he pulled the zip to the top of his Carrera jersey, straightened himself and smiled. For a second it seemed he was going to throw his hands in the air and say, 'that's it, my last performance.' No sooner had he taken his hands from the handlebars but he replaced them, leaving us to form our own impressions. This was it, he *was* making his exit.

And nothing in his career became him like the leaving of it.

5

1

THE JOURNALIST'S TALE
Harry's Game
HARRY VAN DEN BREMT

1. Harry Van den Bremt
2. Because journalists no longer see the Tour de France, the pre-race interview has gained a new importance. Harry Van den Bremt talks with a rider from the Lotto team
3. Director General of the Tour, Jean Marie Leblanc is part of a distinguished line of journalists who have controlled the race

It makes a startling sound; the thud of driving rain on thick canvas. Gives the impression the rain is heavier than it is. Underneath journalists stand around, mostly discussing the weather. It excites them for they know Miguel Indurain dislikes racing in the wet.

Any other day, it mightn't have mattered but today's 59-km time trial is a big day. Ten days into the Tour and time for Indurain to show his strength. But the rain brings uncertainty and the press room hope that, at the end of the day, the race will be less certain.

He sits far from the busier corridors in this converted tennis hall. Looks about 52 or 53, could be less. Bronzed, overweight; he draws constantly from the cigarette in his right hand. Occasionally he checks his notes or a reference book, mostly he sits upright before his word processor: this is Harry Van den Bremt, cycling writer for Belgium's leading newspaper *Het Nieuwsblad* (circulation 400,000).

The big hall can seat a thousand or more journalists. So different from the little rooms they called the *Salle de Presse* when Harry started. Everything changes. But Harry has moved with the times. He talks about his portable computer which can transmit 5000 bytes in three seconds on an average telephone line, 10,000 on the best line.

He first covered the Tour de France in 1968, a time when he was one of about 50 journalists. They penned their stories and called them in by telephone. Lines were unreliable in the Pyrenees and the journalists were especially nervous when the Tour over-nighted in Luchon. Thirty minutes delay to Brussels, the lady would say. Now the phones lie in cubicles: one to 24, each with direct access to the world.

In that first Tour, Harry drove the *Het Nieuwsblad* car close behind the riders, near enough to see the breakaways, to be excited by the pursuits. When some fell behind he waited a few minutes before overtaking, slowing to assess the pained expressions.

In 1975, he was in the car just behind Eddy Merckx at the moment of his collapse on the stage to Pra-Loup. Merckx led the race and seemed on his way to a sixth Tour de France victory. But he suddenly lost his powerful rhythm and the pursuers, Bernard Thevenet and Felice Gimondi, began to close. As he overtook the champion, Harry saw Merckx's eyes and recognized the beginning of the end. Merckx put it down to hunger knock, Harry knew better.

Eddy Merckx, the greatest cyclist of all time, had reached the end. He would compete for another two and a half seasons but, that afternoon, Harry saw the curtain begin its descent.

This year he follows the Tour but not as before. There are so many journalists now they cannot all get close to the modern race. But Harry is no old fogey. Things weren't wonderful when he was a young reporter and he likes the efficiency of the modern race. Radio Tour narrates each day's story, pedal stroke by pedal stroke, and then two hours before the stage end, he tunes into the live television coverage.

When television ends there is an audio-visual link-up to a studio by the finish line and the stage winner is interviewed by journalists who may be as many as five kilometres away in a press room. Everyone hears the winner's responses and after that there is the rush of official results; stage placings, general placings, mountains, points, teams and even a summary report of that day's race. All the reporter could ever need.

Thinking about the way it was and the way it is, Harry has one lament.

Today's young journalist on his first Tour must follow the race on television. What he sees are celluloid images of athletes competing in one of sport's toughest events, not men pushing themselves to and beyond their limits. And the images are of the leaders: those who appear to suffer least. Television distances its viewers from the humanity of the race: the pain, the desperation, the heroism, the will to survive.

Rather it shows all the important moves, replays where necessary. There is more to the Tour than this, says Harry. For one day at least, the young journalist must forget the leaders, ignore the television and stand on the side of the mountain where he can see for himself the true severity of the race and the courage of its participants.

When Harry first followed the Tour, every rider in the race was considered a hero. Now, they are seen as mere competitors.

Could it be the efforts of the racers, through the filter of television, are less heroic? In our armchairs, we are encouraged to see them as winners and losers. Maybe the old reporters, telling what they saw on the mountain, showed us much more than television can?

Harry Van den Bremt has done it both ways: from the mountainside and from the press room. 'You have to taste the race. Unless you see it, experience the atmosphere, witness the riders' difficulties, then there will be no taste in the report. When you stay in the press room, you can't have this. You don't get it by talking with the rider at the start and the best story is the one with taste in it.'

He thinks it was the Tour of '73 or '74, his sixth or seventh. It happened on the Col du Tourmalet in the Pyrenees. He was driving the *Het Nieuwsblad* car himself, weaving his way forward from the back of the bunch. As he overtook those left behind, he glanced across, trying to measure their exhaustion. Suddenly there was Eric Leman, a Belgian rider. Twice a winner of the Tour of Flanders, Leman was good in the one-day classics but not so good on the big mountains.

As Harry slowly overtook Leman, the rider grabbed the aerial of the car radio and held it. Unaware, Harry continued driving. Soon there was an announcement over Radio Tour: 'A rider is being towed by the car of *Het Nieuwsblad* and it (the car) must stop immediately, otherwise the driver will have his accreditation withdrawn.' Harry was shocked. He was also confused. If he stopped his car, it would block the narrow road, slowing the group of riders who were close behind.

'I drove fast, very fast because I thought he cannot hold on at this speed. But he did hold on. The *commissaire* was now shouting over Radio Tour: "*Het Nieuwsblad*, can you not see it, the rider is still holding on." I was trying to shout at Leman, telling him to stop but he hung on for about five kilometres until he just couldn't do it anymore. I was very, very upset about it.

'I waited for Leman at the finish and he arrived in the boot of the autobus, you know we call it the bus, the guys who are always behind. I saw Leman there and I said, "Look, you mustn't ever do that again." And he showed me his hand from the aerial. There was a deep incision across the palm, just like you had cut it with a knife. I saw that and I could not say anything.

'When I say you must taste the race, this is what I mean.'

Jean Marie Leblanc walks through the early morning throng, smiling on all who smile, stopping to chat with those who offer a *'Ca va?'* A Frenchman, in his mid-40s, Leblanc has controlled the Tour since 1989, responsible for its £20 million budget and its reputation as the world's best bicycle race. He moves lightly under the weight. Leblanc is especially comfortable in the company of the Tour's journalists. He has worked with most and would count many as personal friends.

Before 1989, he was a cycling correspondent; first with *La Voix du Nord* in Lille and later with the sports daily *L'Equipe* in Paris. From the position of chief cycling editor with *L'Equipe*, Leblanc was appointed director general of the Tour de France. To the outsider, unfamiliar with the Tour's beginnings and its relationship with *L'Equipe*, Leblanc might have seemed an unlikely choice. Within the Tour family, his succession was unsurprising.

For it was Geo Lefevre, chief cycling reporter for the fledgling newspaper *L'Auto-Velo* who first mooted the idea of a continuous bicycle race around France. Lefevre proposed this to his editor Henri Desgrange in January 1903. As his journal needed new readers, Desgrange was receptive and six months later, the first Tour de France left Montgeron, just south of Paris. Desgrange organized it and is justifiably recognized as the Tour's founder.

Circulation of Desgrange's newspaper soared as the Tour de France became popular. Desgrange himself guided the Tour up to the Second World War. He died in 1940. After the war *L'Auto* re-emerged as *L'Equipe*, Jacques Goddet and Felix Levitan became the Tour's co-directors. Goddet was editor of *L'Equipe* and Levitan was editor of its sister newspaper, the *Parisien Libéré*. They controlled the race for almost half a century before Levitan was pushed to one side and Goddet retired. Leblanc is the fourth chief of the Tour de France and the fourth journalist to hold the position.

A race conceived by the need to sell newspapers would, in time, look to other means of turning sport to profit. Now the Tour has become a commercial giant. Revenue from television rights and sponsorship (officially, the Tour has partners not sponsors) far exceeds the cost of staging the race. Yet for all the change, the *raison d'être* retains some relevance. The Tour de France continues to sell newspapers.

At the height of the extraordinary Bernard Hinault/Greg LeMond dual in the 1986 race, *L'Equipe* sold something around 450,000 copies which was 150,000 more than its average daily circulation. So, too, on the day following Eddy Merckx's sensational defeat on the Grenoble to Orcières-Merlette stage of the 1971 Tour, *Het Nieuwsblad* sold 20,000 extra copies. Which, of course, also proves that disasters sell newspapers.

Harry Van den Bremt and Jean Marie Leblanc are friends of long standing. For many years they covered the Union Cycliste Internationale (UCI) Congress and from that their friendship developed. On Leblanc's first day as director of the Tour de France in 1989, he and Harry met in the press room in Luxembourg. Leblanc was angry. Pedro Delgado, wearing the yellow jersey as the previous year's winner, had missed his starting slot in the prologue and, as a result, lost over two and a half minutes. Leblanc was upset this should have happened on his first day in control.

Harry told Jean Marie not to worry, that Delgado's mistake was to the Tour's advantage, arguing that the Spaniard would attack early and often in his efforts to recover the lost time. As others reacted and counterattacked, the pace accelerated and the racing was brilliantly exciting. It happened as Harry predicted.

Maybe his 20 years experience had taught him to take the broader view, to look at the disappointment of the day and see beyond.

Mid-morning and the wind rises, the rain continues to lash. Lake Madine in eastern France is host to this leg of the Tour and it can never have looked greyer. The early starters, those on the bottom of the second page of the classification sheet, are soaked and buffeted as they race the 59 rolling kilometres against the clock. For most of them there are no thoughts of glory, just the certainty that it will end and the promise of a warm shower.

Their efforts are not noticed in the press room, for even though journalists arrive early for work they are concerned only with the bigger battles. Harry Van den Bremt needs to clear decks before getting into the time trial and is writing about the impact of the time bonuses on the first week of the Tour.

Through the first nine days of the race, the bonuses have been a recurring theme. Twenty seconds to the stage winner, 12 to the second, eight to the third and smaller (six, four and two) bonuses for the sprints sprinkled along the way. Sometimes the yellow jersey would stay with one rider or leave another because of a bonus and, for the sprinters, they matter.

Within the greater story, they are a minor sub-plot. As *Het Nieuwsblad* daily devotes three pages to the race there is scope to assess the importance of the bonuses. Harry writes that Mario Cipollini won 86 seconds in bonuses, Wilfried Nelissen 80 and Djamolodin Abdujaparov 60. Of the Tour favourites, only Indurain picked up a time bonus and that was an insignificant four seconds. The conclusion is that there isn't a story: the bonuses helped animate the first week's racing but their influence does not stretch beyond that. It is generally but not always thus.

Underpinning Harry's journalism is his starting point: he came through his profession to the Tour de France, not the other way around. He is journalist first, a cycling enthusiast second. His father owned a factory which manufactured bicycles and actually built bikes for some Belgian professionals. The young Harry saw them come for their bikes and developed an interest in the sport.

He didn't compete himself and when it came to a career, he wanted journalism. Harry's love for the journalistic life has not diminished over time. 'I still see it as the most beautiful job in the world because you have the opportunity to be creative. And you travel a lot, making friends in different places, I couldn't imagine myself in an office all the time. That's not me.'

Sean Kelly, the great Irish champion, once said that, for the riders, the Tour de France is the 'one hundred percent race'. It is equally important for the cycling journalists. What they write from the Tour matters more than anything they write through the year and they remember their Tour experiences long after other races and stories are forgotten.

Harry Van den Bremt's Tour memories cover 25 years. So many miles and so many stories. Can he remember his first? Could he forget? That was 1968. There he was, a neophyte with the good fortune to be reporting on what was likely to be a great Belgian victory. For Harry began in the year when it seemed sure Herman Van Springel would win and give Belgium its first victor since Sylvere Maes in 1939.

Harry reported on Van Springel's progress through that Tour, talking to him every day, writing how the race might unfold and feeling vindicated when Van Springel moved into a winning position. At the start of the final stage, an individual time trial in Paris, Van Springel led his only remaining rival Jan Janssen by 18 seconds and, as he was better than the Dutchman against the clock, it seemed only an accident could undo him.

On that Sunday morning Harry got to the press room early. Because Van Springel's victory was close to certain, Harry got on with it. As the early birds flew in the time trial, he wrote about Van Springel's background, about the implications of the victory, about the reaction of other riders to his triumph. As he did, 10,000 Belgians people boarded special trains in Brussels, determined to be present when Van Springel pushed his head through the last yellow jersey.

Twenty-five years later, it is the picture of Van Springel's head which the journalist continues to see. Never before that day had Janssen beaten Van Springel in a time trial, never afterwards would he better him but on that one day, Janssen beat his rival and beat him well. The Tour was his.

'Belgians are not a chauvinistic people,' says Harry. 'Not at all comparable with the British, or the Germans or the French who all love their own guys. But, everyone of us, we were feeling for that poor guy Herman. You just had to see the look on his face, just like Fernandel, the French comic, the same look with the long teeth. Like the head of a horse who has been beaten.'

Because Van Springel's defeat was so unexpected, Belgians found it difficult to accept. It was said Janssen must have taken dope, that Van Springel was given an incorrect time. Although disappointed for Van Springel whom he liked, Harry Van den Bremt thought the time trial explainable.

'Janssen rode that Tour in a weak Dutch team and because of this he was never considered one of the favourites. But, through the race, he improved his position and was very strong in the final week.'

That evening Harry rewrote every story and the songs of hallelujah became laments.

He followed Van Springel's career afterwards to see how this defeat affected him. People used to say Herman was a bit stupid but Harry didn't believe that. What he saw was an intelligent and simple man. From that Tour defeat, Van Springel became a better rider. Three months later he competed against Janssen in the Grand Prix des Nations time trial and beat him by five minutes. He won many classics and was always at his best in bad conditions.

If Van Springel learned from that Tour so, too, the young Belgian journalist. Twenty-one years later he sat in the offices of *Het Nieuwsblad* on the final day of the 1989 Tour. Colour photographs of the almost certain winner Laurent Fignon were processed and the production people wanted to close the colour pages. (Fignon led Greg LeMond by 50 seconds with only the final 24-kilometre time trial to be completed.)

'Wait,' said Harry, 'wait, wait. You never know what will happen.' So true. LeMond beat Fignon by 58 seconds to win the Tour by eight. At *Het Nieuwsblad's* offices, the photographs of Fignon were replaced by those of LeMond. As the colour pages had not been closed, the newspaper saved money and inconvenience.

Van Springel's long face may have reflected the Belgian mood but that would soon change. At that time a young cyclist was setting out on the greatest journey the sport would ever know. Harry Van den Bremt remembers his first interview with Eddy Merckx: the young cyclist was then an amateur, 19 or 20 years of age and expected to do well at the World Championships in Sallanches.

At the time Merckx's amateur career suggested he was going to be one of the great riders of his era. Harry met him at his house and found him introverted and difficult to interview. With Merckx there was no possibility of getting close, of being taken beneath the surface. They would work together for 14 years and this would never change during that time.

'I didn't ask to be his friend and I think that was the right thing. He was hard to approach and he was always surrounded by a lot of people. When he moved one step to the left, there were a thousand people who went one step to the left. But, as soon as he retired, we became close friends. Today we can't wait to be together. And all those guys who were too close when he was riding, he looks at them now and says "phew!" He doesn't have the same respect for them. It's crazy.'

Harry came away from that first interview with one overriding impression. 'I knew I had been in the company of a man who would never be born again. You could see his enormous strength and his results were unbelievable. In every victory there was a story, he always seemed to win with panache. He had the ability to surpass himself again and again and again.'

Harry has no doubts about Merckx's place in the sport: the greatest cyclist of all. And by a distance. Three times the world news agency United Press International (UPI) voted Merckx its sportsperson of the year. No other world sportsperson won this award three times.

Merckx's greatness lay in the breadth of his talent. He could win the one-day classics and the major tours, more often and more emphatically than any other rider in the history of cycling.

Bernard Hinault followed Merckx and, in the Tour de France, emulated him by winning five but even so Harry argues Merckx was in a different class. 'It's not difficult to say that. You only have to take the record of both riders. When you see Merckx's *palmares* (record) and the *palmares* of Hinault, you always see the difference.

'You can have the same rider as Merckx, with the same force, the same ability and things like that but you will never have a guy who will win so many races. Merckx started on the first day of January in the six-day track races, two weeks later he made a cyclocross and then he started his preparation for the road season. He was on the top level for 12 months of the year. Today you never see Indurain in the classics, you never see him. It's only the Giro and the Tour, that's all.'

In 1969 Eddy Merckx rode his third Giro d'Italia. It was Harry's first. Even though Merckx was young, he was expected to beat more experienced rivals. Things went as Belgians anticipated. Their young rider won a number of stages and the *maglia rosa* (pink jersey) of race leader. With a week to go he looked certain to win. Then, on the evening that the race stopped at Albisola, there was an announcement that Merckx had failed an earlier drugs test.

The shock vibrated back to Brussels. There, the wagons circled in defence of Merckx. One Belgian politician, convinced that the race organizers had conceived this scandal, proposed that diplomatic relations be severed with Italy. Many newspapers urged other forms of protest, some suggesting that Italian emigrants working in Belgium be deported.

Harry Van den Bremt was a young journalist working on his first dope story. He was *Het Nieuwsblad*'s man on the race and from him they expected direction. He wrote that if Merckx had taken illegal products, as the drugs test indicated, he should be punished like any other rider guilty of the same offence.

'Our newspaper received a lot of letters in reply, some were against me but more letters said "Bravo, that's good. You have made a stand against the problem." I got messages from Merckx's entourage that he was upset about what I wrote but he never told me personally. When we met I found him cool so I said, "Listen, when a little rider is positive I say he must be punished. So, when a big rider is positive he has to be punished also."

'He said he didn't take anything but I said you were positive and you remain positive.'

Merckx was dismissed from the race but the controversy lingered. Italians believed Merckx guilty and felt he had cheated their great favourite, Felice Gimondi. With Merckx banished, they directed their anger at the few Belgian journalists covering the race. Supporters of Gimondi threw bottles and other objects at the Belgian cars. *Het Nieuwsblad*'s wasn't spared.

One picture stays with Harry. 'When the news came that Merckx was positive I had to go to his hotel to interview him. I went to his bedroom, he was sitting on the bed crying, the *maglia rosa* alongside him. Every year afterwards I passed the hotel when following the Milan–San Remo classic and I could always see a crying Merckx on his bed, the jersey lying there.'

At the time Harry did not publicly say what he thought. Twenty-four years later, he is less constrained. He believed something was going wrong within Merckx's team. Medical people were trying things and Harry's hunch was that somebody gave Merckx something which they thought was safe. Two weeks after the Giro one of the doctors associated with the team was fired. Harry believed and still believes he was the one held responsible.

The controversy heightened interest in Merckx's first Tour de France. Belgians willed Merckx to prove how good he was, the rest of the cycling world wondered about this champion and Merckx himself desperately wanted to show what he could do. That first Tour de France was Merckx's greatest, says Harry. He won the race by almost 18 minutes. As well as the yellow jersey, he won the green jersey as best sprinter and the polka dot jersey as the best climber. He also won six stages.

On the big Pyrenean stage to Mourenx-Ville Nouvelle he attacked on the Tourmalet and broke clear on his own. Out in front, he increased his lead over the Aubisque. At the finish he was seven minutes ahead of the second-placed rider. All the questions were answered.

Harry Van den Bremt followed Merckx, from victory to victory, admiring the athlete but not knowing the man. And even if there was an exciting extravagance to Merckx's talent, there was only so much the journalists could say. Before the big races, they knew he would win but they daren't write that. For sportswriting demands a little suspense.

'We tried all the tricks. We wrote stories about the other riders, what they thought, how they thought they could beat Merckx. Of course, for a journalist it was not easy.'

Long before the end, the biggest stories were not the victories but the defeats. Like Merckx's sensational defeat by the Spaniard Luis Ocana on the Grenoble to Orcières-Merlette stage of the 1971 Tour and then, four years later, the similarly sensational weakening on the climb to Pra-Loup in the Alps. In '71 Merckx recovered from the loss to Ocana to win the race but in '75 he could not regain the time lost to Thevenet.

Harry Van den Bremt was there for the last race. An inconsequential event in the Belgian town of Kemzeke at the beginning of the 1978 season. He finished seventh or eighth, not many cared at the time but Merckx was upset. He thought he should have been better. After the race he asked Guillaume Michiels, his *soigneur*, for his training top and even though he had just ridden 220 kilometres, Merckx punished himself by riding a further 60 kilometres to his Brussels home. The official announcement of his retirement came four weeks later.

He stayed too long? 'Yeah, yeah. He couldn't accept. He couldn't see that every man has a career, he gets to the top but then there is a decline. It was very difficult for *him* to accept that. He would try different positions on the bike, different training methods because he could not accept that it was over.'

One champion leaves the stage, another enters. That year, 1978, Bernard Hinault won his first Tour de France, the first of five. Harry can't forget this one, either.

It was so hot that day on Alpe d'Huez. As he remembers he nods towards the canvas roof and the sound of driving rain, 'Indurain won't like it' he says before returning to this infamous afternoon on the Alpe. He was in the non-denominational church of Notre Dame des Neiges which served as the press headquarters and feeling the tiredness a Tour reporter feels at the end of a long day.

That afternoon his compatriot Michel Pollentier rode the race of his life to break away from his principal rivals and finish alone at the top of the mountain. Pollentier also won the yellow jersey and had a good chance of holding on to it to the very end.

Harry's story had been sent when his friend Jean Marie Leblanc sought him out. 'Most of the journalists had finished and returned to their hotels, only a few were still in the chapel. Jean Marie came over and said, "Harry, you are going to have to re-write your stories."'

Leblanc, then a cycling writer with *L'Equipe*, had heard that race leader Pollentier was caught trying to cheat his drugs test. He would be expelled from the race. In that quiet chapel, all hell was about to break loose. What could be bigger than a man taking the yellow jersey in the Tour de France? A man taking it and then losing because he was afraid to pee.

The Pollentier affair was a mixture of tragedy and comedy. Not certain that his urine sample would pass the test, Pollentier armed himself with a rubber bulb and tube contraption. The bulb, concealed in his armpit, contained urine which was not his own and the adjoining tube was taped down his back, under the buttocks to emerge below the penis. Pollentier intended to squeeze the bogus urine into the doctor's flask.

It might have worked were it not for Antoine Gutierrez. A French rider, Gutierrez was giving a sample at the same time as Pollentier and found to be in possession of a similar if less sophisticated contraption. Once he was discovered, attention turned to Pollentier and when the doctor pulled down his shorts he discovered private parts which the rider would have preferred to remain private. For *Het Nieuwsblad*'s three journalists the story could hardly have been bigger. One went to Pollentier's hotel, another to race director Felix Levitan's and Harry worked from the press room. Adding to the story was the widespread accusation, made by Pollentier and others, that the French organizers wanted Hinault to win and that the removal of his chief rival facilitated them.

Fifteen years on the old reporter believes that was a part of the story. 'That feeling was very strong in Belgium. You see at the time there was never much problem at the medical control caravan. Then there was this very thorough test. Something must have been said to the doctor, like "you have got to do this very carefully". Maybe it was an organizer, maybe it was the sports director of another team. But you can't prove it, of course.'

Pollentier left in disgrace, accused by the organizers of having besmirched the name of the Tour. Harry couldn't help liking him. 'I liked him for his honesty. He was considered a cheat by everybody and most people in his position would not have dared to appear in public. But the day after he came out and said "I was stupid, I did a stupid thing. Even though many other guys do the same thing, I was the one caught." He would not name the others. He was the kind of guy you liked.'

A little after mid-day and the rain continues to fall. Because each drop carries a threat to Miguel Indurain, the journalists grow more animated. Every human huddle considers the implications of Indurain not gaining his customary advantage in the time trial.

His story on the time bonuses filed, Harry Van den Bremt talks to a young woman who has travelled from Lans-en-Vercors to distribute publicity material about her region.

'What's the weather like in the Alps?'

'Bad,' she says, 'it's cold and raining down there. It has been for the last couple of weeks.'

In two days the Tour would be in the Alps and Harry is encouraged by the new possibilities. Maybe there would be another winner of this race. Chiappucci? No. Very aggressive with a big heart but a *picolo motore*, he says choosing the Italian expression for a small engine. Rominger? No. At 32, he thinks it too late for the Swiss rider to begin winning this race. There is one rider who can take on Indurain, Gianni Bugno. He has started the race well and Harry thinks he is physically capable of beating the champion.

How many times has he done this? Used rain, or a crash, or a puncture, or a minor stomach bug, once again to weigh the possibilities. And what fuels *his* engine? Love for the Tour? Love for the sport? Both are factors in his motivation but not the principal one. Harry is a journalist, his duty is to his profession. He wouldn't see anything noble or romantic in this and idealism doesn't come into it. It is simpler than that: a job, one that he wants to do well.

Most journalists following the Tour admit to a love of the race. As enthusiasts, they want the race to become more popular. Drugs are a question they will happily leave to one side. Far better to write about angels on wheels.

But that's not Harry. He was in Albisola when Merckx cried and later a witness to the humiliation of Pollentier. His starting point is that there is a problem, because drug-taking has always existed and will always exist. It is part of human nature to look for solutions wherever they can be found. A truck driver, faced with a 600-km, journey and feeling tired, reaches for a stimulant.

In sport, the temptation to seek chemical assistance is much stronger. Those who govern have serious responsibilities and Harry Van den Bremt is sure that cycling's authorities are failing their sport. He watched with incredulity when the controlling UCI decided in 1992 to discontinue the

In the prologue to the race Miguel Indurain made his first mark, his rivals saw it and feared what was to follow

The calm followed the storm. Strong and aggressive as he prepares to celebrate his victory at Verdun, Lance Armstrong's mood is pensive two days later in Grenoble

The Tour's first sprint at Les Sables d'Olonne was ominous for Jean-Paul Van Poppel. Third from the left, he trails Mario Cipollini (the winner) by two bike lengths, a deficit he would not make up in later sprints. In this finish Cipollini is more concerned with, from left, Jaan Kirsipuu, Wilfried Nelissen, Laurent Jalabert and Johan Capiot. Van Poppel quit in the first mountain stage. Edwig Van Hooydonck (inset) kept riding even though he disliked the attention he received as the last-placed rider in the Tour

For an *équipier* like Neil Stephens, time trials are endured rather than enjoyed. The two spectators show no more than a passing interest. Bernard Hinault, on left, did not merely endure time trials, he won them

On every Tour there are occasional and all too fleeting moments when tranquillity reigns and the riders get some peace. Sean Yates expresses his appreciation with a smile. At his right shoulder Neil Stephens doesn't look quite so comfortable, a sign of things to come?

Chazal came nineteenth of 20 in the team time trial but getting the team on the road was Vincent Lavenu's greatest achievement. On the right Once's doctor, Nicolas Terrados, sits on the steps of his mobile laboratory. Terrados provides a medical back-up service which low-budget teams like Chazal can only dream about

Twenty-five years ago there were 50 journalists and constant worries about phone lines. The race has grown and so too the Press Room. As a speaker of six languages, no rider is better equipped to help the international media than Tony Rominger

Bicycling down the Champs Elysées for the final time, Stephen felt both sad and happy: sad to be leaving, happy with the style of his exit

Claudio Chiappucci likes being called *El Diablo* (the devil) and his helmet furthers the association. He said he was 'a good devil' but, for him, the Tour was sometimes hell

**Indurain's dominance was never seriously threatened and the serenity he shows
on the final podium had been apparent for three weeks**

practice of releasing the names of those who fail drug tests.

'The UCI is not right. They decided only for the money, commercialism, the relationship with the sponsors of UCI teams. It is very bad when, for example, the cheese-manufacturer who sponsors a team has a rider who is positive. The product becomes associated with dope. So, the UCI decided not to mention the names of those who are positive.

'Under UCI regulations, the positive rider gets a three-months suspended sentence, they have an amount to pay and they lose 50 world ranking points. As a journalist, it is not normal that the only way I discover a rider is positive is getting the FICP (Federation of International Cycling Professionals) rankings each month and seeing if any rider has been taxed 50 points. In my computer at home I have a system where I can find this but the UCI gives no names, it gives no races and it does not tell which dope product was discovered. This change is very bad for the sport.'

Ten days into the Tour de France there is not the whiff of a dope story. Five years have passed since the Tour's last scandal and three years since the last positive. Three hundred tests and not one failure. Within the race there is now a sense that dope is yesterday's problem, a part of the race's less sophisticated past. Harry does not accept the problem has gone away.

'So, we've had three years of no positives in the Tour. That gives the impression of credibility and everyone says "ah, that's marvellous". But when you see how this race is developing, you wonder. Every day the riders are beating records, the stage to Amiens which Bruyneel won was the fastest in the history of the Tour.

'The roads are better, the materials are better but I think the preparation, the medical preparation, is also better. I am talking about what they take. The doctor plays a big part in how riders prepare. We know there are new products but you can't prove it. And the only way I can find out if there is a positive is to check the FICP rankings on my computer.'

Harry wonders how today's riders will be 20 years from now. Maybe then we will understand what they were doing during their careers.

'People talk about how bad it was in the time when riders were taking amphetamines. Now you can see Rik Van Looy, he is over 60 but you would say he is only 40. That is all he looks. I see Kubler. They say he began with amphetamines at breakfast, though it was never proved. He's 71 now and he looks like a guy of 50.

'But what will happen with the champions of today. Twenty years down the road, how will they be? That's when we could see the Glory of Sport.'

Harry's warning is rasping and unmistakable. It comes from an old watchdog. One who hasn't lost his bite.

The rain stopped early in the afternoon. The wind which buffeted the morning starters died away. Miguel Indurain, a late starter, made the best of the improved conditions, winning the 59-km time trial by over two minutes. This performance jumped him from 27th place to race leader, one minute 35 seconds ahead of second-placed Erik Breukink. Two weeks of racing remained and although few were saying the Tour was over, most felt it.

The press room was a quieter place. However impressive, Indurain's victory in the time trial drained much of the suspense from the race. Without suspense, long tours seem longer. And even then few realized that Tony Rominger, who would emerge as the only serious challenger, was the rider most hurt by the wind and rain.

Quite the moment of the day came long after the racing ended. Prudencio Indurain, four years younger than his brother, finished last of the 171 starters in the time trial. He was 17 minutes 48 seconds slower than Miguel and close to the limit which would have meant automatic elimination. Those with an eye for the finer details suggested to Jose Miguel Echavarri, manager of the Indurains' Banesto team, that he might have lost Prudencio if Miguel had not punctured on the way. The 30 seconds which Miguel lost in changing wheels had kept his brother on the right side of the time limit.

To this Echavarri replied 'From the summit, one can see everything.'

And Harry Van den Bremt wrote another story for *Het Nieuwsblad*. A difficult piece because in telling of Indurain's prowess, he was writing of a race running too true to expectation. Difficult also because Harry does not find Indurain easy to write about. 'He rides like Jacques Anquetil. Very, very good in the time trials and he uses that to dominate. He is supposed to be a very nice guy and I imagine he is. But you can't feel it. And for me it is hard because I don't speak Spanish and he doesn't speak French or Dutch or German or English.'

All the stories are filed. The press room is empty. Harry has gone to his hotel. Another Tour day ended. One which began with possibilities had faded into certainties. Indurain. Indurain. Indurain. The whispered expectations, the clever theories; they counted for nothing. Even Harry went with the talk of Indurain slipping a little. What had it all been about?

It was then an old admission came to mind. Merckx, Harry had said, was difficult for the journalist. What could they say about the man who always won? So they spoke to other riders who talked of Merckx's weaknesses, the ways in which he might be beaten. 'We tried all the tricks,' Harry had said.

Twenty years after the old champion, Harry tries the same tricks with the new champion.

He thinks he will do two or three more Tours and that will be it. He doesn't want to be covering the Tour de France at 65. Because for all the fun of the race, the working days are long and tiring. When *Het Nieuwsblad* finds a younger reporter, he will show him or her the ropes and willingly move to one side. Without regrets.

Because Harry Van den Bremt has enjoyed the life. Liked the work. Loved being on the Tour and never minded change. As the race grew it opened its arms to commercialism. The tented village is, for Harry, the symbol of the new age. It provides breakfast for the sponsors and their guests but has nothing to do with cycling or the cyclists. Yet without it, he says, the modern Tour is not possible.

Merckx, you imagine aloud, must have been his hero. 'No, no, no. I'm a journalist, for me a man is a man. Heroes cannot be found in sport. In sport you have some riders who are better than others, some sportsmen who are better than others but a hero, sorry you must look elsewhere for him.

'Merckx was a man of flesh and blood. He had the ability to win a lot of races but a hero, not in my eyes. A hero is a guy who does something special for mankind. Maybe the scientist who will produce the cure for cancer. He would be my hero.'

Like many travelling reporters, Harry has depended on his partner's generosity. Lutgarde, his wife, accepted he would be often away. Without her support, everything would have been different. He thinks back to when his two children, Wim and Els, were young and he covered all three major tours. He spent May in Spain, June in Italy and July in France. So rarely at home and so reliant on Lutgarde.

Once, she demurred. It was a New Year's Eve and they were enjoying it at home. Harry thinks it must have been the mid-70s because the children were still young and that was the time he was travelling to every race. Lutgarde gave him an envelope, which he took to be a gift. Inside the envelope was a calendar of the year about to end. Encircled were the nights that Harry had not slept in their bed. Totalled, they numbered 175.

Lutgarde wasn't complaining but wanted Harry to understand that if he wanted to increase the size of his family, he would have to do better.

Harry looked at all the circles and thought it was crazy. He couldn't have been away *that* much. But he was. It was he who was crazy.

And, still crazy after all these years.

6

1

THE EQUIPIER'S TALE
Nature has its Way
SEAN YATES

1. Sean Yates
2. Yates — 'The last of the great *équipiers*' according to Stephen Roche
3. On the extreme right, Yates leads the Motorola line-up

2

3

The frog and the scorpion were talking by the river. Both wished to get to the other side. Although there was a strong current, the frog knew he would be able to swim. The scorpion asked if he could take a ride on the frog's back. He was so light, the frog would hardly know he was there.

Afraid of the scorpion's venomous sting, the frog was reluctant. 'If I carry you,' he said, 'you'll just sting me and I'll die.' 'Don't be silly,' answered the scorpion, 'if I were to sting you while I was on your back, I would be killing myself because I can't swim.'

Swayed by this logic, the frog agreed to carry the scorpion across the river. They were over halfway and going well when the frog felt the scorpion's long tail slide into its flesh. Seconds later he could feel the poison work. As he sunk, the frog saw that the scorpion was going down with him.

'Why did you do it,' yelled the frog.

'It's in my nature,' said the scorpion.

Strange that this story should call Sean Yates to mind for no human could be further from the scorpion. Yates is a big but gentle man, quiet but affable and utterly without venom. The single ring in his left ear bespeaks a softness at odds with his profession. Most unusual for a pro cyclist, he is liked by all. 'A lovely guy, a real nice and reliable man,' says Martin Earley who shared hotel rooms with Yates when both rode for the Fagor team in 1987.

He has been a professional since 1982, 12 seasons and already signed up for a 13th. When he thinks about it, Yates can just about believe it. He earns a good salary now, something around £80,000 a year and says if he lived in his native England, he would be in the top five per cent of that country's earners. But then Yates is one of the best team riders in the *peloton*.

'The last of the great *équipiers* (team-riders),' says Stephen Roche. A line of praise which may not be far-fetched.

Allan Peiper rode with Yates for two years at Peugeot. They roomed together, trained together and became close friends. Time passed, Peiper found a new team and then a new career, Yates moved from Peugeot. On this Tour Peiper works for Australian television and Yates rides for the American-backed Motorola team.

Each morning Peiper comes early to the tented village. He was always an early riser and even if Yates didn't like the dawn training spins they had together, he knew they were good for him. Now Peiper comes early to catch interviews. At the village, he watches out for Yates. He doesn't need to talk or even greet his friend, just wants to see him there. At the finish, it's the same. Peiper's eyes x-ray the *peloton* as it passes, searching for one face. And Peiper knows where the feeling comes from.

'Sean's always been a caring type of guy, that's why we got along so well. I needed someone to lean on. Like a big brother, if I needed a hand or a shoulder, he was always there. I think he has been like that for everybody.'

The only criticism heard about Yates was that he didn't care enough about himself. So busy looking out for others that he neglected himself. 'He was good enough but wasn't selfish enough to be a top rider,' says Roche.

What is undisputed is Yates' prodigious talent.

It was obvious from that first year in the *peloton* back in 1982 and a spring afternoon in the north of France. Jan Raas, then one of the great riders, attacked five kilometres from the finish of a stage in the Four Days of Dunkirk. Those near the front when Raas accelerated had seen this before, the fierce attack to establish the advantage and then the sheer power to sustain it.

And many wouldn't bother about a serious pursuit because, with Raas, you weren't going to catch him. Innocent in the ways of the *peloton*, Yates went after the Dutch rider. Those who knew Yates, and there weren't many, thought this would be interesting. Yates devoured the daylight which divided Raas from his rivals and the race was decided in a big sprint.

Yates didn't win but he had made his point. Very displeased, Raas spoke to him at the finish. 'Young guys don't normally do that to me and when one does it, he does it only once.' Yates wondered why Raas was so upset. It was a race, wasn't it?

Over the years there have been some notable Yates performances. His victory in the long individual time trial at Wasquehal in the 1988 Tour de France stands out. This time trial, placed at around the same point in every Tour, separates the wheat from the chaff. Indurain's race begins in earnest at the time trial and he has won it for three consecutive years, LeMond won it in '89, Roche in '87, Hinault in '86 and '85, Fignon in '84. And Sean Yates, he won it in 1988.

His peers were not surprised. Yates can shift. You don't see what he does in races, they say. All the riding for his team; getting to the front of the pack and controlling the race for 20 kilometres. Do you know what it takes to do that? But at the end the winner stands alone on the podium, accepting the applause, telling how good *he* is. And Yates cannot blow his own trumpet. He doesn't even have a trumpet.

Of course he wins a few races every year and he likes that. He jokes that when you win as seldom as he does, you forget what it's like to put your hands in the air. But something has always struck him about the euphoric feeling: it passes too quickly. Enjoyed for an instant and then gone. The next day someone else wins, his hands go up in the air, he's in the news and you, you are yesterday's hero.

Hard to say if he consciously decided to become an *équipier* or if he just freewheeled into service. 'I like to win but I'm not motivated to win. I never go into a race saying "I want to win this". The thing that motivates me is riding for someone, either leading out a sprinter or helping a climber or defending a jersey. And when I'm in that situation, in any of those situations, then I perform much better because I'm motivated.'

It is more than a simple desire to work for others. It is better, he says, to be a worthwhile team rider than a below average leader. Good team riders get good reputations and good contracts. And even if the satisfaction of helping a team-mate is not the same as that of winning, the former is easier to achieve.

At the end of a racing day what matters is self-respect. When Yates joins his team-mates at the evening meal, he likes to feel he has done his job, made his contribution. To sit before them knowing he has done what was expected of him. This is what he most wants from life on the bike.

Sometimes it bothered Allan Peiper. Yates worked for him even when it was clear that he, Yates, was the stronger rider. So Peiper would round on his friend: 'Hey Sean, you're the man that can do it. You've got so much ability why don't you get out and do it.'

Yates would shyly demur, not agreeing, not disagreeing and not changing. 'He always called me the master of the job,' says Peiper, 'that was because of my desire to be good but unfortunately I only had a limited amount of ability. Sean had much more depth as a rider. In the mountains he would be three or four groups ahead of me and he would think, "what's the difference between finishing 60th and 160th" and he would wait for me, then stay with me all the way to the finish. If I was getting dropped, he'd go slow for me.'

Peiper reckoned it wasn't just that Sean liked riding for his team-mates. Part of his selflessness came from the fear of responsibility. 'I think there's a bit of scariness there, he never wanted to face up to his own desires. When he rode for me I felt he was hiding behind me, like it gave him a corner that he could stand behind. There was no pressure because he didn't want pressure.'

Roger Yates watched his son's progress from boy to man, from amateur to pro and, where he could, he helped. He sees the evolution differently. 'I don't know if Sean is laid back, I think he is slightly lazy although he will hate me for saying that. He didn't have the killer instinct and still doesn't have it.

'He was never totally convinced that he had what it takes and maybe he was right. I don't think he was good enough for the first *echelon*. As it turned out what he loved doing was being a top team man and he loved riding for people that were good.'

His friend believes he was fearful of responsibility, his dad reckons he knew he wasn't good enough to be a frontline rider and settled for something else. Fetching bottles, giving a wheel to a team-mate, shielding another from the wind, pacing a team-mate up a mountain, guiding another on the descent. Twelve years of this and he has loved every week of it.

And you know why he does it this way?

It is in his nature.

It is now 20 minutes after eight, the meeting was set for half-past but fearing the conversation will run late, Yates shows up early. It had been a long day in the Alps, he could feel it in his legs, another mountain day to follow; he will need his sleep.

He waits outside the Hotel Olympic in Chantemerle. Massaged and fed, he chats with his team-mate Phil Anderson. He has got to know Anderson over the previous three years and they get on well. Don't ask him to room with Phil for they cannot agree on lights-out. Yates likes to turn in at around 10, Phil, later, much later.

Anderson's victory in the 1992 Tour of Ireland pleased him for it was one of the days when Yates was inspired by his *équipier's* instinct. Before the start of the final stage to Dublin, he decided nobody was getting away. Physically, he didn't feel so good but there was a yellow jersey to defend and one day to survive. On the road to Dublin Yates maintained such a high pace that most were discouraged from breaking away and those who did escape were recaptured. Anderson held his jersey. Yates enjoyed his food that evening.

There was another day on the Tour of Ireland: a winning performance in a 1987 stage through the hilly countryside of the southwest. He rode with Fagor then and without a strong leader, he *had* to think of himself. That day he attacked just after the start.

They saw him escape and worried. That's Yates, be careful, he's too good to let go. Because this was the most difficult stage of the race, the big men weren't prepared to give Yates leeway. The chase was furious. He raced about 300 yards clear of the pack, once or twice he was sighted, going over the brow of a little hill and because they could see him, they thought they were sure to catch him.

For almost 30 minutes the pursuit continued. Then the leaders of the pack looked up: he was gone. They lost heart and he won the race by 13 minutes.

That was Stephen Roche's great year and his return to Ireland meant an unusually high media interest. Many journalists unfamiliar with cycling were present. Afterwards one of them interviewed Yates, offered congratulations and asked what seemed to him the obvious question.

'Sean, you began today's stage 26 minutes down, you won by 13 minutes today, do you think you can do the same tomorrow and take the yellow jersey.' Yates had just ridden the hardest 100 miles of his life, given 20 interviews in 30 minutes and then this.

The expression on his face never changed. There was no incredulity, no exasperation, no hostility. As politely as anybody could, he explained that although he had ridden hard to get clear, the winning margin of 13 minutes happened because his rivals had stopped chasing. It is not often that happens, he said.

And, he went on, there was no chance it would happen on two successive days and therefore no possibility of him winning the race. 'Thank you,' said the journalist, who went off with his quotes and a better understanding of bicycle racing.

Benoit Faure rode in the '30s, a very good climber but not complete enough to win the Tour de France. He placed 13th in the 1931 Tour, one place below the Australian Hubert Opperman. 'I saw a great deal of Oppy in that Tour,' Faure recalled in a conversation with cycling writer J B Wadley, 'and I particularly remember a burning hot day on the Esterel hill along the Mediterranean coast.

'Yes really burning – the sun had set the trees on fire. Some Australian friends handed Oppy a bottle on the climb – champagne. He liked the stuff but was worried how it would affect him in the heat. He was going to chuck it away, the chump. So I grabbed it, had a swig, filled my old tin *bidon*, and handed the rest to a pal. Didn't do me any harm! Don't get the idea that I was always drinking, though. Far from it. I refused water and beer, but it broke my heart to see champagne thrown away.'

Since Faure, glucose has replaced champagne. When Yates looks back on his 12-year career he wonders at the rate of change. A great evolution within his sport and much change in himself. He didn't plan it but found himself swept along by the prevailing winds. But Yates did like the higher wages and he accepted the new demands. He trained harder, he raced harder and he rested more conscientiously.

He remembers how it was when he started, down in the south of France with the ACBB amateur team preparing for the season. He won his first race, thinks it was the Grand Prix de St Tropez and then went rapidly downhill. His weight increased by over 20 pounds and he failed to finish 14 consecutive races. In fact he didn't much care if they sent him home because he preferred home.

But ACBB persevered and by the end of the season he achieved enough to be offered a professional contract with Peugeot. That was 1982 and he joined a team that already had Roche, Anderson, Gilbert Duclos-Lassalle, Jean-René Bernaudeau. It was a high-powered team but, back then, Yates wasn't ready.

He lived in Joue-les-Tours with John Herety, an English-born professional who rode for the Coop-Mercier team. Stephen Roche, then an ambitious young professional, knew Yates could ride but he couldn't fathom the man. 'He and John (Herety) stayed together and whenever you went looking for Sean in the bunch, you only had to find John. They spent a lot of time at the back of the *peleton,* chatting away while the race went on up front. I used to wonder did they not talk enough down in Joue-les-Tours?'

Yates remembers the five years at Peugeot with mixed feelings. They were good times because he had a happy-go-lucky nature and, as he was paid badly (circa £200 per week), he didn't feel any obligation to produce big performances. There was less pressure then, team budgets were small and the demands on the riders were considerably less than now.

Often he and other Peugeot riders would decide before a race that they were going to pull out at the first feeding station. They would climb off at that point, hide behind the *soigneur*'s car until the *directeur sportif* passed and then travel to the finish on four wheels. 'Half the team was going to pack, so it was easy to be one of them. Nowadays if you pack, you're likely to be the only one and how can you then show your face at dinner?' he asks.

For the first five years, he waited until the very end of the season before knowing if he was to be retained for another one. At the end of his second year, he thought he was on his way home but Roche and the Peugeot sprinter Francis Castaing spoke on his behalf. Roche once asked Yates what he would do if Peugeot fired him. 'Go back home and do a bit of gardening,' he told his bewildered team-mate.

Peiper's coming to Peugeot helped. He was a serious professional and their friendship developed quickly. Through the two seasons they spent together, Peiper impressed his team-mate and as the Australian moved forward, Yates stayed close behind. When Peiper won the Tour of Sweden, his friend was third; when he won the Tour de l'Oise, Yates was fourth and when Peiper was third in the prologue of the 1984 Tour de France, Yates was sixth.

Yates put down his own marker as well, winning the prologue of the 1984 Four Days of Dunkirk, a performance which might have been forgotten were it not for the list of the vanquished: prologue specialists Bernard Hinault, Eric Vanderaerden, Alain Bondue and Jean-Luc Vandenbroucke.

He was, of course, still underachieving. Although he trained hard, he didn't understand his body and so didn't train effectively. And, as Peiper says, he hid behind the mask of the *équipier,* fearful of the pressures which personal ambition brings. And then there was his health.

More specifically, his teeth. Through the first six years of his pro career Yates was forever suffering from neuralgia, never sure which tooth pained until it seemed that every one of them ached.

There were countless nights when he couldn't sleep and soon after the onset of pain came the abscesses. Sometimes the infection spread through his body and this happened most frequently during stage races when his immune system was at its weakest.

He suffered from poor health, picking up whatever bug was going and recovering less quickly than his rivals. Then, his teeth began to fall out. Roger organized for him to see a dentist who practised at Harley Street in London.

In the winter of 1987, the treatment began. Yates appreciated the dedication of the dentist and didn't mind the cost. He knew what his teeth had already cost him. The treatment went on for five years; he paid £15,000 and now has 22 reconstructed teeth. Shortly after the treatment began, the bouts of neuralgia decreased and the infections ceased. His general health improved enormously. Now he is hardly ever sick.

At the end of five years at Peugeot, Yates searched for a new team and wasn't deluged with offers. He joined Fagor, with whom he spent two years. Although frustrated by Fagor's lack of organization, he rode well and had his greatest win in his second year: the 1988 Tour de France time trial, a performance which showed what he could do and it set him up for the rest of his career.

But Yates desperately wanted to get away from Fagor and when the American team 7-Eleven made him an offer, he signed. That was 1989 and he has not moved since although the team now races in Motorola's colours. Life has been good with the American team, they pay on time and they organize correctly. He loved especially the first year when the team raced innocently but very successfully.

Based in America, they hit Europe at different times in the season and good results fell their way. Beginners' luck maybe, but no less satisfying for that. Dag-Otto Lauritzen, a Norwegian, was with 7-Eleven and he and Yates struck up a friendship that would deepen and last. He's been lucky in his friends. From Herety to Peiper to Dag-Otto. People who at different times were there for him.

7-Eleven was a good team. Andy Hampsten rode well, Davis Phinney could sprint, Ron Kiefel was also there, Bob Roll was a character. They survived with an attitude which, if not cavalier, lacked the grim seriousness of their European rivals. But as the budget grew, the pressure to win increased and with this came the realization that the team would have to become more European.

So they spent more time in Europe and adopted racing programmes similar to their rivals. Motorola replaced 7-Eleven as team sponsors and the success was sustained. By now Yates was better paid than he ever imagined and his attitude to the sport became more professional. For six years he had lived from season to season but that changed and now he talks about how much money he will need to give himself a start in life after cycling.

Within the Motorola team he is *the* team-rider, a respected man. In the stage races he takes care of Hampsten and, more recently, Lance Armstrong. Armstrong has been hugely impressed. 'Sean doesn't talk much at all, so I kid him sometimes, call him my security blanket. I just like being around the guy in the *peloton*. I know if I'm ever in trouble or if I'm ever in a bad position, I'll be at the front as soon as I ask.'

Yates has watched Armstrong's arrival and seen a kid who could not be more different from himself. Confident, assertive, impatient and without an ounce of fear; Armstrong wants to win every-time he races. He is good for Yates because *équipiers* need winners in the team. 'Sean is at his best riding for the very best, he has to have frontline leaders to ride for,' says Stephen Roche.

Yates' admiration for Armstrong betrays a little envy. 'He's got that killer instinct and he's got the legs to back it up so he's a lucky guy you know. He gives me something to work for. If you've got leaders who are not the best you are out there saying "sod this for a game of soldiers." If you've got say Cipollini in your team, you're laughing.'

Yates doesn't laugh easily but he smiles often, the milder expression reflecting his liking for understatement. Pressed on what makes such a good *équipier*, he explains as a postman might describe his rounds.

'When you've been riding as many years as me, you get to know the races. The terrain is the same and if you have a good memory, you'll know where the climbs are. So if it is Lance or Andy or Max (Sciandri) and he's got a winning chance I know where he's gotta be at a certain point. By getting him there, I can make it easier for him. Say in a stage of Paris–Nice that goes up the Col du Tanneron, I'm not going to win over that so I make sure to get our guy to the bottom of the Tanneron in the right position. So I do that, it's not so bloody difficult, and when I have that done I can sort of have a bit of peace.

'If I don't do it, then our guy must do it for himself and that makes it a bit harder for him. And he is competing against somebody who has had this help. I do it and I know I have made my con-tribution. I get x-amount of salary to do a job and I must do it. It's that simple.'

Ask Roger Yates about his childhood and he laughs nervously, playing for time. He says he doesn't want to go into that. 'My youth is a very sad memory.' He picks up the story of his life from the day he first went to art school where he studied painting and sculpture. He concentrates on sculpture now, carving stone to produce pieces which are neither representational nor abstract. 'They are what I call pure form,' he says.

Ask Sean Yates about his childhood and the memories flow. Happy days. Retrieving old bikes from a tip, patching them up, racing through Ashdown Forest with his younger brother Christian and his two friends, Paul Dival and Richard Turner. Then, a little older, they went on long rides together and, invariably, the day ended in a race.

He played soccer, too, and fancied himself playing goalkeeper for England. When the seasons changed he was away on his skateboard or going rock-climbing with Roger. Sean's was an outdoor life; fast and fun.

Things evolved with the innocent purchase of a cycling magazine, Christian and himself reading it and thinking this could be them. From money given to him by an uncle, Sean bought his first rac-ing bike and soon he was winning. Roger watched from a distance at first and thought he saw unusual talent.

As a boy Roger had been a good runner but a little lazy and he didn't pursue it. As he grew older he wondered how important it was that he didn't have a relationship with his family, didn't have the encouragement of his parents. When his own children arrived, he wanted them to have more.

Roger's way was gentle, encouraging Sean with his enthusiasm. It didn't matter how far away the race was, Roger was game. 'Sometimes we used to leave at two or three in the morning. I took the passenger's seat out of the car and made a bed in its place so Sean could get out of his bed, get straight into the bed of the car, go back to sleep and wake up three or four hours later halfway up the M1.'

Sean has his memories. 'Once Dad drove me from bloody Sussex to Glasgow and back in one day for a Kellogg's criterium, that's 16 hours driving for a one-hour crit. Poor guy. He was just looking after me, that was his motivation. He liked to see me do well. There's no way I would have done anything without him.'

Other riders came to Roger and told him if they had a Dad like him, they would do much better. After races he would clean Sean's bike, working into the small hours of the morning, washing and drying with the fervour of a fanatic. He prided himself on the fact that Sean Yates rarely punctured because his tyres were always immaculate. Whatever the latest equipment, he checked it out to see if it could be of use to his son.

'When I reflect on those years I was living through him, that's what it was. It was a phase I went through. I realized for a father to do that, there were great dangers. While I got angry once or twice, I never pushed him.'

The important decision came when Sean finished school and started a part-time gardening job. 'My wife Jennifer and I spoke to Sean and said if he was prepared to show real discipline at his training, we would keep him for as long as it took him to make it.' Sometimes Sean wasn't that bothered about training but was driven by his parents' belief in him. He owed it to them to give it a serious shot.

In 1981 he left home for ACBB in Paris but the support continued. Roger, Jennifer and the four other children holidayed in France during the Tour so they could be close to Sean during the most difficult race. Each year they came for the Pyrenean and Alpine stages because it was there they would be most appreciated.

Having seen and cheered Sean on the climbs, they went to his hotel in the evening and how he loved to see them come. Much of the disappointment at having to abandon the '87 Tour came from having to pull out at the very moment his family were making themselves comfortable out on the course.

'It was the morning of the second last stage, a time trial at Dijon. I had an infection in my hand which was as big as a boxing glove. What upset me about pulling out was knowing they were out on the *parcours*, expecting me to come past.'

Roger Yates has been a witness to his son's career. He says the win in the Tour de France time trial would have to be rated the biggest but, for him, it wasn't the greatest. No. Roger's greatest moments were on the mountain sides in the Tour, watching his boy struggle upwards, sometimes 20 or 30 minutes behind the leaders.

'People are motivated by and linked to winners. It's typical of all sports. But I am a great lover of the workers, the underdogs, the team-riders. The great riders cannot exist without the lesser ones. I don't think the public realizes the protection given to the top riders, especially in a race like the Tour. Everything is done for them, I don't think the public's imagination can grasp this.

'When you wait up a mountain for two or three hours it is marvellous to see what's happening at the front but when you see the poor buggers struggling . . . I feel more for them because they are putting more into it, because they have done all the donkey work as well. It's fantastic really. That gives me the greatest thrill, seeing them and hoping they will make it inside the time limit. Yeah, yeah, it's a hard bloody sport.'

Roger is proud of what his son is rather than what he has achieved. 'Some people are givers, some are takers. Sean is one of the rarest givers.'

Hereditary, maybe? Dad encouraging his boy to train, driving him to races, listening to the anxieties, suggesting solutions. Being there. You suggest to the son that his Dad has been a giver.

'Yeah, yeah,' he agrees. 'It could run in the family.'

Yates knew they wouldn't stay in a better hotel, the Chateau de la Commanderie; nice atmosphere, outstanding food. They would be gone in the morning. Worse luck. But they had stayed two nights and it was a good place to spend a rest day on the Tour de France. Eleven of the Tour's 23 days had passed. Almost halfway.

As he faded off to sleep he wondered if his roommate Steve Bauer would be okay on the next day's race through the Alps. First day in the mountains was always hard and Steve had a slight infection. That afternoon he had been first to turn back on the team's training ride.

He has never needed a wake-up call or an alarm clock: the watch inside his head is reliable. With the next day's race beginning at 10, he has to be out of bed at seven. Once that information is assimilated, he can fall asleep.

Breakfast is notably quiet; always is on the morning of a mountain stage and Yates, never the perkiest at dawn, adds to the sombre mood. His team-mates are a lot like him: mostly a group of serious bike riders and middle of the road characters. Cycling has discovered, as other sports did before it, that big salaries hasten the death of flamboyance.

Once he accepted the new ways and thought about the future, Yates discovered that his body was the key. If you understood it, you could mind it and he began to listen to its messages. It didn't function well on certain types of food and the amount had to be strictly controlled. He listened to his heartbeat and it told him whether he was fresh, tired or in-between. He trained accordingly.

He laments this is his last breakfast at the Chateau. His mental arithmetic is straightforward: three hours to the start of the stage, five hours to the first climb, the Col du Glandon; Yates rides best on a light stomach and so settles for a bowl of muesli and two croissants. He has to be strong on the Glandon.

For his job is to get over it in a good position and then shelter Andy Hampsten in the Maurienne Valley which comes after the Glandon and before the Col du Telegraphe. He has ridden this valley many times and expects a troublesome crosswind.

Since joining the American team in '89, he has regularly ridden for Hampsten. Andy is not the

easiest guy to work for but Yates understands that the calm and articulate Colorado boy is more public persona than real Hampsten. He knows Andy's nervous and sometimes quick-tempered side, has seen the vulnerability but he appreciates Andy's willingness to acknowledge the help.

Yates climbs the Glandon well, riding hard to stay with the main group which includes Hampsten. He succeeds and then earns his pay by shielding his team-mate from the wind through the Maurienne Valley. It is difficult and when the group arrives at the foot of the Col du Telegraphe he steers away to the quieter side of the road and lets the climbers pass.

This is when he gets a little peace. He prefers to climb on his own. Aware that he has 30 kilometres of mountain before him, he begins slowly and soon realizes he is going okay. He overtakes five or six riders on the Telegraphe but doesn't even notice who they are. On the longer and equally difficult Col du Galibier he rides for a while alongside Miguel Indurain's team-mate Marino Alonso. One minute he is in front of Alonso, then behind him and near the summit Alonso falls behind and stays behind.

Near the top of the Galibier, he sees a big group 400 or 500 metres in front of him. He reckons his friend Dag-Otto Lauritzen is in it and vows to overtake them on the long descent into Serre Chevalier. He smiles at the thought. Yes, he will catch them on a long straight and, freewheeling, he will simply glide past.

For as long as he can remember, he has loved racing downhill and is addicted to the exhilaration of speed. His big body generates a formidable momentum on the descent which is not tempered by fear. He flies, speeding past the loners who separate him from the group.

Halfway, he sees his prey and waits for a long straight. Body crouched, legs locked into a fixed position, he travels so recklessly fast he knows that Dag-Otto is nodding his head, saying 'Yates, bloody madman.' He gains a minute on the group and then runs out of descent. On the flat approach to the finish he is not bothered to stay in front of the group and so he eases, they join and he rides the last five kilometres in their company.

He has finished 62nd of the 171 starters, 21 minutes, 42 seconds behind stage winner Tony Rominger. Hampsten finished fourth on the stage and moved up to sixth overall. Yates knows he has helped and, this evening, he will feel comfortable in the company of his team-mates.

Back at the hotel he showers, has something light to eat and sorts out his dirty clothes. Through the season Motorola riders wash their dirty jerseys, shorts and socks at the sink in their rooms but, during the Tour, the team does the washing for its riders.

After massage he goes to evening meal, takes care not to eat too much and then he looks for a telephone. For this isn't the Chateau and there is no telephone in the room. He likes to ring his wife Pippa every day, just to find out how she is, especially as their first child is due in three months. They know it is boy and will call him Liam, the Gaelic name for William.

Does his daily contact with Pippa underpin his good morale?

'No,' says, Yates. 'Good morale in cycling comes from good legs.'

It is appropriate that Andy Hampsten should be his roommate on this evening because they have been a team within a team on the road. Hampsten, the leader, had got through it, not in a way which suggested he could beat Miguel Indurain but well enough to keep his place amongst the top

7

THE MANAGER'S TALE
A Man with Ame
VINCENT LAVENU

1. Vincent Lavenu
2. Vincent Lavenu's achievement was to prove that a low-budget, modestly talented team had a place in the Tour de France

In Vincent Lavenu's childhood memories, his father doesn't crop up very often. His parents divorced and dad left home when Vincent was five. But there was one thing his father did before he left which helped shape the boy's life. It was a July afternoon in Briançon, sometime in the late 50s, when Monsieur Lavenu took his young son to see the Tour de France. So long ago that Vincent can picture only one scene from the day: there are riders with spare tyres looped around their torsos, pedalling uphill. Something about them gripped his imagination. It was their suffering. He was amazed that men should willingly submit to this and wondered what made them do it.

Such was the impact that when, two or three years later, his PE teacher at school did a quick poll on the career ambitions of his charges, young Lavenu said he wished to be a 'Champion de ski et champion de velo.' In the Alpine town of Briançon, where the Lavenus lived, most kids dreamt only of being ski champions.

Introducing his son to the Tour may have been the starting point but, in *absentia*, Monsieur Lavenu continued to have an influence. Vincent and his brother were reared by their mother, Genevieve, a social worker. Mum did a good job but Vincent knew there were times when he needed a father, somebody to put his foot down and say no. Without that, he developed a tendency to always do what pleased him.

There were other consequences. Vincent became more tenacious, developing a resilience which he might not have needed had he had the support of a father. He loved cycling from the first day he raced. As a schoolboy, he was hopeless but that didn't discourage him. If anything, it sharpened his motivation. He set goals for himself, little targets well within his scope and once realized, he then reached higher.

Vincent dreamt of being a cyclist, but it was no more than a dream. He decided to be a Physical Education teacher. That was until he compared the academic requirements with his likely results. So, towards the end of his school years, he studied accountancy in which he planned to work full-time. It never happened, he couldn't let cycling go.

His original ambition had been to become a first category amateur, to prove to himself that a racer with modest ability could compete against the best amateurs in France. That led him to the national team and having represented his country, the next goal was to become a professional. The quest excited Lavenu and each year he compressed his accountancy career into three winter months, leaving spring, summer and autumn free for cycling.

This he did for six years but in the winter of '82, Vincent Lavenu felt it was time to grow up. He was 26, a month short of his 27th birthday, and he resolved to get on with the rest of his life. For four years he had been one of the better French amateurs but nobody, except himself, rated him good enough to be a professional. Now he was too old. So he said, right, time to concentrate on accountancy and work towards the future.

Out of the blue, Saint-Etienne-Pelusin gave him the chance to race as a professional. Formerly a highly successful amateur team, it entered professional cycling through the basement, working from a small budget and making do with the less talented. Within the *peloton* Saint-Etienne-Pelusin was known as *l'équipe des chomeurs* (the team of the unemployed), ridiculed because they were seen as amateurs who could not get professional contracts. Vincent Lavenu didn't care, he was a pro at last and he set himself just one further ambition. He wanted to ride the Tour de France.

He could have earned more as an accountant but money never motivated him. His pro career would run from 1983 to 1991 and for nine seasons he was a prisoner of the road. He won three road races in that time and moved through the nether regions of professional cycling. A world where next week's pay might not arrive, where it was better to live in the present than contemplate the future and a world in which success rarely intruded: but Vincent Lavenu didn't worry. He was cocooned in his dream world. It was what he wanted and he loved it. Still loves it.

Saint-Etienne-Pelusin lasted a year and, at 28, he was unemployed. Excited by his first taste of the pro life, he wouldn't give it up and for two years he raced as an individual. That ranked as the lowest form of professional existence as, alone and unpaid, he raced against the teams. They were bad years but during that time he won a national track championship, a victory he cherishes.

At the end of 1985, Miko-Carlos offered him a place and he accepted. But that team lasted only seven months before he was again out of work. RMO then came to his rescue in 1987 but, at the end of his first season, they let him go. He was now 32 years of age and again unemployed. Unsure of the future, Lavenu sensed it was time to leave the *peloton* so he got a job with the Look organization. Responsible for the company's cycling products, he worked with retailers and dealt with the professional teams which used Look accessories.

For the first three months of 1988, Vincent Lavenu lived a normal working life. He enjoyed it but the longing for the *peloton* was still there. At the beginning of April he went to the two-day Criterium International race to arrange deals for Look. While there he met Patrick Valcke, *directeur sportif* of the Fagor team. Valcke complained about injuries which left him short-staffed and said he could do with an extra rider. Lavenu immediately offered his services and lied about his physical condition.

'Yes, yes I am training regularly,' he said to Valcke. 'I would really like to join the team.' Although sceptical, Valcke's need was great and he agreed to think it over. A few days later he rang Lavenu – it was a deal. Vincent told Look he was returning to the *peloton*. The boy who grew up doing as he pleased had not changed.

Stephen Roche, then the world champion and team leader at Fagor, liked Lavenu. 'Vincent did not have great class as a rider but he gave everything he had. He was a worker and even though he didn't have much racing ability, he was the kind of fellow who was going to make the most of it.'

He rode well at Fagor, winning a stage in the Tour of Portugal and placing fourteenth in the French professional championships. The team renewed his contract for 1989, a first such show of faith in his professional career. Encouraged by Fagor's confidence, Lavenu enjoyed his best year and realized his one remaining ambition by riding the Tour de France. He finished sixty-fifth and rode well in many other races that season, seventh in the French championships being his highest placing.

At the end of 1989, Fagor withdrew from cycling sponsorship and Lavenu waited for other teams to sign him. The telephone never rang. Somehow that surprised him: it left his dream world a little shaken. But to prospective employers, he was an old pro of average ability. 'The only person who believed in Vincent Lavenu was Vincent Lavenu,' says a former team-mate at Fagor. 'That is what saved him.'

Hurt by the lack of interest and unsure about the future, he kept alive the dream by racing as an individual in 1990. His contemporaries would have considered him a sad case: so much in love with the bike he allowed it to humiliate him. He would never agree. Lavenu won a stage of the Route du Sud in 1990 and raced through the season; one week in an amateur race, the next week against the pros. At the end of the 1990 season he was almost 35 and the great adventure of his life neared its end. Not that Vincent saw the signs; in his mind he simply needed a backer. His friends would have laughed but Lavenu had sharp survival instincts. 'I have enough energy to take an idea forward and my strongest point is that I am never beaten.'

It was an autumn afternoon in 1990 and he was competing near his home at Chambery in the Alps in a 'Gentleman,' so called because this event pairs a professional or first category amateur with a veteran (or gentleman) to form a two-rider time trial team. They race against other teams, with the pro or first category amateur riding strongly at the front and providing shelter from the wind for his 'gentleman.' On this autumnal afternoon, Vincent Lavenu sheltered a gentleman called Alan Chazal. Owner of a *charcuterie* (processed meats) business in Chambery, Chazal sponsored the local amateur cycling team.

Alan Chazal was also a keen cyclist and after the race he and Lavenu ate together. Lavenu told his story and said he would like to race as a professional in 1991 but he couldn't find a backer. For small money, Chazal could be his sponsor. Alan Chazal must have seen something in this hopelessly obsessive biker for he agreed to fund Lavenu for the year.

But at the age of 35, Vincent Lavenu's dream died. Alan Chazal's money gave him a weekly wage but it could not make his legs turn faster. Left behind too many times through the first four months of the '91 season, Vincent recognized that he could no longer do it. He would not have been the first to see it but, once he did, he quickly decided to move on. He accepted the end because he could see a new beginning. The achievement of involving Chazal in his career fuelled a new ambition.

Vincent Lavenu would form his own team and be its first *directeur sportif*.

Through the last two decades, professional cycling has achieved unprecedented levels of popularity. Television has played an important part in bringing the sport to a wider audience and the Tour de France is now seen on every continent. A predominantly European sport has been internationalized.

As well as helping to attract the public, television also enticed big business to the Tour. Vying with each other to be associated with success, companies have invested heavily in the sport and there has been a revolution in the organization of teams and in the amounts of money paid to riders. Miguel Indurain and Tony Rominger, the two highest earners, now make in excess of $2m per season. Twenty years ago the very best riders did not earn that over an entire career.

Equally indicative of the new age is the investment in professional teams. Banesto, Once and GB-MG, three of the best teams in the *peloton*, all consume annual budgets of around $8m and most of the front line teams cost at least $5m a year. This money has come through sponsorship.

Banesto, the Spanish banking conglomerate, is a good example of the modern sponsor as it backs Spain's greatest sportsman, Miguel Indurain, and associates with his consistent success.

After two weeks and over 2500 kilometres of racing, the Tour arrives at Andorra in the Pyrenees. At the Hotel Xalet Ritz, Jim Ochowicz is noticeably good-humoured. *Directeur sportif* of the US-backed Motorola team, Ochowicz has just heard the team's principal sponsor has reversed a decision to withdraw from the sport. Motorola's decision to continue for at least one more season is, in part, based on the team's outstanding performance through the first two weeks of the Tour. Their change of heart is a relief as Ochowicz does not now have to search for a replacement. It is no simple matter to find a company willing to invest betweem $4m and $5m each year in a bicycle team.

Ochowicz knows this first-hand for he has already been to the market. Officially the *directeur sportif,* he is much more than that. More like the chief executive who is responsible for the team's survival.

All except the very biggest teams can, he says, be funded by a budget somewhere between $3.5m and $6.5m annually. Salaries eat up a substantial part but there are considerable operational expenses. Insurance is a significant cost as is the cost of transporting a team through the nine months of the racing season. The latter includes food, lodging, ground travel and air travel. Providing the vehicles for ground transportation is another serious cost: the better-equipped teams need two big trucks and about seven cars.

Bikes and clothing are also important as each professional team needs at least four bikes per rider and the amount of clothing is staggeringly high: jerseys and leisure-wear, shorts, skinsuits, headbands, hats, gloves and socks. Almost all the teams do deals within the industry to cover the cost of their bikes and most do clothing deals as well. But these have to be worked out and that takes time. 'I handle the administration, the fundraising and the business side as well as being *directeur,*' says Ochowicz. 'I would say the administrative part of my job takes up about 40% of my time. There are times when your time could be better spent with the team rather than travelling somewhere to make a presentation but that's a part of keeping a team like this funded.'

Motorola has 18 riders and employs 10 full-time staff to provide back-up services. Many others are employed part-time. At the busier times of the season Ochowicz will have two teams racing simultaneously, almost always in different countries and often on different continents. In Motorola's immediate preparation for the Tour de France, one team competed in the Giro d'Italia and, at the same time, a second team competed in an American stage race.

Motorola is the team's chief sponsor and contributes seventy-five per cent of the overall budget. But the success of the team depends also on the auxiliary sponsors. The sponsors' names fall easily from Ochowicz's lips: Volvo (trucks and cars), Giordano (clothing), Eddy Merckx (bikes), Shimano (bike accessories), American Airlines (air travel), Polar (heart-rate monitors), Specialized (accessories), Oakley (sunglasses), Cinelli (accessories), Vittoria (tyres), Selle Italia (saddles), DT (spokes), Park Tool (bike stands and mechanical accessories).

'The deal may be product and dollars, just product or just dollars,' says Ochowicz. 'It can be complicated. Does the sponsor want logo space on the jersey, on the car? There are a number of items that are negotiated and they determine whether money is paid or not.' These auxiliary sponsors contribute around $1.5m to the team's budget.

Ochowicz devotes October, November and December to the organizational needs of the team and draws on the administrative skills of Mary Wiezzork, Noel Dejonckeere and Jody Wallner to set up the programme and then make it work. By the middle of December he is thinking racers again. 'That's when the riders get their programmes for the coming season. Every rider is evaluated individually and his programme is worked out to ensure he gets enough racing, enough recovery time, enough training and then racing again.

'I am not going to put some rider in the Tour de France if he doesn't belong there and there are riders in our 18-man group who should not be put in the Tour de France. I don't give them any illusions, I just build their programme in another direction.'

The personal sacrifices are not inconsequential – Ochowicz averages six weeks at home during the nine months of the racing season. 'If there is somebody in my story who deserves thanks,' he says, 'it's my wife.'

A racer of modest talents and a man of extremely modest means, Vincent Lavenu was undaunted by the challenge of setting up his own professional team. For his new dream was to build a team that would race the Tour de France. It would be sponsored by small to medium companies, it would be mostly French and would be a team with *ame* (soul). Running alongside the ambition to win races and generate publicity was the determination to show there had to be a place for the smaller, less well-off companies in world cycling. 'It is now a fact that you cannot run a show like the Tour de France without Coca-Cola's money,' says Tour reporter Harry Van den Bremt. Fine, thought Vincent Lavenu, but you mustn't close *la petite porte* (the small door).

Through the second half of 1991, Lavenu raced by day and worked by night. He wrote a long report on the viability of a small team and arranged meetings with potential sponsors. Energy flowed from him, so desperate was he for the team to happen. Alan Chazal was swept along by the force. He saw potential in Lavenu's idea and committed his company to a major sponsorship. Eurotel, the hotel chain, said it would be a co-sponsor but later backed out. Vanille et Mure, manufacturers of child cosmetics, replaced Eurotel and Vetta, the cycle accessories firm, came in as a third sponsor.

On 15 December, Lavenu announced that his team was a reality and would race in the 1992 *peloton*. That allowed six weeks to contract riders, hire staff, build bikes, buy cars and design jerseys.

Vincent Lavenu sensed how the established teams would react to his new formation. They would expect it to be badly equipped and poorly organized and would laugh if their expectations were realized. But Lavenu swore that nobody would laugh at his team. It would be professional and it would look professional. For six weeks he worked 20-hour days and when the team turned up on the Cote d'Azur for its first race of the season, everything was in place. The riders of Chazal-Vanille et Mure rode good bikes, travelled in good cars and wore nice clothes. Nobody laughed. The first battle had been won.

Lavenu raised six million francs (around £750,000 or $1.1 million) to put his team on the road. Those with high-powered squads said that Chazal-Vanille et Mure was ridiculously under-funded; Lavenu replied that it didn't seem ridiculous to the owners and employees of the small companies who had invested. The team was a reflection of their status. Vincent Lavenu saw nothing wrong with the big, multinational teams but he stood for something smaller, something different. His team was, in effect, a self-portrait. Modestly talented but committed, poor but not shoddy, often beaten but never demoralised; the team moved in the circles the *directeur* had known as a racer.

Judged on results, Chazal-Vanille et Mure did reasonably well in its first year, winning nine races. But the successes had to be set against the disappointment of not getting a place in the Tour de France. 'I never promised the sponsors we would be accepted into the Tour, but once we were up and running, the management and riders began to hope. At the last minute they refused to take us. We were worth our place and after being turned down it was hard to get the riders motivated.'

Lavenu realized the future of his team depended upon participation in the Tour de France. Without it, sponsors weren't interested and to keep his team afloat, he gambled. Vanille et Mure withdrew their sponsorship and in the search for a replacement, Lavenu promised the team would ride the Tour de France. 'Every sponsor is reluctant to hand over money until he is sure about his return and in French cycling, the only sure return is participation in the Tour de France. While I felt we were mature enough for a place in the Tour, guaranteeing that to a sponsor meant taking a risk but then life is a game of risks and those who are afraid of taking one achieve nothing.'

And, for once, Vincent Lavenu found his lowly status to be an asset: he had nothing to lose.

The lure of the Tour attracted a new sponsor: MBK, the bike manufacturer. In its contract with MBK, the team committed itself to riding the Tour. Lavenu's years of living close to the outer margins of the *peloton* taught him much and he aggressively went after a Tour place. He told the riders they should be riding the race and, in every media interview, he said the Chazal team 'wanted and needed to ride the Tour de France.'

Pressure mounted on the Tour organization as Lavenu publicly argued that to refuse the Chazal team would be to discourage small and medium-level sponsors. It would also hurt French cycling at a time when Spanish and Italian teams dominated the best races. The Tour's answer was that theirs was an international event and their first responsibility was to the status of the race. For weeks before the start, Chazal's fight to be included developed into a Tour sub-plot. Towards the end the organizers said they would amalgamate them with the American team, Subaru-Montgomery, and allow a combined team.

That didn't suit Chazal, but it suited Subaru even less and they publicly spurned the offer. Chazal thought they were there but were then matched with the Spanish team, Kelme, in another combined team. Lavenu didn't want to join forces with any team, not Subaru and especially not Kelme with whom there would be language difficulties. But Kelme, like Subaru, were not prepared to link with Chazal and they withdrew. The Tour de France organization did not have any other strays and Lavenu's squad had what it most wanted.

Vincent Lavenu was delighted for his riders and especially for Alan Chazal. He has never needed a contract with Chazal, they work on the basis of re-assessing at the end of each year. Alan Chazal, says Lavenu, is that rare specimen: a boss who respects his workers.

Four days into the race, Alan Chazal called Lavenu to say that even before the Tour began his company had benefited from the publicity about the team's participation. A supermarket chain, Provencia, ordered 10 pallets of its meats. Within three weeks Chazal's turnover with Provencia had risen to one million francs (£125,000) and it looked like growing. Alan Chazal wanted a favour from Lavenu.

The boss from Provencia was a cycling enthusiast and he would love to travel with Lavenu in the Chazal team car on one stage of the Tour de France. Small price, thought Vincent.

So much about the Chazal team reflects Vincent Lavenu's experiences as a racer. It gives a chance to riders discarded by other teams. Lavenu looks at these riders with sensitive eyes; recognizing their little strengths, understanding their weaknesses. It is a squad of modest talents, something which the *directeur* does not try to conceal. He assesses his riders with that mixture of empathy and honesty which comes only from the kindred spirit.

Eric Caritoux is the team leader; a quiet, serious professional whom Lavenu respects. Bigger teams would dismiss Caritoux as too old, not Lavenu who had his best year in the *peloton* at the age of 33. In Caritoux he sees an intelligent and correct professional, one who shows good example to the younger riders and helps to create the right team ambience. Lavenu says Caritoux is paid properly but is the only rider to be so.

Laurent Biondi is slight and very fragile. When in good condition, his engine ticks like a watch but like most under-powered engines, it breaks down easily. Lavenu puts Jean-Pierre Bourgeot and Oleg Kozlitine 'in the same basket' as they are both solid riders who know how to get deep into themselves. The *directeur* thinks both will finish the Tour and gain from the experience.

Then there is Pascal Chanteur, fragile like Biondi, capable of enjoying one big day but not certain of going all the way to Paris. Jean-Pierre Delphis is different, likely to finish the Tour but without the zip to make an impact on any one day. 'Something for him to work on,' says Lavenu. Patrice Esnault has talent but, if you read between Lavenu's observations, there are questions about his temperament. 'With him it is either all good or all bad, everything depends on what side of the bed he gets out of in the morning.'

Jaan Kirsipuu is from Estonia and, according to his boss, a sprinter for the future. He needs to be more serious and to control his weight better. 'He's a trackman at heart,' says Lavenu, 'and trackmen generally have heads like mules – afraid of nothing but stubborn.' Franck Pineau is the ninth Chazal rider, nominated by Lavenu as road captain because he communicates well and understands the subtleties of racing.

Kirsipuu from Estonia and Kozlitine from Kazakstan are the only non-French riders in the team. The balance was deliberately struck. 'The team is still a French team with a French identity,' says Lavenu. 'These riders (Kirsipuu and Kozlitine) have adapted to our way and that was important. I didn't want to take a Belgian or an Italian and make it too cosmopolitan. I wanted this team to have a soul and the foreigners to adapt but, at the same time, having their own culture and traditions respected by us.'

In the Tour, the team performs well, even if it wins nothing. Caritoux is its highest-placed finisher at thirty-seventh and the only Chazal rider to place in the top 70. There was no surprise stage win, no stunning performance to catapult the team into the limelight. Vincent Lavenu appreciates the little feats: his team did not finish last in the team time trial and did not place last in the team classification. Three have finished beneath them and Lavenu notices that the vaunted and costly WordPerfect team is one of the three. WordPerfect's budget would fund five teams of Chazal's size.

But Chazal's greatest achievement was to justify its inclusion in the Tour. The team competed. Each day they jostled for positions at the front of the *peloton*, especially as the race entered its final 40 kilometres and live television began. Jaan Kirsipuu's parents, watching Eurosport in Estonia, telephoned their son each evening and told him how prominently he raced that day. More importantly, Alan Chazal could sit before his television any afternoon sure that his company's name was going to appear before the nation.

Vincent Lavenu didn't expect his team to achieve wonders or, as he says, to explode the TV screen, but they proved themselves worthy. 'My riders acquitted themselves with honour, they had their place in the race.' As *directeur*, Lavenu was constantly interviewed by journalists and he could sense a growing regard for what he had created. 'We are seen as a little team pushing up and in France, people like that.'

The creation of the Chazal team is Lavenu's greatest achievement. He doesn't expect recognition because results will not merit it but he is proud of what he has managed. On the evening before the Tour began, its 20 competing teams were introduced to the public. When Chazal's turn came, Vincent Lavenu could barely contain his joy. Midway through the race, the riders pedalled through Briançon and his Savoyard region. Once again he felt the satisfaction of having beaten the odds. Lavenu, poor old Lavenu, came back to Briançon with his own Tour de France team.

On the final day, Chazal's seven surviving riders took their place in the Champs Elysées parade and their manager followed in a car close behind. The provincial boy had not just come to Paris. He had arrived.

Lavenu knew then that this was his triumph. 'I think that we do things well when we have a feel for them.'

Vincent Lavenu wants it known that he does have a life beyond cycling. His daughters Megalie and Aurelie mean the world to him. He does not mention his wife and anytime the conversation moves towards his partner, he diverts it. How does one integrate an obsession into everyday domestic life?

'The passion that I feel for my children is emphasized by the fact that I have a job where I am often away. I miss them each day but I love my job and so long as I am not forced to make a choice . . . . All of the love that I miss from the children and all of the love they miss from me means that when we are together, the bond between us is all the stronger.'

Early in the Tour Lavenu met Philippe Jeantot, the French yachtsman. They spoke about how their respective professions had devoured them. Jeantot planned to tour the world for seven or eight years with his family and Lavenu thought he too would like to take a year or two off and give to Megalie and Aurelie what had been denied them over the years.

There were times in his cycling life when Vincent Lavenu asked himself 'why the hell am I doing this?' He never had an answer. 'I don't know. It's instinctive, I've drifted toward what attracted me. I haven't sat back and wondered why. Because if I had thought about it in a logical way and if I had followed the normal path, I would never have got involved in cycling.' He says it goes back to his mother, Genevieve. She wasn't strict, she never forced him to do what he didn't want to do. And if there was something he liked, she encouraged.

'Maybe if she had been more strict, I would have gone higher in life. Who knows? I'm raising Megalie and Aurelie as I was raised. I'm giving them a long rein.'

8

1

THE CLIMBER'S TALE
Paradise Lost
CLAUDIO CHIAPPUCCI

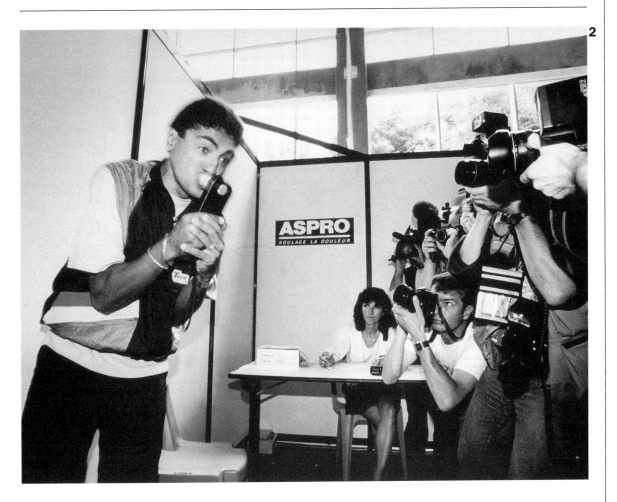

1. Claudio Chiappucci
2. Recording his lung capacity for the gallery, Chiappucci would have preferred to have had this attention during the race

'You've got to be somebody,' Arduino Chiappucci constantly told his son. Claudio wanted his parents Arduino and Renata to be proud of him. But, at first, he was timid and unsure of himself. Team-mates remember him as a quiet but willing *équipier* (team-rider). Anyone suggesting that Chiappucci would one day be a successful leader of the Carrera team would have been ridiculed. Claudio proved them wrong.

Now he *is* a respected leader. Changed from the uncertain *équipier* of old, but not unrecognizable. His team-mates see the old Claudio in his constant need for reassurance, most of which he provides himself. For days before a mountain stage he talks of what he is going to do, convincing himself it will happen. He makes little attacks, inconsequential except for the effect on his morale. 'See that,' he will say after winning an unimportant little sprint to the summit of a third category hill, 'I beat him three lengths, could have been four or five.' And the team-mates agree. 'Sure you could Chiappa, sure.'

They watched him through the first 10 days of this Tour and because he didn't make so many attacks, they wondered if it was the same old Chiappucci. He still talked as ever, said he was concentrating on the yellow jersey and wasn't wasting energy. But they knew Chiappa, always wanting to show off. He did attack at the foot of the Douaumont hill on the day into Verdun but was overtaken and left behind before the summit.

Maybe he wasn't going well. But he was still up-beat and it was more difficult than ever to distinguish belief from bravado. Doubts were not assuaged by his performance in the long individual time trial at Lac de Madine. He finished a disappointing 16th, over five minutes down on Miguel Indurain.

Before his mates could ask what was up, he said he was fine. And anyway the mountains were *his* terrain, medical tests showed he was in excellent shape and his second-third-second record of the three previous years was there for all to see. As the race moved closer to the first mountain stage, Chiappucci was confident. The stage to Serre Chevalier was for him. No one need worry.

A few kilometres up the Col du Glandon, the first climb of the day, Stephen Roche is worried. Mario Chiesa is pacing Chiappucci at the front of the *peloton* and the team leader is puffing. Chiesa is no climber but as he has only to pull for five kilometres, he gives it everything. Roche glances across at Claudio who is now swaying from side to side to generate more power.

Damn Chiesa, fumes Roche. Why can't he slow down a little? Others can see he is putting his own leader in trouble. Discreetly, Roche tries to get Chiesa's attention but it is hopeless. For even if Chiesa slows, someone else will accelerate. Chiappucci is having a bad day and with the Col du Telegraphe and Col du Galibier to come, things are going to get even worse.

As they climb the Glandon many are shed from the leading group. Long before the summit Chiappucci loses his place. Rolf Sorensen, another team-mate, stays with him and they work to limit the losses. The race intensifies and the story changes quickly. Tony Rominger makes his move on the Col du Galibier and only Miguel Indurain and Alvaro Mejia can match his infernal pace. Behind, the Tour hopes of many are destroyed.

Claudio Chiappucci finishes over 12 minutes down, losing all hope of a place in the top three. He is the day's great loser and defeat raises new questions. That morning he was a Tour contender, now he is a casualty. How will he react? Since becoming Carrera leader three years earlier, he has never been through a day like this.

Roche is the first to see: two kilometres from the top of the Galibier, he and Chiappucci find themselves together. Both on their last legs. 'Come on Steve, keep going. You're okay,' says Claudio. Roche thought this is some guy, down and out but only in the minds of others. They make the descent of the Galibier together, Chiappucci encouraging his friend all the way, as if Roche is the fallen one.

The evening at the team hotel in Briançon is difficult. Tito and Emerio Tachella have flown from Italy hoping to be cheered by Chiappucci's performance. Owners of the Carrera jeans company which sponsors the team, they are anxious that the team do well following bad publicity, forced lay-offs and a failed investment in Russia. They come to escape from bad news and walk in on a calamity.

Carrera riders Sorensen, Chiesa, Roche, Artunghi, Roscioli, Tafi, Pulnikov are all a bit down: they can add. Chiappucci's collapse will cost them around £8000 ($13,000) each: their share of the money he would have received for second place overall. But now there will be no place on the podium and for the *équipiers,* no changing car, no moving house, no new motorbike. This is a significant blow and yet they sympathize with Chiappucci. Even though he can more easily afford the financial setback, he loses most. He has said goodbye to the Tour.

More than that, the climber has failed in the mountains. Claudio senses what his team-mates are thinking, knows their sympathy is forced. He puts on a brave face but he has let them down. They continue to joke, to pretend that all is well. His silences grow longer. It hurts him to look back and he cannot look forward. For one night the racer they call *El Diablo* (The Devil) is in hell. Paradise has been lost.

What is it that makes climbers? How is it that two of the best racers, together at the foot of a mountain, can be divided by 10 or more minutes at the summit? Genetics? Suppleness? Lightness? Attitude? Training? There is no one quality which makes the difference. Dr Michel Ferrari, physician to Tony Rominger, may be right when he says it is easier to carry 64 kilos (Rominger's weight) to the top of a mountain than it is to carry 78 or 79 (Indurain's weight). Yet, as Indurain climbs at Rominger's side, the difference doesn't seem to count. Then the contrast is between Rominger's punch and Indurain's powerful tempo.

Ten years ago, lightweight racers from Colombia came to the Tour in great numbers. Herrera, Parra, Rodriquez and their *équipiers.* For them, the race began on the climbs and, often, they were first to the top. Their supremacy in the mountains shook the race. It was not Lucho Herrera's two stage victories in '85 which astonished but his panache: combing his hair with his fingers, fixing his hat, tugging his jersey until it was straight and then raising his arms in victory. Later in that Tour he and compatriot Fabio Parra were well ahead of the pack as they climbed to the finish at Lans-en-Vercors. 'I have done this before,' Herrera seemed to say as he slowed and let Parra cross the line first.

This Herrera, we thought, he will be the first South American winner of the Tour. Not this year, but next year or the year after, allowing time for the Colombian climber to improve his time trialling. But it didn't happen. The European riders reckoned the slightly built mountain men would not be so good on the climbs if forced to ride harder on the flat.

They were right: the Colombians lost the strength which allowed them to dominate the mountains. Soon the South American threat receded and now just a few continue to ride in Europe and they do so as ordinary riders.

Still, it is the climber who excites. Pedro Delgado's popularity is a reflection of his unassuming nature but it is also a tribute to his racing style; to the moment of his sudden acceleration on a Pyrenean or Alpine pass and to the wonder of such speed on so steep an incline. It is a spectacular sight. On the roadside or in our armchairs, we marvel at the audacity of the breakaway: will he keep it up, has he gone too soon? Whatever the outcome, there is applause for his courage.

Routinely, the greatest moments on the Tour occur in the mountains: LeMond and Hinault hand-in-hand on Alpe d'Huez in '86; Stephen Roche's collapse at the summit of La Plagne a year later; LeMond's weakness and Indurain's punching of the air on the stage to Val Louron in '91. That afternoon marked the end of one era, the beginning of another. And then there was the 1992 Tour. Long after the details of Indurain's second victory are forgotten, Claudio Chiappucci's ride to Sestrière will be remembered. It was an amazing performance. In its way, beyond compare.

For 200 kilometres Claudio led through the mountains. He galvanized the breakaway group through the morning and burned them off when they threatened to slow him down. Behind, Indurain's Banesto team led the pursuit, riding fiercely and then dropping away like lemmings. But they did their job, Claudio was reeled in and left to their leader, Miguel. They were now on the final climb to Sestrière in Italy: Miguel in the yellow jersey, Claudio wearing the polka dots of mountain leader.

What would Miguel do with the audacious breakaway? Attack and thus punish Chiappucci for making every rider's day so hard? Or he could just sit at his shoulder and remind the Italian that, in the end, he could never get away. Either way, Claudio would learn that it was no use; he could break away anytime he wished, but he could never win. Claudio's legs ached and Indurain's presence deflated him. Six and a half hours of torturous effort only to end up in the shadow of the rider he most wanted to beat.

But all around, Italian fans were going crazy: *Chiappa, Chiappa, Forza, Forza*. And Claudio began to notice. Maybe he had something left. This was *his* country. *Forza, Forza*. Okay, he thought, try again. One more attack, just to show this guy doesn't control you. And the fans, they want you to try. Claudio went faster and Indurain began to drop back again. Those on the side of the road saw something they would never forget. It was Indurain who cracked.

Hundreds of journalists watched the big screen at the *Salle de Presse*. When Indurain cut down Chiappucci's lead, they thought it sad. Chiappucci deserved better. They too waited for the race leader to put the breakaway in his place. Then the gap opened and Chiappucci was drawing away. At first they gasped, astonished at what was happening. Almost immediately those who sat were on their feet, every one of them cheering and clapping. Seasoned reporters who thought they couldn't be emotional about this sport stood with tears in their eyes. No one had ever seen anything like it.

But then no one had seen anything like Chiappucci, a true angel of the mountains.

Funny that he can seen as an angel for he prefers to be known as a devil. *El Diablo.* 'A good devil,' he says, 'not a bad devil.' As self-assessments go, Chiappucci's is passable. He sports the head of a devil on his racing helmet and encourages the link with the prince of darkness. But there is nothing sinister in Claudio, rather a yearning to be seen as the racer who likes to break away in the mountains and animate the race.

El Diablo attacks and the devil takes the hindmost.

But maybe there is a little more to it. Claudio needs to be noticed and devils, no matter how benign, attract us.

He became a leader after four years of riding for others. His rise astonished his peers and he felt they resented him. 'Because I was once a nobody, they didn't like it when I became a leader.' In the mountains, he would win their respect by attacking and hurting them.

Arduino and Renata conceived Claudio 10 years after the first two boys, Giovanni and Emilio. Maybe that gave him privileges his brothers did not have. As well, the family's small textile business prospered and there was more money to spend on the third of the Chiappuccis' three boys.

Giovanni and Emilio tried the bike but didn't have the passion, which was a quality Claudio had in abundance. He first raced with the Pedale Saronnese, a club named after Guiseppe Saronni, one of the great Italian riders of his era. From the beginning, Claudio liked the hills and could never resist the temptation to accelerate and leave his friends behind. Before long they said 'go to the hills, but go on your own.'

Arduino Chiappucci loved the sport although he hadn't raced. 'It was in our blood,' says Renata. As a soldier in World War II, Arduino fought in Ethiopia alongside Fausto Coppi, the most celebrated of all Italian cyclists. They became friends and as rations were meagre Arduino, concerned about the health of the great cyclist, sometimes passed his food to Fausto. Years later, he bought his son a racing bike, choosing a Bianchi because that was what Coppi rode.

Claudio says he was 14 at the time, Renata says 13. But they agree on the colour, pink. 'Like the jersey of the Giro,' says Claudio. 'It was my first competition bike and my parents made a great sacrifice to pay for it. It would be the same as a motorbike today. A month later I competed in my first race and I attacked them from the start. I was already like that. I had no tactical sense, no team and I didn't win a single race that season.'

Cycling was then a distraction. He loved the hills in his native Lombardy and when he wearied of his electrician's studies, Claudio rode away from it all. Although a free-spirited racer, the youngest Chiappucci was earnest in his attitude to life. Gradually developing into a good amateur, he would not consider a pro career until he got his electrician's diploma. And his choice of team, Carrera, also reflected his good sense. 'There were other teams interested but I thought, "If I am going badly, will they stick by me?" I knew Carrera would and I joined them.' He has been with Carrera ever since, an unusually stable relationship in a sport where change is constant.

He joined Carrera in 1985 and Arduino was pleased. He was at Claudio's first race but, shortly afterwards, he died suddenly. Without pushing, Arduino had enthused about the sport and encouraged his son to do well. Years later, the victories came and Claudio regretted that his dad was not around to see them. 'He was so much into cycling, he would have loved to see one of his boys become a champion.'

Mindful of the long hours his parents worked and their generosity towards him, Chiappucci feared failure and, later, he worried that he might fritter away his wealth. He has a reputation for miserliness but laughs at the accusation. The laughter is hollow; for having seen his parents scrimp and save, Claudio cannot be cavalier with money. 'In two years I have earned more than my parents earned in their life,' he says with a hint of resentment.

In his early years at Carrera he worked for Stephen Roche, Roberto Visentini and Urs Zimmermann. To his team-mates he was likeable but lightweight, a decent climber but not a leader. They wanted him in the team because he was a willing worker and no threat. Chiappucci's career almost ended in the middle of his second season when he crashed into a car on the Tour of Switzerland. He was lucky to escape with a broken leg and a fractured collarbone.

A year later, he returned to competition but two seasons passed before he rediscovered his best form. The improvement in his station came about when Roche left and Visentini and Zimmermann retired. Carrera cried out for a boss. Flavio Giupponi was hired as a potential leader but he didn't work out. Nobody considered Chiappucci officer material but all changed in the 1990 Tour de France. Claudio got the break he needed or, more precisely, he made the break.

It was on the first kilometres of the opening stage that he attacked. Mostly he was motivated by the mountain points to be won on two hills inside the first 25 kilometres but there was also his natural inclination to ride away from his companions. Three riders followed Chiappucci's lead; Ronan Pensec of France, Steve Bauer of Canada and the Dutchman Frans Maassen. They hurried to the climbs.

Riding at a pace which acknowledged that it was a three-week and 4000-kilometre race, the *peloton* allowed the breakaways to increase their advantage. From two to four, then, eight, 10 and right up to 13 minutes. Just then there were only 15 kilometres to race and though the pack tried frantically, they could knock only two minutes off the lead. The quartet flew to the finish, 10 minutes 45 seconds ahead of their pursuers. This was a turn nobody expected and it caused a furore. Of the four, only Maassen couldn't win the Tour with a 10-minute start. Pensec certainly could, so too Bauer and, at a pinch, Chiappucci. Not that many believed in Claudio; not his adversaries, not even himself.

Bauer was the first to wear the yellow jersey but he eventually fell away. Then Pensec, but he too wilted. That left Claudio in the *maillot jaune*. He was thrilled but scared and lay awake at night wondering if he could win. Few considered it possible. Past the halfway stage in the Tour, Chiappucci's lead on Greg LeMond and the other serious contenders was seven minutes.

Then on a shortish stage between Villard-de-Lans and Saint-Etienne, Claudio blew it. Reacting to Pensec's presence in a breakaway group, Chiappucci rode like a man possessed. Driven by fear, he led the Carrera pursuit and spent the strength he would need for later. Pensec was not a serious rival and Chiappucci did what a leader must never do: he thought and rode like an *équipier*.

LeMond, a team-mate of Pensec's, watched this, knowing Chiappucci was destroying himself.

Carrera recaptured Pensec but left the door open for LeMond. The American soon made his exit and driven by LeMond, a small group gained five minutes on the *peloton* and Chiappucci's lead was down to two minutes. Because there was a time trial two days before the end of the race, two minutes would not be enough for Chiappucci. In the time trial, LeMond was much stronger. Claudio had lost the Tour and he knew it.

His naivety on the stage to Saint-Etienne confirmed every suspicion of weakness and re-established Chiappucci as an *équipier*. It might have remained that way if he hadn't attacked on the Pyrenean stage to Luz-Ardiden a few days later. At the time it wasn't easily fathomed.

Here was a jumped-up *équipier,* catapulted into the yellow jersey and given a chance to win the Tour. Because of inexperience and lack of judgement, he blew his opportunity. He led the race by two minutes but on sufferance. He was expected to surrender his yellow jersey in the Pyrenees and if not then certainly in the final time trial.

That morning Claudio sensed the general perception. But early in the mountain stage, he saw others suffering. Why not attack? Surprise them. Make them realize they couldn't laugh at Claudio. So he broke away and gained two minutes on the Col du Tourmalet, stretching his overall lead to four minutes. But his legs couldn't match his heart and LeMond caught him at the bottom of the final ascent to Luz-Ardiden.

After a few kilometres of the climb LeMond tried to distance him. But each time the American accelerated, Chiappucci countered. 'I rode up to him and looked in his eyes. I wanted to say, "You see, I'm still here, you're not getting rid of me like that."' Close to the top, there was one surge too many and Claudio was left behind. He finished over two minutes behind LeMond and held his jersey by a handful of seconds.

As was expected, the yellow was handed over to LeMond after the time trial at Lac de Vassiviere two days before the end. Claudio finished second overall but achieved much more. For in his outrageous attack in the Pyrenees, he won new respect. It might have been foolish but it showed stubborness and a refusal to accept second place. At last, Claudio was somebody.

The irony was that in proving himself, Chiappucci lost the best chance he would ever have to win the Tour de France. In learning to be a *patron*, he had to ride like a gallant and not so clever *équipier*. It was for his team-mates to chase the Pensec group to Saint-Etienne and he should have simply followed LeMond in the Pyrenees. Like a willing *équipier*, Claudio took the initiative on both occasions and played right into the American's hands.

It was, wrote Samuel Abt in his book *Three Weeks to Glory,* as if he was 'expecting Roche or Visentini to come along, ruffle his hair and tell him he had done just fine.'

Sils, Switzerland, 17 June, 1993

Should he have won that Tour? Did he throw it away? They think yes. Claudio, his Carrera team-mates Stephen Roche and Mario Chiesa and assistant *directeur* Sandro Quintarelli all sit around a lunch table at the Hotel Giovanoli and discuss the Tour he might have won. Since that race, Claudio has become one of the sport's best. Third in the Tour de France of '91, second in '92, winner of Milan–San Remo in '91 and currently fourth in the official world rankings.

Quintarelli says he should have won it. Claudio argues he was aggressive then, that was his style and, anyway, he didn't plan to attack on the stage to Luz-Ardiden. It was something which just happened. He was inexperienced and too brave. But, yes, if he had let his team-mates do the work behind Pensec, that might have saved him. Back and forth the arguments rage . . . what the hell, it was three years ago and old Tours cannot be changed. Still, says Claudio, LeMond won three Tours, two of which he might easily have lost, that 1990 race and 1989 to Fignon. Lucky guy, says Claudio as he asks who's for cards. Rita, his wife, will play, his team-mate Pulnikov and Misha his *soigneur*.

It is 9 a.m. the following morning. Claudio Chiappucci walks from the hotel wearing his Carrera training gear, picks up a bike lying against a wall and pushes it before him. In a minute Stephen Roche comes along, takes his bike and joins Chiappucci. Vladimir Pulnikov and Mario Chiesa make it four and all are prepared for a training ride to the Swiss Alps. The plan is to go for five hours although Pulnikov and Chiesa are less than enthusiastic. Like the boys in Uboldo who refused to ride to the hills with the teenage Chiappucci, they know what they're in for.

Attracted by Chiappucci, a crowd gathers in the little square. He chats, signs autographs, poses for photographs before easing himself free. Their affection for him is obvious and he likes to take the time to please.

Chiappucci and Roche have heart monitors strapped to their chests which are linked to mini-computers fixed to the handlebars of their bikes. From this they get a reading of their heartbeats throughout the ride. Each has a threshold beyond which his body produces too much lactic acid which quickly destroys the efficiency of the muscles. They understand the temptation and the danger. Both are competitive and cannot train without racing and, without the monitors, they would push themselves too far. Chiesa and Pulnikov have seen all of this before. Chiappucci and Roche train at racing speed and sometimes faster. Worn to keep them in check, the monitors don't always do their job.

Six minutes after 9 a.m., the four ride out of Sils. Sandro Quintarelli drives the team car behind them with Misha Pivovarov alongside. Chiappucci and Roche are at the front, just behind them Pulnikov and Chiesa. From the first kilometres, they speed. Wanting to loosen out before the climbing begins, they ride up and then down the valley between the towns of St Moritz and Maloja. Roche sits motionless on his bike, conveying an impression of ease which cannot be real. Chiappucci sways a little and the body language from Chiesa and Pulnikov suggests foreboding. This is not going to be a fun day.

A light rain begins to fall. With 10 days to the Tour de France they cannot take chances. A fall on a slippery road or a bad chest could destroy their Tour and Chiappucci wonders if they should turn back. Chiesa agrees too eagerly but Roche is for continuing. 'See that car,' he says, 'it's coming from where we want to go and it's dry.' Chiappucci accepts, Chiesa doesn't. At a roundabout he does a complete circle and heads for home. He leaves without warning, like a boy stealing out of class while teacher's back is turned. Just 30 kilometres and the four are now three. Later in the evening Chiesa will say it was the rain. 'Sure,' Chiappucci and Roche will reply, 'we know.'

Beyond the town of Pontresina they meet the first slopes of the Bernina Pass. The order rarely changes; Roche and Chiappucci at the front, Pulnikov behind. As the gradient steepens, Chiappucci slows, removes his gloves and shuffles them into the back pocket of his jersey. Roche does likewise. The gloves are off.

They are now pedalling harder. Pulnikov strains to keep his place, spitting to his right every 500 metres or so. Roche and Chiappucci play a silent game, each trying to edge his wheel a few inches in front of the other and the pace increases all the time. Pulnikov can't keep up and about five kilometres up the climb, he lets them go. Someone shouts 'Chiappucci' and Claudio waves in reply. He and Roche talked constantly through the first hour but conversation has now ceased.

Four kilometres from the top Roche feels his team-mate is going through a bad patch. He steals a glance at Chiappucci's heart monitor, it is at 155. Five over his limit. Time, says Roche, to go. Stretching himself upwards and out of the saddle, he forces down on the pedals and away he flies. Got to make this count, he tells himself. The acceleration is explosive. Chiappucci doesn't watch but concentrates on keeping a good tempo of his own. Quintarelli is surprised that Roche has left him and he drives alongside.

'Claudio?'

'Si.'

'Fredo?' (Are you cold?)

'No, bene.' (No, I'm okay.)

He recovers, chases Roche all the way to the summit and finishes about 150 metres behind him. Pulnikov arrives a minute and a half later. Misha jumps from the car and fills the *bidons* with the water of melting snow. Claudio is slightly subdued, so too Quintarelli. They don't give much importance to events on the Bernina Pass; it is only a training spin, just the first of three mountain passes, no need to be bothered. But they are. On his terrain, *El Diablo* hates to lose.

Roche would pay on the next climb, the Julier Pass. Pulnikov lets them get on with it as he settles into his rhythm on the early slopes. In the team car Quintarelli worries. Ten days before the Tour and they ride like crazy. 'Tranquil, tranquil,' he screams but it has no effect. Halfway to the summit Chiappucci goes clear; 20, 40, 60 metres. Roche waits, the gap widens to 100 metres, then 150. He counters. Quintarelli yells at them to calm down but neither listens. Roche chases furiously, bearing down on his team-mate. Now within a couple of lengths of Chiappucci, Roche slows to draw breath and recover strength. He surges past. 'Tranquil, tranquil,' shouts Quintarelli but no one is listening.

Chiappucci doesn't feel good but cannot bear to see Roche ride away again. Digging into himself, he regains the lost ground and outsprints his rival to the summit. This is enough for Chiappucci and Roche. On the third climb they listen to Quintarelli and obey their heart monitors. Riding side by side, they keep up a good pace and Pulnikov falls behind again. But there is no battle now and they finish with 30 kilometres of speed training behind the team car: a brutal conclusion to a 185-kilometre day.

Worries about Chiappucci's form for the Tour are not aired. A training spin, no one should make too much of that. Lunch arrives and Pulnikov smiles for the first time since the previous day. Misha tells Chiappucci he should race in Russia, that he would be well received.

'Do you have television in Russia,' asks Chiappucci.

'Of course.'

'And girls too?'

'Plenty of them.'

'Good.'

'But you could never afford them.'

They all laugh. Maybe Claudio wasn't at his best but there were 10 days before the Tour. He would come round. They believed that because it was what they wanted to believe.

Following his bad day to Serre Chevalier, Chiappucci was down. But those ready to count him out were not given the chance. Claudio could explain. One bad day, that was all. He would get better. You want to know how it happened? 'After the Giro (d'Italia), I needed another race to stay sharp. But I went to Switzerland to train and it was a mistake. My form is coming, just a week late.' 'Sure Chiappa,' said his team-mates. 'You'll be better next week.'

On the second Alpine stage, from Serre Chevalier to the ski-station at Isola 2000, Chiappucci was more like his real self. More like but not quite. On the first two passes, the Col d'Izoard and the Col de Vars, he hung out at the front of the pack, setting a strong tempo, without ever making an attack. Claudio wanted his rivals to know he wasn't going away. Because he was almost 20 minutes down on overall time they would have noticed but not worried. He began the race as a threat, now he was a minor irritation.

Those at the lower end of the race would not have seen Chiappucci's showmanship but they felt its effects. On those first two climbs many lost contact with the *peloton*, never to regain it. More would be eliminated that afternoon than on any other stage and Chiappucci was mostly responsible. Not all his peers smile at the mention of *El Diablo*.

Though he improved, Claudio never quite rediscovered himself. He could lead on the Vars and Izoard passes but when the race intensified on the Bonette pass, he was overtaken by Rominger, Indurain and the others. He kept going, caught up with the leaders on the descent and felt strong again on the final climb, finishing third behind Rominger and Indurain at Isola 2000. The improvement raised his morale. 'See, I was stronger. In the Pyrenees I will be on form.' The Pyrenees came and he improved a little more. The final mountain race crossed the Tourmalet and Aubisque passes.

Claudio attacked on the Tourmalet, as did Rominger and for the first time in the Tour, Indurain was left behind. The race leader crossed the summit 50 seconds adrift but raced furiously on the long descent from the Tourmalet and recaptured Rominger. Chiappucci counterattacked with his old Carrera team-mate Massimo Ghirotto. They rode together from there to the end of the race.

Behind, the Ariostea team of Bjarne Riis feared Chiappucci might take fifth place from their man and so they chased the two leaders. Just Chiappa's luck thought his Carrera team-mates, on the day he escapes, the powerful Ariosteas are on his trail. After crossing the Aubisque pass, Chiappucci and Ghirotto had 70 kilometres to the finish. Could they possibly outride the Ariostea team? They did. Only those swept along by Ariostea's pace appreciated what it took.

'I didn't give them a chance,' says Roche. 'Every time there was a time check, I expected their lead to be cut. But they increased it. They did an unbelievable ride.'

Well clear coming into the town of Pau, only the stage victor had to be decided. Ghirotto or Chiappucci? Opinions would have been equally divided but Claudio's need was greater. Inside the final kilometre he slowed, forced his rival to take the lead and then passed him decisively in the final 200 metres. It wasn't how the big climber was expected to win but, at this point in the Tour, Claudio didn't mind. He would not leave the Tour empty-handed.

Afterwards he was exuberant. This proved what he had been saying. The Tour had come a week early for him. 'Sure Chiappa, that's what you said.' One more week and these guys would have suffered. 'They sure would, Chiappa.' 'You know what,' said Claudio, 'next month, I'm going to win the classic at San Sebastian, my form will be just right for that.'

'Sure you will Chiappa,' they said. 'Sure you will.'

9

THE ABANDON'S TALE
A Fair-dinkum
Aussie

NEIL STEPHENS

1. Neil Stephens
2. Bags packed, ready to go. This hurts more than the physical pain which brought about the abandonment
3. The names are sorted out for the final time trial. On this end are the ones that didn't make it and won't be riding into Paris

Everybody understands. His team-mates come to say goodbye. 'Take it easy for a few days and then start back.' Herminio Diaz-Zabala, friend as well as team-mate, says it isn't the end of the world, not even the end of the season. Riders from other teams at Montpellier's Hotel des Pins wave sympathetically when, an hour before the start, they see him in civilian clothes. 'There goes Stephens, on his way home.'

Nicolas Terrados, the Once team doctor, tries to cheer him. He tells him he is surprised he got this far. Terrados hadn't expected him to make it through the Alps and that was four days ago. Pablo Anton, Once's organizer, tries to find the best way of getting him from Montpellier to San Sebastian. Not a simple matter on this quiet Sunday morning.

His suitcases lie apart from the rest and when the loading of Once's team bus finishes, they remain behind in the lobby. Soon his team-mates are gone, then the team truck and bus roll away and, finally, the cars. He is the only cyclist left in the hotel and he feels like a mourner after the sympathizers have gone. His Tour number, fixed to each suitcase, is the only visible reminder of what he has been.

The race is now on its way to Perpignan and Neil Stephens has to get back to his home in Spain. Settling into life after the Tour is difficult: yesterday he had only to pedal as every other decision was made for him, today he cannot pedal but must do everything for himself. He asks the hotel receptionists for help and, knowing his situation, they can't do enough.

Hertz, Eurocar and Avis are telephoned but, on this Sunday morning, all are off duty. Montpellier Airport is awake but a flight to San Sebastian, *ce n'est pas possible*. If Monsieur Stephens is prepared to fly to Lyon, he can connect with a flight to San Sebastian. And a journey which should take an hour would take an entire day.

His mother will know from Australian television that he is out of the race so he rings to say he is fine. 'You made the correct decision,' she replies. 'If you had continued you might have damaged your health?'

'Basically Mum, it was past that. I got to the stage where I didn't have a choice.' He wants to convince her that he didn't voluntarily quit. So he asks her to imagine a day when, feeling so bad, you can't bear the sound of the television. A day when you just want to lie in bed but it is on this day someone tells you to go out and ride a bike for 200 kilometres in 35 degrees of heat and if you don't, you will be unemployed from now on. Unemployment it would have to be.

Less than 24 hours have passed since Neil Stephens abandoned the race. Already he is beginning to come round. The illness is receding and, granted a reprieve, he could have started today's stage. In this sense his recovery does not make him feel better.

He rings his Basque girlfriend Amaia and says he doesn't know for sure when he will be home but he is on his way. She worries that he is not strong enough to drive and asks him to be careful. He organizes a ride to the airport and has loaded his suitcases when he remembers he hasn't paid for his phone call to Amaia. Back at reception, he is told one of the car hire companies is now open for business.

That settles his means of transport and he will soon begin the seven-hour drive back to Ventas de Astigarraga, a little town near San Sebastian. But Stephens anticipates his week at home without enthusiasm. He will sit before the television, waiting for the camera to pick out the pink jerseys of his team-mates. It will stop at Erik Breukink and he will think 'I should be with him.'

It is an empty feeling and one that will come and go on the long journey back to Spain.

Neil Stephens is as Australian as could be. Each winter he takes off for Canberra and spends Christmas with his Mum and family. In Europe he listens constantly to a shortwave radio which links him to home; still feels an allegiance to *his* rugby league team, the Canberra Raiders, and likes to keep in touch with what is happening in Australian politics. Allan Peiper, his compatriot, says Stephens is 'a fair-dinkum Aussie'.

Yet the fair-dinkum Aussie has become a cosmopolitan. Sometimes he comes to the Once table and notices there are two groups; the Spaniards at one end, the foreigners at the other. It is a natural division, ordained by language and Stephens invariably chooses to sit with the Spaniards. He rolls the double r in Leanizbarrutia and pronounces the name Diaz-Zabala like a Spaniard.

Stephens lives in the Basque country and has fallen in love with a Basque woman, Amaia. They tell him he speaks Spanish with a Basque accent and his business card lists his address in Australia and his address in 'Euskadi', using the name Basque people give to their country. On the question of separatism, he says he understands Basque aspirations.

His rented house is called *Casa Perurena* , a villa once owned by Vicente Perurena, a member of the separatist organization ETA who was killed by the Spanish police. Stephens has long been a friend of Txomin Perurena, a brother of the late Vicente. Spanish police came to the house looking for Vicente, he fled to the Basque country of south west France but was pursued and killed. This happened in the years before Stephens moved to Spain but he has often heard the story.

A profile in the Basque newspaper *Egin* described him as half-Basque. Stephens was flattered. But Once, the national lottery which sponsors his team, is right wing and very Spanish. So he is careful. 'I have a lot of sympathy for the Basque cause but I can't say which side's right. I can understand both sides you know.'

This Spanish adventure astonishes him. For he was the kid who complained about French being forced down his throat at high school in Canberra. Why should an Aussie kid learn the language of a country so distant? Shouldn't we be learning Japanese, he once asked a teacher? And he never saw sports in his future. He deserted the athletic life once he discovered women and beer, and anyway cycling was for fitness freaks. One evening he was out with his mates, one beer followed another and the hours rolled by so fast he was always going to be late.

As late as 4.30 the following morning. He knew Fin, his Dad, would be upset and he can still see him vacuuming the swimming pool as he approached. Expecting anger, he was surprised by his Dad's calmness. 'I was going to give you a licking but your brother says you plan to ride the bike race this afternoon.' Shit, was Brian clever! 'Of course,' said Neil, unaware of the race and without any enthusiasm for it. But, if it squared things with his Dad, he would ride. He competed and enjoyed it; not so much the 10-mile race as the beers afterwards. He came back for more beer and gradually got into the racing.

Three years later Stephens left Canberra for England to join the ANC racing team, an opportunity set up by an Aussie in ANC, Shane Sutton. This was 1984 and it was the start of a professional career which would stumble forward. Fin died in 1985 and Neil returned home to help sort out his business affairs. The year in England had been enjoyable but it didn't convince him he could be a pro cyclist. After selling his Dad's haulage business he needed some space before deciding what to do and so he returned to the bike.

He rediscovered good form and rode well in Australia's premier race, the nine-day Sun Tour at the end of 1985. That performance earned him a place in the small Italian team, Santini, and being young, Australian and adventurous, he thought 'What the hell!' Off to Italy he went. Stephens lasted four months but in that time rode the Giro d'Italia and learned much about European cycling. 'I got so much of a kicking I thought "Well, that's it. I'm not good enough to be a bike rider in Europe." I just thought I wasn't at that standard. I was quite willing to hang it up and to go home.'

Back home, he continued to race and won the Australia King of the Mountains Championship. Ironically the prize was a trip to Europe. Stephens opted to return to England where he had friends. While there he rode a few races with the Ever Ready team and was offered a place on the Belgian team Lotus. He didn't want to race in Belgium, especially not in a small and almost certainly disorganized team and so asked for an exorbitant salary.

To his surprise, Lotus agreed and in January 1988 he recommenced his professional career with them. However he left in March, disillusioned by the team's inability to pay him. But this time the young Australian wasn't going to give up and he joined a team called Zero. As its name suggested, Zero's resources were thin. It was a group of individual racers who could not get places in sponsored teams and banded together in the hope of getting backers on a race-to-race basis.

Stephens rode some races and was promised payment. It never came. 'Some Dutch rider whose name I can't remember was the boss. He just ripped us off.' At the end of 1988 he was broke but not unrated. A few teams offered places for 1989. Caja Rural, the Spanish team, offered an illegally low £4000 a year. However, they were ranked sixth best in the world and he was eager to be part of an organized squad. He sold his car and accepted.

Stephens began the 1989 season well, finishing fourth in the Tour of the Mediterranean but the following month he crashed and broke his leg. That finished the season and, without the intercession of Txomin Perurena, the fall would have ended his career with Caja Rural. *Directeur sportif* of the team, Perurena said he should be re-signed and his faith was rewarded when Stephens rode well in 1990 and showed he could earn his living in the *peloton*.

At the end of 1990, the team split in two and Stephens joined the group sponsored by Paternina and controlled by his friend Perurena. It was an exciting time. Perurena made him one of the team's leaders and opened up possibilities which Stephens never expected. 'It was great to talk about, to say "I'm one of the lead riders" but when you got into the nitty gritty, it wasn't so good. I'm a very realistic rider. I know I'm not a bad rider but I'm not a super rider. I prefer to be known as a good *domestique* rather than an average leader. Now I have a reputation as a good *domestique* and I'm quite proud of that.'

Doubts about Paternina's continued involvement in the sport forced Stephens to look for a new team for 1992 and when Once offered, he signed immediately. He felt he would do better away from Txomin Perurena as his friend was not a demanding enough *directeur sportif.* Because of the doubt about Paternina he could look elsewhere and not feel he was being disloyal to Txomin.

He remembers his friend calling to say he should not commit himself to another team as he now had a sponsor. It was the day after he signed for Once.

Stephens settled quickly into life as an *équipier* with the highest ranked team in the *peloton.* Eight years of varied and mostly demoralizing experiences of the sport convinced him he couldn't progress in small, low-budget teams. 'They say it's difficult to soar like an eagle when you're surrounded by turkeys. If you're in shitty teams, getting paid shit, your morale's shit as well. Then if you go where you can feel respect for yourself and people treat you with respect, things will pick up.'

He is proud to be in the Once team and his performances did rise with his self-esteem. He rode the three major Tours in 1992; the Vuelta a España, Giro d'Italia and Tour de France. Few riders attempt all three and fewer still finish them all: Stephens proved himself a very tough rider by finishing them and performing well. It was expected he would wilt in the last, the Tour de France, but there he rode particularly well and established himself as one of Once's best *équipiers* .

He never wants to leave the team. Alex Zülle, Laurent Jalabert and Breukink are the riders for whom he works and he discusses them with the easy confidence of the respected *équipier.* Breukink is quiet and easy-going, Alex is very nervous and neither is good at maintaining a place close to the front of the bunch. This is important for when there is a sudden acceleration Stephens must search for them and guide them to the front. That kind of effort saps the strength. Jalabert is different, he tells exactly what he wants and is always well-positioned.

Zülle is billed as the brightest of cycling's young stars and Stephens thinks if he can keep his nice, unassuming nature he will mature into a very good rider. Because he does not consider himself a star, Alex works at his profession. But there are no certainties. 'Physically, Alex is young. Mentally he's very young. It is not a question of years, Jalabert is the same age. Alex has just started to go out with his first girlfriend and Jalabert is married with a child.'

Stephens is contracted to ride with Once until the end of 1994 but he would like to see out his career with them. 'After so many years of being stuffed around with shitty teams, it means a lot to get into a team with such good feeling and to be treated so well. If they said to me "we'll give you x-amount of dollars to the end of your career", well I'd stay unless someone came up and said "we will pay twice that amount of money". That is what it would take to get me to leave this team.'

Athletes have an instinctive sense about their physical condition. They know when they are not quite right and can usually identify the reasons. From the beginning, Neil Stephens was uneasy about his fitness for the Tour de France. His problem went back to the Tour of Murcia in March and the excruciating pain in his lower abdomen. Although he didn't know it, he had a hernia and as he pushed himself, the hernia got bigger and pulled on a testicular nerve. The pain was violent. Between the operation and recovery, Stephens was two months off the bike and didn't have the time to achieve the physical fitness necessary to do himself justice in the Tour de France. Manolo Saiz, Once's team *directeur,* accepted the fact, but selected Stephens in the hope that he would ride himself into the race and be strong in the final week.

Which sounds fine in theory but the Tour de France does not allow a rider to ease himself in. Through the first 10 days Stephens suffered and lost the strength which might have protected him from the viral infection that, early in the second week, attacked his lungs. The infection took up residence on the day before the first mountain stage.

Neil Stephens feels poorly. He hates the thought of the day which lies before him. Please God, he thinks, let there be no attacks before the first mountain. Hardly has this thought struck when 18 riders break clear and provoke an acceleration in the *peloton*. They are racing up the Maurienne Valley, on their way to the Col du Glandon, when Once's *directeur* Manolo Saiz orders his team to assist in the pursuit of the breakaways.

Stephens and Alberto Leanizbarrutia are the two *équipiers* posted to the front of the *peloton*. They help Miguel Indurain's Banesto team-mates to keep the breakaways within reach but the effort drains Stephens' energy. He is wrecked. Miserable, he sees only torture before him: three mountain passes and 150 kilometres of racing.

He forces himself to think positively, tells himself that, today, survival will do. All he wants is to reach Serre Chevalier on the right side of the time limit. The air grows cooler on the higher slopes of the Glandon and he starts to cough. Feeding on itself, the coughing bouts intensify until they make him vomit. Three times he slows to get sick. But the coughing persists and he finds it hard to breathe. His stomach contracts, suddenly and involuntarily, and he winces with pain. At the summit of the Glandon, he is alone. This is the worst day of his cycling life.

On the flat road between the Glandon and Col du Telegraphe he catches the Belgian Jim Van de Laer and they help each other until the first slopes of the Telegraphe. There, Stephens is told by his Once team that he is a long way behind and liable to be eliminated. They don't want him to stay with Van de Laer if he can go faster, and he understands. Slowly increasing the pace, he leaves Van de Laer behind. It would have been nice, but it would have been dangerous to stay with the Belgian.

On the climbs of the Telegraphe and Galibier, the stomach cramps persist but he keeps going and finishes seven minutes inside the limit. Back at the hotel Dr Terrados examines him and thinks it unlikely he can survive another day but does not say so. Knowing Stephens is a fighter the doctor jokes about him being soft and likely to quit. It is a ploy to harden Stephens' determination to survive. Before leaving, he gives his patient some salt replacements.

That evening Stephens checked to see if Van de Laer was still in the race: last to the finish at Serre Chevalier, he had arrived 30 seconds inside the limit. Too close for comfort.

Even though Dr Terrados felt Stephens would not complete the next day's stage, he was not certain about the rider's rate of recovery. Stephens himself expected the worst, for he would not suffer as he had the previous day. The memory was too vivid, too painful.

On the first climb, the Col d'Izoard, he started to cough and feel dizzy. 'Ah shit, here I go,' he thought but kept pedalling. Remarkably, others lost their place at the back of the *peloton* before he did. He was surprised and encouraged, he wasn't the worst. Hanging on for as long as he could, Stephens got himself into one of those small groups that work for collective survival. He climbed steadily and after scaling the highest mountain pass in Europe, the Bonette-Restefond, he breathed a little more freely on the final climb to Isola 2000.

Next morning the Tour moved out of the Alps and raced south to Marseilles. Stephens felt better and, in his own mind, he re-entered the race again. Little things unnoticed by others pleased him; he went with a few attacks, did all the jobs he was expected to do as a Once *équipier* and generally began to look beyond mere survival. That evening he spoke with Manolo Saiz and cheerfully told him he was over the worst of his illness. He was now going to be able to do what he was brought to do: to be one of the strong men in the final part of the race.

So enthused was he that Stephens rang his family in Canberra and told them not to worry. 'I've been crook for a few days but it's over now, I feel good,' he told his mother. It was 11 p.m. at Marseilles' Residence Ste-Anne when he offered this reassurance. His view of the immediate future was soon to change.

Oh God, this is the worst. Not daylight yet, must be early. Five o'clock and so sick. The bed alongside is empty, thank goodness. Lucky the team-mates who are paired off in other rooms. Nico (Dr Nicolas Terrados, Once's doctor) wouldn't want a call at this hour. Come on Neil, don't panic, a bad stomach can be cured in the toilet. Find the light, get sick and you'll feel better. Now back to bed and wait for things to improve.

Oh no this is serious. I feel so hot . . . I'm burning up . . . sweating like crazy. My stomach is churning. Back to the toilet. Get sick again, and again. But I'm not getting any better. Nico will come soon. Please Nico come soon.

'How are you this morning?'

'Terrible doc, terrible. Been vomiting for two hours and feel bad.'

'Okay, this is an injection to stop the vomiting and I will bring some liquid food.'

Liquid food. I have to take it. Nothing in my body and 180 kilometres to Montpellier. How am I going to do it?

Gentle sips. Sick again. Get dressed first, pack your suitcases, you can sip this stuff later. Bending is so hard, head is spinning. Come on, try harder, pull the shorts up, jersey down.

Team-mates and soigneurs must have heard because they come to the room. 'How are you, feeling okay?'

'I'll be fine.'

'See you at the team meeting.'

The room is warm, Manolo is telling us what he wants. Keep your eyes open, don't fall asleep. Concentrate, concentrate. But the dizziness, the drowsiness. Manolo is talking to me. Look at him, act normal. 'Neil, we know you aren't that well. Just try to hang in there. It will be hard for you today.'

Boss, you don't know how hard it's going to be!

There are thousands at the start. Having breakfast, waiting for friends, some picking me out. Leave me alone, please. 'Hi Neil.' Pretend you haven't seen him, move on. A journalist approaches. He sees my expression and diverts, pretends it wasn't me he wanted.

'G'day Neil, I'm from Aussie, saw the Tour on television and decided to come over. Howya doin'?'

This is awful. This bloke's come from Australia. He wants to talk. He'll think I'm a shit.

'I'm sorry mate, can't talk this morning.'

Somebody says the race is neutralized for the first nine kilometres – that will help. Time for my liquid breakfast. Riders are talking and laughing but the slow pace is killing me. God, I must be bad. They joke, I sweat. Drink from the bidon, go on you need to drink.

It flows down. Surges back up. Wait, take it easy, try another sip. But back it comes. Forget it. Just take the water. Down it goes, oh no, up again. Each time the road rises and I give a little extra the urge to vomit gets worse. Five hours of racing, but on what? They're watching me getting sick. They think I haven't a hope but they don't say. Don't worry, it will pass. Some pat me on the back, others pour water on my neck. You'll be better in a hour, hang in. Don't give up.

Herminio (Diaz-Zabala) stays close. 'Come on Neil, you can get through this.' He goes back to the team car and tells how bad I am. They tell me to keep drinking. Herminio pushes me, all the time encouraging. Herminio is a devoted team rider. He wants me to make it. I tell myself this is just five hours in my life, five hours when I suffer like never before. Tomorrow will be better.

Herminio asks if I can ride with him. He has to help Jalabert at the first sprint. He wants me at the front. Better be there when the acceleration comes. But I can't do it. He understands. Says he's sorry for increasing the pace, hopes things calm down afterwards. The sprint must be close, everyone's going faster. Riders pass me on all sides.

There's the 1000m sign. Keep your place, it might ease. They are going faster, shit I can't hold this. The 500m sign, there is a gap. I'm on my own. God, they're travelling twice as fast as me. I'm giving it everything. Forget the tiredness. Think, think, think. Don't give in. They may soon ease up. Stay calm, don't go too hard, keep them in sight, they can't keep this up.

The gap widens. I don't see them anymore. You're on your own now Neil, don't drop the bundle, keep riding, you'll get better. Take a drink. Come on now, don't get sick again. Oh no, I can't stop this. It's getting harder to think. I want to stop.

'Neil,' says Sebastian. (Pozo, Once's assistant directeur sportif who has driven alongside.)

'Yeah?'

I'm happy he's here. He knows I'm no quitter.

'Neil, keep drinking, keep going.'

'Yeah.'

But I know he knows.

'Neil, what do you think?'

Happy he's asked, I shake my head, I signal that I can't continue. I don't think about what it means. Don't realize I'm quitting the Tour. So exhausted. So thirsty. Maybe if I stay still, I can drink. It's all unreal, I'm out of the Tour and I feel nothing.

The ambulance stops, and the broom-wagon. Cameras come from nowhere, French television, Channel Four from Britain. Someone tears off my race number. The ripping sound has the effect of the first clay on a wooden coffin. Suddenly I realize what's happening. I have just abandoned the

Tour de France.

Sebastian's arm is around me.

'Don't let it get to you Neil, you didn't have a choice.'

I have abandoned the Tour but it is I who feels abandoned.

Sebastian takes my bike, I walk to the car. Someone tells me I must travel by ambulance or broom-wagon. I can't argue but no way am I going in any broom-wagon. Once was enough. Humiliating.

Inside the ambulance a woman asks how I feel. I try to talk. I'm so tired, so drowsy. I sleep, I think, for two hours, waking as the ambulance comes to the feeding zone. Sebastian will be there, I'm now allowed to transfer.

Sebastian takes me to the hotel in Montpellier. Straight to bed.

Minutes after the *commissaire* peels the race numbers from Neil Stephens' jersey, his abandonment is announced over Radio Tour. Journalists lean towards the list of riders taped to their dashboards and draw a line through his name. 'Stephens. That's the Australian with Once.' Driving two or three miles in front of the race, they have noted the latest casualty and wonder where they will stop for lunch. So far from the race, they can't begin to empathize.

What was it veteran Tour reporter Harry Van den Bremt said: journalists don't taste the race any more.

Before the Tour ends in Paris, 44 of the 180 starters will have been lost. Some eliminated through injuries sustained in crashes, others forced to stop by illness, some defeated by sheer exhaustion and quite a number disqualified for finishing outside a time limit. In many cases they did not have a choice but that doesn't mean elimination is easily accepted.

Quite the opposite. For most the experience is traumatic, especially for those eliminated for the first time. It is not uncommon for cyclists to weep at the moment of exit. As boys they dreamt of riding the Tour de France and then through the first week of the race it is everything they imagined. Exhaustion comes in the second and third weeks and with it the difficulties of survival.

Sean Yates is not an arrogant man but he permits himself one boast. Once it is known he is a professional cyclist, Yates is asked an inevitable question. 'Have you ever ridden the Tour de France?' 'Yes,' replies Yates, pausing to allow the fact to sink in. Then he says '10 times.' Next question will be 'how many times did you finish?' for the achievement of completing the Tour confers status and Yates will say proudly 'eight.'

Each Tour has its sub-plot of torturous eliminations. This one no less than others. Jaan Kirsipuu, the Estonian sprinter with the lowly Chazal team, surrendered his place on the terrible stage from Villard-de-Lans to Serre Chevalier. A first-timer, Kirsipuu rode with a group of stragglers well off the pace. One by one, they abandoned. He carried on, riding alone in front of the so-called broom-wagon which travels at the end of the race and sweeps up those who abandon.

Kirsipuu refused to surrender but so far behind and so exhausted, he didn't have a hope of arriving within the time limit. He finished five minutes outside but didn't realize it. When Kirsipuu crossed the line he was surrounded by journalists. An Estonian in his first Tour, they saw in him a footnote to the day's report. 'Jaan, how do you feel about being out of the Tour de France?' Kirsipuu didn't understand. *'Moi?' Moi, hors delai? Non.'* ('Me? Me, outside the time limit? No.')

However, he would have soon realized he was out: from his *directeur* Vincent Lavenu's expression of sympathy and from the sombre mood which falls on a team when one of its members is eliminated. Official confirmation would have been in the day's official results. Just one reference; KIRSIPUU, JAAN – *hors delai*. Then there would be the difficulty of finding transport back to his French base. A small team like Chazal is not going to encourage him to rent a car. Pascal Chanteur, a team-mate, watched Kirsipuu pack his bags.

'When you see one of your team-mates eliminated, it is sad. You put yourself in his place, you wonder how you would react. When Jaan left that evening, it wasn't funny. He told us about his day, riding with four or five others who, one by one, abandoned before his eyes. But he wanted to continue. The Tour is joy, it is suffering, it is disappointment.'

In his book *A Rough Ride*, Paul Kimmage vividly describes the moment of his abandonment in the 1987 Tour: 'I pass the statue of the Tour founder Henri Desgrange. It's as good a place as any to get off, but there are too many spectators. Allochio, an Italian and Gorospe, a Spaniard, pass me just before the summit and leave me. The broom-wagon is now directly behind. The descent of the Galibier is twisting and dangerous but I take no risks.

'There is an icy wind blowing up from the valley below and it freezes me as I drop. Down through the village of Valloire and then the short five-kilometre climb of the Telegraphe. Oh God, that feeling of jadedness when I am asked once again for effort. There is nothing in my legs. I look for a place to end it. A place void of people so that I can retire with dignity. I stop on the right-hand side of the road after a kilometre of climbing.

'I have cracked. It is over. The broom-wagon and ambulance stop behind me. I stand, head bent down over my bike, as a nurse descends from the ambulance and offers her sympathies. A *commissaire* gets out of the broom-wagon and unpins the two race numbers from my back. *"C'est dure,"* (it's hard) he sighs, as he completes this unpleasant duty. People further up the mountain come running down to witness the excitement. There are ohs and ahs as I climb into the bus, and then cheers as I am driven away. I feel numb and dazed and cold.'

Not all who are eliminated suffer as Kimmage did then. Two years later he abandoned the 1989 Tour without regret. In this race Laurent Fignon, twice a winner of the Tour, arrived at the foot of the climb to Isola 2000, did a little bit of mental arithmetic and stopped pedalling. 'I knew I was going to be outside of the time limit, there was no point.'

Fignon departed without tears, as did others. For each rider sees his exit in *his* way. To Fignon it was natural: he wasn't riding well and saw no value in simply finishing. Jaan Kirsipuu desperately wanted to finish. Somewhere between the emotional upset felt by Kirsipuu and Fignon's calm acceptance lay Neil Stephens. This was his second Tour and he did want to finish — for himself and for the Once team.

But his disappointment was tempered by the circumstances. Stephens was too ill to continue. If he hadn't been vomiting and unable to eat, if the doctor had not told him how bad he was, if he had not felt so hopelessly weak, his surrender would have been so much harder.

On the day he retired, Sebastian Pozo brought him to the hotel in mid-afternoon. He went to bed and slept. He awoke in the late evening but went back to sleep for another 10 consecutive hours. Next morning he was still weak and in need of more rest. He knew then he had been right, the Tour de France was not the place to be.

Around 11.30 on that morning, Sunday 18 July, Neil Stephens left Montpellier Airport in a rented car. He left a Tour that still had a week to run. His journey through south west France towards the Spanish border was difficult because he was weak and sleepy. At different times he thought of pulling into a hotel, hiring a room and resting but the urge to be at home was greater. He was near Pau when he picked up radio commentary of that day's Tour stage and was pleased by his team-mate Johan Bruyneel's presence in a five-man breakaway group.

Amaia called round that Sunday evening. It was good to see her. Whenever he came home from a race early, it lifted her spirits. She saw it as one of the perks of his career. Amaia would say how sorry she was that he had to abandon and then immediately how thrilled she was to see him.

But Neil found it hard. The further he got away from the Tour the more depressed he became, upset by the feeling that he was not where he should be. But Amaia's mood was so different he couldn't help being affected by it. She made it easier to cope with the disappointment.

Friends offered to visit but he discouraged them. He knew if he discussed his abandonment, describing how sick he was, they would sympathize. That was something he couldn't take. He wanted nothing to dilute his determination to make a swift and effective recovery. For it was his plan that on the day the finishers in the Tour de France rode down the Champs Elysées, he was going to ride the Villafranca de Ordizia race in San Sebastian.

For three days Neil did nothing except rest and eat. He slept soundly; 12 hours each night and a three-hour siesta in the afternoons. On TV he saw his team-mates Leanizbarrutia and Jalabert abandon the race, ill. Although sorry for his mates, he felt reassured others had got sick. When he wasn't sleeping or watching the Tour, he waited for Amaia to call round. She worked from morning until 1.30 in the afternoon, then from 5 p.m. until 7.30 and visited twice most days.

Neil cooked for Amaia, as he generally does, for when at home he is the one with more time. Because he had been so sick, he worried the bug might still be in his system and so ate lightly. He is fastidious about food, foregoing the pleasures of taste for the sake of athletic correctness. Amaia would look at his sauceless pasta and his unsalted fish and ask how he stomached it. But after eight years of this, his taste buds have adapted well.

He went for his first training ride on Wednesday but still felt weak. On Thursday he was much better, on Friday he rode the Classica de Sabinanigo and realized he was fully recovered. He would be competitive in the Villafranca de Ordizia and that pleased him. There were many reasons why he wanted to do well in this race. Most importantly, he remembered that on last year's Tour de France, he and the Spanish riders heard the result as they raced towards Paris and the Champs Elysées finale. He wanted his team-mates to know he had not idled since abandoning.

There was also Amaia. They had seen a lot of each other since his return and it had been good. And now, for the first time, she would come to watch him race. He woke on that morning feeling strong and confident, certain he was going to have a good race.

Sixty kilometres from the finish he attacked and a breakaway group formed. They were caught and his team-mate Leanizbarrutia counterattacked, initiating another split but, 15 kilometres from the finish, that group was recaptured. Then another group got away and Stephens was there. Not many would have given him a chance against Angel Edo in the sprint but on a slightly rising finishing straight, he passed Edo with 150m to go and won decisively.

This was the start of his end-of-season campaign and he was elated. As Herminio had told him, dropping out of the Tour de France was not the end of the world, not even the end of the season.

10

1

THE DOCTOR'S TALE
Exercising his Influence

NICOLAS TERRADOS

1. Nicolas Terrados
2. Inside his mobile laboratory the doctor rules. 'Teams with doctors do better than those without,' says Nicolas Terrados

Tall and athletic, he moves with the ease of the trained. Noon, this is his time of the day and he runs. Always for an hour and his pace is dictated by feeling. When he feels good he pushes himself along, on other days he moves at a saunter. Sightseeing runs, he calls them. Whatever his mood, he stays within his limits. Nicolas Terrados earns his living treating those who go beyond, and it wouldn't do for him to complain of tiredness. He slows to a jog in the car-park of the Hotel Ibis on the west side of Pau and estimates how much time he has before the day's first arrivals.

Terrados is doctor to Once, one of cycling's best professional teams. He travels with the squad to the important races and none are more important than the Tour de France. Just three days remain and it hasn't been a good race for the team. Erik Breukink, the leader, is on his way home to Holland; Alberto Leanizbarrutia and Neil Stephens are already back in Spain. All sick and tired. This afternoon Terrados expects Laurent Jalabert to become the team's fourth casualty.

He traces the trouble to Marseilles. Something in the food that was slightly off. Anyone else would have withstood the destructive bacteria, but 2000 kilometres into the Tour de France, the cyclist's immune system is weak and his defences easily breached. Stephens abandoned the morning after Marseilles, Leanizbarrutia went a day later and this morning, five days after the suspected food-poisoning, Breukink did not start. Now Dr Terrados waits for Jalabert.

He says the Ariostea and Lotto teams which shared the same hotel in Marseilles had similar troubles. But the others have not suffered as badly. Only Andrea Ferrigato of Ariostea had to abandon. Another explanation for Once's difficulties is that the team burned itself out in the first five months of the season when it achieved a string of successes and its young star Alex Zülle came within an inopportune crash of winning the Vuelta a España.

But all that seems inconsequential now. Johan Bruyneel's victory on the sixth stage to Amiens and likely 7th or 8th place overall isn't enough for Once. Nicolas Terrados does not admit to disappointment but he feels it. He is part of the team, having adopted a role which is more than that of doctor. An old basketball pro, he cannot help getting drawn into the ebb and flow of the team's life.

Now it is a time for tending the wounded.

Laurent Jalabert has arrived, two hours before the *peloton*. Illness forced him to abandon early in the day and he has travelled to the hotel by team car. As he gingerly gets out, Terrados is there to meet him. He expresses sympathy with a touch on the rider's shoulder. Jalabert is very down and Terrados says what needs to be said. 'You tried as much as you could to stay in the Tour, you had an infection, there was nothing more you could have done. You have had a lot of victories this season, you have been good for the team.'

They walk towards the hotel. The doctor has already made sure the rider's room is ready and they disappear into the lift together.

They are a new breed of tourist, the doctors. Nicolas Terrados is just one; his friends Sabino Padilla and Benjamin Fernandez are others. Padilla is doctor with the Banesto team, Fernandez treats the Clas riders. Terrados got his primary medical degree at the University of Oviedo in northern Spain and later received a PhD in exercise physiology for a thesis on the effects of training at altitude. Padilla, another Spaniard, studied exercise physiology in France and Fernandez worked as a grant student with Terrados at the Department of Sports Medicine in Asturias.

On the tour they travel with their mobile laboratories, built into the team buses. Their language is the jargon of sports medicine and they see their roles as making an important contribution to their teams' performances. At one level they are conventional doctors, treating athletes who pick up the same infections and sicknesses as the next man. On another level, they are exercise physiologists helping cyclists to achieve optimum performance.

To this end, they take blood samples and analyse them. They measure the red cell count, the lactic acid level, they check the glycogen stores. Too few red cells may mean the rider needs iron, too much lactic acid reduces the efficiency of the muscles and must be tackled and low glycogen stores highlight the need for a glucose supplement. Some riders produce a high level of toxins, causing problems for the liver and that, too, must be treated.

Terrados looks upon his patients as athletes and tries to use his knowledge of exercise physiology to improve their performances. This may be as straightforward as suggesting a course of weight-training for a rider or as complex as working out for how long Alex Zülle could effectively exceed his anaerobic threshold during a long time trial.

The anaerobic threshold is the point at which the athlete works at maximum efficiency. Should the athlete go beyond his anaerobic threshold his body secretes far more lactic acid than it can dissipate and the build-up leads to chronic fatigue and diminishes performance.

'From working with the rider Melchor Mauri I learned he could perform beyond his anaerobic threshold for 20 to 25 minutes. My medical friends could not believe this was possible. Now we are trying to see how far Alex could go in this respect.'

Once's riders call him Nico, for here there are no formalities. Men with a job to do; he, no different from the rest. Nico, Sabino and Benjamin are friendly with the Ariostea doctor and Dr Testa of Motorola and, through the grapevine, they know the Carrera doctor works pretty much as they do. They believe the teams with doctors are achieving the best results in this Tour and that the French teams Gan and Castorama, who don't have doctors, could do with them.

Terrados believes the sport benefits from the involvement of exercise physiologists. 'We are involved in the riders' training, also with the care and health of the rider and, of course, they need medicines like everybody else.' He entered the sport with his eyes open, aware of its link with doping but without reservations. 'Ethically, it is for each doctor to decide. If some people do things unethically, it's their problem.

'I have got my ethics. But the ethical problems existed more in those days with no doctors or with doctors who just came to particular races to provide particular medicines.'

The old days were different and not so long ago. Doctors were uncommon and all kinds of drugs were administered by *soigneurs* or taken by the riders themselves. They got their hands on the favoured drugs of the day and hoped they would work. Riders needed to believe they had the same advantages as their rivals and this, more than anything, led them to the medicine cabinet. Vitamin injections, iron tablets and glucose drinks were routine and legal; there were other substances, taken less often but illegal.

At the beginning of his professional career, Jean-Paul Van Poppel demurred when told he needed injections. His reluctance stemmed from squeamishness and he asked could he take his medications orally. Okay, said the doctor but it wasn't efficient because oral ingestion taxed the stomach and the liver and this led to other problems.

Problems which changed Van Poppel's attitude. Most of his illnesses originated in his stomach and he eventually agreed to injections. He got used to them quickly enough and his stomach problems diminished. Although it was fear which put him off needles, Van Poppel is not dismissive of the moral question.

'People see injections as doping. They think if you take one before the race it has to be illegal, even though you have just taken something for an infection. A man riding the Tour de France needs more vitamins than the normal person. In my mind what is not on the [banned] list is not doping. But there are riders who ride the Tour de France without vitamins and all that stuff. It's possible.

'I know Paul Koechli's team: they never rode with any vitamins or anything else. He was against all of this. He doesn't like injections, just Supradine. No needles, never. It's possible for a strong rider like Steve Bauer, who rode in Koechli's team, but when you're like Jos Van Aert or Martin Earley, then maybe it's a problem. They are skinny, they haven't much reserves and they are more likely to get ill.

'But I am against doping, I don't like cortisone and that. I am in favour of controls and having a good list. I hear a lot about EPO [Erythropoietin, a drug which produces red cells and thus increases the blood's capacity for transporting oxygen] and they talk about more things that I don't know. It's not my problem but we will see in 30 years. I know a team which says you can take testosterone, that the risk is very little. But there is a risk and when you take it, you cannot put the blame on anybody if you get caught at control.

'I don't think testosterone is bad for you but if you take too much, it is bad and that is why I think it is right to have it on the list. When everyone takes a little, maybe it is okay. But there are always guys who take too much. I have never been positive in my career. Please, don't let's talk about this. If you were positive, people would look at everything you've won and say you were once positive.

'What happened to Paul Koechli's idea?' asks Van Poppel.

According to Koechli, it worked. 'I founded a company in Switzerland which controlled the team and I ran that team from 1988 to '92 without one needle. The process was more important to me than the results and I could do it because it was my team and I owned the company. I had the freedom to do it. We had less money because that was the price I had to pay for absolute freedom but we had very good results. We had the yellow jersey in the Tour de France for 10 days, Steve (Bauer) was fourth in the 1988 Tour and the riders in my team became convinced it was possible to do this job without doing what so many told them they should do.'

Koechli's life in cycling was shaped by his short career as a pro. He rode for three years in the *peloton* before health problems forced him to stop. This made him curious about the medical back-up for cyclists. During his training to become a cycling coach, he studied physiology. He quickly earned a considerable reputation for his coaching ability and in 1983 he became *directeur sportif* of the powerful La Vie Claire team. Backed by wealthy entrepreneur Bernard Tapie, La Vie Claire was a highly successful team.

It placed second (through Bernard Hinault) in the 1984 Tour de France; first and second (Hinault and Greg LeMond) in the '85 Tour; first, second and fourth (LeMond, Hinault and Andy Hampsten) in the '86 Tour. Although he is reluctant to be specific, Koechli was not impressed by everything at La Vie Claire. 'About my experience in France, I cannot say no one ever took drugs. I never saw it but I know it might have happened. I started to change the team because of this reason. The difficulty was that at the time I went to La Vie Claire, the team was already built.'

Central to Koechli's philosophy is the belief that cyclists take drugs because of a psychological dependence. Physically, they don't need them, a view confirmed by the performance of Greg LeMond. 'I know that Greg, when he was in my team, did not use any stuff. I say that two hundred per cent certain and he won the Tour de France. So you can win the Tour de France without taking drugs. This is important because many riders are dependent. It is like a ritual, they cannot live without them.'

As a former professional, Koechli understands the cycle: a rider turns pro, struggles to adjust to the increased demands and is tacitly advised to take certain substances. Anxious to produce results, he accepts what is suggested and then attributes all progress to the drugs. 'The rider loses all confidence in himself, he is drawn into the dependency culture and one day he finds he cannot do anything without drugs.'

Koechli says you cannot convince riders on the basis of drugs constituting a danger to their health. 'Because many of the dope products are not dangerous. We take other risks in our lives which are much more dangerous.' Neither can the *directeur sportif* appeal to the riders' sense of fair play or honesty. 'Life itself isn't fair so you cannot tell them they must behave fairly.' Instead Koechli tries to educate.

'I tell them they should not become dependent upon anything. Not on drugs, not on their coach. The biggest trouble in life comes if you lose confidence in your character and in your capacities. I encourage the riders to be themselves. I try to give them more knowledge, I tell them to develop stronger personalities, to accept their own limitations.

'Not everyone can win the Tour de France but this is not a reason to be unhappy and it is not a reason to use drugs. I consider it a basic problem of life; not so much a cycling problem. In other words, faced with a similar situation in life, what would you do? I don't like the dope control system but it is something we need. And it must be done correctly, very severe and very professional.'

Because he educated himself about the body and its physiological needs, Koechli could answer riders' questions. When, for example, they asked why he allowed them to take an iron supplement but wouldn't permit them to take testosterone, he could provide an answer beyond the simple, 'Iron is not banned, testosterone is.'

'Iron,' says Koechli, 'is not a substance produced by the organism. You must make sure your organism gets it by normal means. If you have an iron deficiency, it might be that while you are taking it in your food, you are not absorbing it. This may relate to the effects of a hard bicycle race. So you have to treat that and make sure the athlete has as much iron as he needs.

'Testosterone is not the same thing because it is produced by the organism and it knows how much it has to produce. It also knows when it has to get the level low to encourage the athlete to slow down. It is the organism's way of telling him to take things easy and you shouldn't interfere with that.'

Paul Koechli believes there is less doping now than in the recent past. A small number of strong-willed riders have come into the sport and challenged the accepted customs. He is thinking of LeMond and Bauer especially, two north Americans who were not prepared to go with the European way.

'They had a different attitude, they had their own knowledge about training and physiology and that kept them away from what should not be done. They also had strong personalities and so they could resist. But if you have grown up in a bad environment, it is very difficult to resist and, in many places, that is still the case.'

Only a year has passed since Koechli's Helvetia-La Suisse team raced in the Tour de France, so he was aware of the trend towards doctors working full-time with teams. He is sceptical about their use. 'I never had a doctor in my team, except in the Tour de France and his only role was to treat those with a real health problem, a flu or an infection. It is important that there is a competent diagnosis and you don't lose time before commencing the correct treatment. But this is only important in a very important stage race where a rider may be treated and helped to continue. In a one-day race it is a nonsense (to have a doctor). If the rider is unhealthy, he must go home. That's it.

'The presence of a doctor in a team is usually a bad thing. Riders are healthy, so why should they need a doctor? In my experience doctors are generally very bad physiologists because physiology is how a healthy organism functions and doctors are more used to unhealthy people. Their perspective is the wrong one.'

What Paul Koechli says about doctors may be true. Nicolas Terrados might even agree. For Terrados sees himself as doctor and exercise physiologist. His work at the Department of Sports Medicine in Asturias and with the Once team involves the treatment of people whose most common affliction is sub-standard sporting performance.

On the Tour his day begins half an hour before the riders rise. That can be as early as 6 a.m. or as late as 7.30. He then does his rounds, calling at the riders' rooms to wake them and to see how they are feeling. Sitting on their beds he checks their blood pressure and their resting pulse. As he does so he chats with them, asks how they are feeling, if they have been coughing through the night or if they feel anything coming on.

Each Friday morning he takes blood samples, drawing blood from a vein in the arm while the rider is in a resting state. He believes in the value of blood tests but, during the Tour de France, they are of limited use. The Once squad had blood tests in January and follow-up tests two months later. Then they have time to act on the results and to make suggestions which might improve the riders' performances.

But two weeks into the Tour there isn't much any one can do when, for example, a blood test shows the rider's hypothalamus drive, which stimulates hormonal production, is not working properly. This can be one of the more obvious indications that the rider is over-raced or over-trained and, unless the doctor is prepared to use banned hormones, there is no immediate solution.

Breakfast is the most important meal and Nicolas advises the *soigneurs* and liaises with the hotel about what the riders should eat. They can expend between 6000 and 9000 calories during a stage of the Tour and so replenishment is important. For breakfast the *soigneurs* prepare a special muesli which is mixed with yoghurt and fresh fruit. Then rice, pasta or an omelette, all taken with bread, butter and marmalade, orange juice and other carbohydrates.

Replenishment also takes place at dinner the evening before and throughout the stage. High-calorie drinks are important as they allow the rider to refuel during the race. For a very hard stage, the doctor insists that a liquid meal is prepared for every rider and given to him during the race. This contains 20% fat, 20% protein and 60% carbohydrates, which represents a well-balanced meal.

Once the riders begin racing, there is little the team doctors can do. If they need medical attention during the race, they are treated by the official Tour doctor, Gerard Porte and his team. Nicolas Terrados likes to drive from the start of a stage directly to the team hotel. After a run to keep his own body in good working order, he may analyse the latest blood tests. By this stage of the season he knows his riders. There is one who produces a lot of toxins, putting extra strain on the liver and causing it to work less efficiently. But the medication which Terrados gives is of limited value because the most effective way to restore the liver to full health is to lessen its workload.

Other riders in the team destroy a lot of red blood cells during competition and so deplete their iron stores. They are given iron. New research suggests that those who take a lot of iron may have health problems in the future and Terrados limits the amount of iron to what is necessary. Another depletes his glycogen store and the doctor arranges for him to have a glucose drip that evening. Still another has too much lactic acid in his system and, even though the rider has been through a long stage of the Tour, Terrados will insist that he spend 20 minutes on an exercise bike to clear up the lactic acid.

By the time the Once riders arrive back to the hotel, Dr Terrados will know what each one needs. But nothing is done until he talks with them individually, for they have just ridden another five or six hours and new problems may have arisen. The doctor has seen enough of the Tour to know that the rider who was so strong that morning may, by evening, be on the brink of capitulation.

Nicolas Terrados was born in the town of Jaen in the south of Spain. His mother teaches the history of art and his father is a businessman. He moved north to Asturias when the University of Oviedo offered him a place in their medical school and he funded his studies through a professional basketball career. Through his early years in college he played in the Spanish first division. It was hard to combine medical studies with serious basketball and he enjoyed his studies better in his final medical year when he dropped to division two.

That allowed more time for his books, a change reflected in his final year examination results. He was awarded a scholarship to study Exercise Physiology under Professor Bengt Saltin in Denmark; Professor Saltin is regarded as one of the world's most eminent exercise physiologists. Having studied for two years with the Professor in Copenhagen, Terrados spent a further 18 months working with him in Stockholm. Much of the time in Denmark and Sweden was devoted to a study of altitude training which formed the basis for Terrados' PhD thesis.

That drew Dr Terrados into cycling as, in researching the subject, he worked with the Swedish national junior team. His first paper on the effects of altitude training was read by members of the Spanish Cycling Federation and they invited him to work with the country's amateur team.

A few riders, Melchor Mauri, Miguel-Angel Martinez and the pro Eduardo Chozas, asked Terrados to be their doctor and their success reflected well on his work.

Even more important was Manolo Saiz's presence as coach to the Spanish team, for when he became Once's *directeur sportif* in 1988 he asked Terrados to join as the team doctor. By then Dr Terrados was working in the Department of Sports Medicine in Asturias and he saw his work with Once as an interesting challenge.

'My job with the team is not my only job, I've got my other position and I think it is better like this. I'm not under any pressure or cannot be pushed to do things I don't want to do. It's the same with Sabino Padilla, the doctor with Banesto. But I know doctors whose only job is cycling and they could be pushed in an unethical way by the team or by the *directeur sportif*. They know on the Once team that I could be out of this tomorrow without any problem.'

Steve Bauer slumps on a sofa in the foyer of the Hotel Xalet Ritz in the Pyrenean village La Massana. Two and a half weeks of the Tour have passed and Bauer is exhausted. Just now he never wants to ride this race again. Too hard.

Within the *peloton*, it is generally accepted that Bauer stayed clear of drugs. Not only was he open in his opposition to all doping but Bauer aligned himself to teams and individuals who shared his ethos. Through the early part of his career he hung out with Greg LeMond when they both rode for La Vie Claire and they challenged the widely held view that doping was an essential part of the rider's lifestyle. At that time Bernard Tapie, chief sponsor of the La Vie Claire squad, said LeMond and Bauer were the only two riders he was sure did not take drugs.

After La Vie Claire, Bauer joined Paul Koechli's Weinmann-La Suisse team, a decision not unrelated to Koechli's vigorous opposition to drug-taking. Bauer is now part of Motorola, the US-sponsored team which takes the old European traditions on an *à-la-carte* basis and refuses to go with the old beliefs about doping. Foremost amongst those is Jacques Anquetil's opinion that you don't ride the Tour de France on mineral water.

At this moment Bauer can't argue against Anquetil's view. He is wrecked. 'See that boy,' he says pointing to a two-year-old boy who toddles across the foyer of the hotel, 'I'd bet every penny I have earned that if you measured the level of testosterone in his body against mine, he would have more than me. Our team doesn't use testosterone but there are teams which do.'

Testosterone is a male sex hormone which stimulates the reproductive organs, encourages growth of bone and muscle and helps maintain muscle strength. It is one of the banned substances cyclists have used and it has the advantage of giving the rider a good chance of avoiding detection. As a body naturally reproduces testosterone and as different people produce different levels, it is not easy to establish what is produced naturally or taken artificially.

The accepted test is to measure the level of testosterone in relation to the level of epitestosterone in the body. Generally the ratio is one-to-one but between riders it varies. Olympic guidelines, which form the basis for the doping laws in all sports, deem a sportsman to be guilty if the ratio of testosterone to epitestosterone is higher than six-to-one. The consensus in cycling has always been that this ratio allows riders room for illegal manoeuvre.

And just now, weary and a little despondent, it irks Steve Bauer to think there are racers out there playing with their testosterone levels.

Dr Terrados, let's consider this hypothetical case. You are doctor of a rider who produces a low level of testosterone. During the Tour de France, blood tests show his testosterone to be severely depleted. You know you can give him some without risking detection. But the rules forbid its use and the rider, while he will almost certainly pass the drug-test, is breaking the rule.

With the example of testosterone, it's complicated. But what about iron, if the rider has low iron and clearly needs iron, should he be given iron?

'Yes.'

Yes?

'Yes. And then testosterone? Should he not be given testosterone? '

That's the question.

'If I think that, ethically, testosterone should not be given, then the thing is out. If I tell you that when they need testosterone, they should be given testosterone, then it's going to be said in a book that "Once is taking testosterone." '

But it is a problem because the testosterone level goes so low in the Tour de France?

'Yes, the rider would be depleted. In some riders, the level [of testosterone] would be very, very depleted. Others are different. Genetically, some have very, very high testosterone levels. Incredibly high levels.'

How precisely can the doctor measure the testosterone level?

'Not very exactly and that's why I don't believe people are playing too much with testosterone. They could be playing but not too much because from the blood test you get a general idea of the testosterone level. The test shows you how much is free in the blood but it could also be with a protein and you only get an approximate measure.

'My impression is that in a serious team, I don't think people are playing around with testosterone. They could be giving a little bit to someone who is really, *really* very down but it would be just a little bit.'

But, as doctor of Once, do you worry that rival teams gain an advantage from drugs which you would not use?

'No. In the old days I know this was what happened but right now we [the doctors] have got the feeling that people are doing the same things. I'm always talking with Sabino [Padilla] and Benjamin [Fernandez] and we don't think other teams are doing anything different. With the dope control, there isn't anything that could make a big difference. And anyhow the teams with doctors are doing better, I don't know why but they are. Maybe the ones without doctors are still using the old methods.'

Terrados' methods are certainly not the old methods. As an exercise physiologist he advises the riders on such things as training, rest and racing programme. It is his view that riders can significantly improve their performances in time trials simply by training correctly. Once's Johan Bruyneel is, he says, a good example.

Immediately after each time trial in the Tour, Terrados takes a blood sample from every Once rider and measures the level of lactic acid. As each rider will have used a heart monitor during his time trial, the doctor can relate the computer read-out from the heart monitor to the levels of lactic acid. Too high a level means the cyclist has ridden for too long beyond his anaerobic threshold; in other words, he has forced himself too much.

'We need to know how much lactic acid they are producing so they can train better in the future. In specific time trial training, the rider can play with the anaerobic threshold, riding a little below it, then a little above it. It is a science but we can really improve people in the time trial. We have tried to apply the same principles to the mountain but lately we have got the feeling that it's much more difficult on the mountains. In climbing, the genetical factor is much stronger. By training you can make a normal cyclist a good time triallist, it's much more difficult to make a *grimpeur* [climber] out of a normal cyclist.'

Paul Kimmage remembers the sequence of events which led to what he calls his first jab. It came a couple of days after the time trial at Nantes in the 1986 Tour de France. Because he was his team's leading rider going into the long individual time trial, Kimmage wanted to perform well against the clock. His descent from the ramp was so fast and his sprint through the first 300m so explosive that he almost overshot the first bend. Through the 61-kilometre test, he pushed himself further than he had ever done in his career.

At the finish Kimmage was close to collapse. He felt he must have done a decent time. In fact he was eight minutes slower than the winner Bernard Hinault. He was shattered by his lowly placing. 'I knew Hinault could not have hurt any more than I did. I couldn't believe he was that much faster than me. What were they doing that I wasn't?'

Two days before the time trial, Kimmage felt his form as good as it had ever been. When a young and unsung Miguel Indurain broke clear on the stage to St Hilaire, he counterattacked and closed the 150-metre gap to the Spaniard. Others followed and the breakaway group remained clear of the pack.

But on the evening of the time trial Kimmage's body ached like never before. Next morning he was stiff and very sore. Every other rider in the race seemed to him fit and well. He complained to different people in the team and some asked how he was 'looking after himself?' Given the effort he made in the time trial, his bad result and his subsequent exhaustion, Kimmage believed there had to be something in the syringes he saw others use.

He was convinced he needed to take something. 'Although this was only seven years ago, everything came out of the *soigneur's* bag then. We didn't have a doctor in our team on that tour and riders aligned themselves with different *soigneurs*. These were fellows with no medical background but they were giving injections.'

He was ready to turn himself over to Emile, the *soigneur*. 'I had been taking multi-vitamins since the start of the race. I had refused all injections, but as I watched Hinault I realized it wasn't possible to continue in this way. I was on my hands and knees. I told Thevenet [his *directeur sportif*] I was knackered. He brought me to Emile's room and suggested a B12 injection. I dropped my shorts and abandoned my virginity without a second thought.'

The B12 injection did not contravene any regulation and Kimmage felt no improvement in his physical condition. He never recovered from the brutal effort of the time trial and made it to Paris only because he doggedly refused to quit. But that injection did improve his morale. For the first time in his cycling career he felt he was competing in the same arena as his peers.

Without realizing it, Kimmage had become a victim of what Paul Koechli calls the 'dependency culture'. It is not that he needed drugs but he thought he could not compete effectively without them.

'The biggest problem the rider has is his own ignorance,' says Kimmage. 'There was no doctor in our team to take a blood test, nobody to say "Hold on, the exhaustion you feel is normal. You produced far too much lactic acid in yesterday's time trial." I mean there was nobody to explain what an anaerobic threshold was and I hadn't a clue. I didn't know what the B12 injection did for me and I only agreed to it because the *directeur* suggested it.

'Bringing well qualified exercise physiologists into teams should bring about an improvement. But they must explain things. Provided they do, the riders will understand their own bodies better and will be less ignorant about what they should and shouldn't be doing.'

Neil Stephens recalls an afternoon at the Australia Institute for Sport in Canberra many years ago. They said they wanted him to do a couple of tests, something to show how he could use his anaerobic threshold to improve his training and, ultimately, his performance. He had to do two 30-minute sessions on an exercise bicycle. In the first he could ride as hard as he liked to achieve the best result. The second session would be controlled; that is, Stephens had to ride just below his anaerobic threshold, at a level dictated by the people at the Institute.

'The interesting thing was that my heart rate was a lot lower on the controlled test but the amount of work, and the performance level, was a lot higher. I suffered much more in the uncontrolled test but, translated into competition, I would have produced a much slower time. It was good for me to have this written into my mind at an early stage of my career.'

Early in his professional career, Stephens rode in teams which could not afford to pay its riders. Teams which regarded medical back-up as an exorbitant luxury. 'I was once in the Tour of Portugal and I got sick. I didn't know what to do. So I just put up with it and kept on riding. But in those days I was racing at a lower level and, to some degree, I didn't need that sort of attention.

'Now I am riding a lot more races, doing a lot more work and it's a lot harder on my body. So the whole question of medical back-up becomes more important.'

As a rider in the Once team Stephens works with Nicolas Terrados and yes, he says, he could ride without medical supervision but not at this level. Certain things he has come to take for granted. For example, after a long and hot stage in the Tour de France or Vuelta a España, the Once *soigneurs* will wait at the finish with a specially prepared mineral drink. 'You deplete your mineral reserves very badly in the heat, Nico knows this and always makes sure we start replenishing immediately afterwards.'

Stephens likes to talk with Terrados about how his body works. A couple of years ago blood tests showed the rider consistently produced low quantities of red cells. That meant he needed to take iron tablets and make sure his diet included foodstuffs with a high iron content. But further tests by Terrados showed Stephens' red cells, although relatively low in quantity, were high in quality. 'What it meant was that the problem was not as great as we first thought. Without this supervision and help, it's guesswork.'

The expertise and professionalism of doctors like Terrados has wider implications. 'When there are team doctors,' says Stephens, 'there is less or no doping. These guys don't need to, they work within the rules. In smaller teams riders go off and take things and can end up being positive simply because they don't know any better.'

The greatest testimony to the influence of the exercise physiologist comes from Neil Stephens. Asked how he, as an Once *équipier*, rides a Tour de France time trial, he says, 'Using a monitor on the handlebars, I keep it at 160 [heartbeats per minute] all the way, that is nine below my anaerobic threshold. At that rate I can dissipate the lactic acid that I am producing and it therefore doesn't tire me for the next day's work. But it is a high enough rate to make sure I don't have problems with the time limit.'

There was a time when it was thought that all a cyclist had to do was put his head down, his backside in the air and simply get on with it.

THE LANTERNE'S TALE
Last but not Least
EDWIG VAN HOOYDONCK

2

1. Edwig Van Hooydonck
2. Van Hooydonck was happy to finish, unhappy to finish last

The cornfield which has been turned into a car park is still empty and the stalls that will serve sandwiches and beverages are not ready for business. A TV crew, making a documentary, waits by the ramp from where the riders will descend but there is no one in sight. Along the barriers the crowd is thinly lined: Bretigny has not quite got into the Tour spirit, has not yet got out of bed.

Hosting the start of a Tour de France time trial may be an honour but Saturday mornings are for late risers and late breakfasts. Neither is there any rush to the start for this will be a long day made interesting by those who ride to gain. Tony Rominger will be followed most closely. Fourth at the beginning of the day, Rominger wants a place in the top three but he will not begin until after 4 p.m. Time is on the fan's side.

Rominger is one of the exceptions. On this second to last day most of the prizes have been won and few can significantly improve their positions. Not Edwig Van Hooydonck for sure; last-placed of the 136 survivors, he trails the 135th-placed Peter Farazijn by almost 22 minutes.

It is now 11.30. The cars are arriving, the stalls opening. And Van Hooydonck is present. As last-placed, he is first off the ramp. In his mind the 48-kilometre time trial to Montlhery is nothing more than the second last step on the journey to Paris. He wants to finish the Tour so this must be endured.

'The thing about the Tour de France,' said an astonished Lance Armstrong after five days, 'is that a rider an hour behind can expect to do 20 interviews each day.' Van Hooydonck is almost three and a half hours down and doing at least that. But then he is unusually interesting: one of the best cyclists of his generation who, in this race, is the lowliest of the also-rans.

Fifteen minutes before starting he is again encircled by journalists as he patiently explains what it is like for a respected racer to be last. A phlegmatic man, Van Hooydonck dislikes the fuss. He is embarrassed about his position but there is nothing he can do.

It is not in his nature to be rude and so he tries to pass it off. 'Rob Harmeling,' he says referring to the Dutch rider, 'won a stage in this race the year after he was the *lanterne rouge.*' That was one angle, a little humour offers another. 'You know I am going to become the first rider in the history of the sport to win the Tour of Flanders twice and then finish last in the Tour of France.'

That's as close as he comes to lightness. Mostly Van Hooydonck is sombre, his answers short. He has no results to speak of and nothing to be happy about. Already he is looking ahead to Paris and being with Christel, his wife. Some of the team are returning directly to their homes but he will spend the final night in the capital. He has promised himself an evening in a nice restaurant with Christel, far away from his team-mates and their talk of attacks, pursuits and tiredness. It has been a long, long three weeks.

Now he is in the little stall, at the top of the ramp where his time trial begins. Looking down the road, he tells himself he is feeling better – he can get through this without bother. He sees heads, arms and elbows leaning across the barriers. All eyes turn towards him. They understand why he is first off and he wonders what they're thinking. Laughing, maybe? There's Van Hooydonck, *la lanterne rouge.*

The starter says he has one minute. His rangy body arched over the bike, his expression one of indifference. *Dix seconds . . . cinq, quatre, trois, deux, une . . .*

At the first flicker of movement, there is a spontaneous and prolonged burst of clapping and cheering from the barriers. Van Hooydonck rolls down the ramp, the sound music to his ears. It continues as his body grows smaller and smaller . . . and disappears into the distance.

Such was the passion of supporters in the early years, Henri Desgrange feared he had created an uncontrollable race. Cheating was commonplace. Fans of one rider tried various tricks to destroy the chances of rivals: they put tacks on the road and physically assaulted riders. Neither were the racers themselves models of good behaviour. Some rigged up elaborate towing devices, others hopped on trains to make up time on their rivals. Desgrange threatened to call it off but then decided the show would go on, once more as a 'moral crusade for the sport of cycling'. Ninety years on, the play still runs, although Desgrange's successors are somewhat less fervent about the morality question.

For all its modernity, today's Tour is a direct descendant of the race founded by Desgrange. The more it changes, the more it values the old customs. Gimmicks conceived in the early 1900s are now traditions; respected, almost revered. Decorate the leader's jersey with all the sponsors in the world but the colour *must* remain yellow. For this three-week race around France survived the early controversies, two World Wars, the rampant rise of commercialism, the tragedy of Tommy Simpson's death on Mont Ventoux and the shadowy sub-culture of drug abuse. Not only did the Tour endure but it now draws strength from its endurance.

The tradition of the *lanterne rouge* (red light) is one of the oldest. He was the last-placed rider and so called because of the red light which hung from the last carriage in a train. To further the association, the rider was sometimes asked to carry an old red lamp on the morning of the final stage to Paris where he was presented before an appreciative crowd.

As a minor celebrity, the *lanterne rouge* received invitations to criteriums all over France and made a lot of money. For a lowly rider likely to finish in the bottom three or four places, it was worth his while to make sure he was last. Less than 20 years ago, the battle to be *lanterne rouge* was sometimes more keenly, and certainly more ingeniously, fought than that for the yellow jersey.

Paul Sherwen rode the 1979 Tour and watched the conflict between his Fiat team-mate Philippe Tesnière and Gerard Schonbacher. 'They were a long way behind the third last rider and they both wanted to be last. On one stage Tesnière, I think, stopped for a pee and Schonbacher stopped with him. They were both left behind and they finished together 15 or 20 minutes behind.

'On another day, one of them hid and let the bunch go by, only starting again when everybody else was out of sight. It ended badly for Tesnière as far as I remember. Near the end of the race there was a time trial and in trying to lose time he finished outside the limit and was eliminated.'

That was the year John Wayne died, but Felix Levitan, the Tour boss, was unimpressed by the cycling cowboys. He felt Schonbacher and Tesnière demeaned the Tour and he disliked the publicity they generated. A year later Levitan imposed a new rule. 'What he did,' says Sherwen 'was to eliminate the last rider on general classification. This was done from the fifth day to the third last day and was meant to discourage riders from being last.

'It was a brutal law and one that the Tour organizers would not get away with today. I remember a rider called Jacques Osmont was last at the start of one stage. He was desperate not to be eliminated and so broke away, gaining a lead of five minutes. He rode very well, stayed clear for most of the stage but was caught near the finish and, at the end of the day, was still last. But seeing how bravely he had ridden, Levitan let him off that evening. He was eliminated after the next day's stage. It was like bringing a guy to the firing squad and telling him you weren't going to shoot him until the next day.'

Levitan's draconian sanction lasted just one year but served its purpose. After this attack on the tradition, the *lanterne rouge* glowed less brightly. Other factors helped the Tour director. The criterium circuit constricted, leaving fewer races and fewer invitations. Furthermore the sport's new popularity brought improved salaries and a reduced dependence upon criterium earnings. Last is now a place to be avoided.

'Eddy would not have wanted to be in the last five,' says veteran Irish rider Sean Kelly. 'As for being last, he would have just wanted to get away from that as quickly as he could. Talk about the *lanterne rouge* would have embarrassed him.'

This was evident in Viry-Chatillon at the start of the final stage. Van Hooydonck waited near the WordPerfect bus, not far away was his team-mate Raul Alcala. The dusty old glass and iron lantern was a photographer's idea but it made Van Hooydonck uneasy. He could do without this silly game. 'Just one little photograph of you holding *la lanterne*?' asked the photographers. 'It's a tradition.' Van Hooydonck's face said no but their enthusiasm needed no approval. They persisted.

He didn't like it and Alcala's laughter added to his feeling of being ridiculed. However, as a conscientious professional, Van Hooydonck complied. After all he earned his salary by getting WordPerfect's name into print. Catching the lantern in his right hand, he couldn't seem to hold it properly. There was something appropriate in that – Edwig Van Hooydonck was cut out for something better.

Five or six years ago Van Hooydonck was hailed as Belgium's best since Eddy Merckx. A judgement which might have been taken with a pinch of salt except that Merckx himself was the judge. Van Hooydonck's parents' home in Ekeren, just outside Brussels, was decorated with the trophies of his amateur career and most of the wins came from lone breakaways. Jan Raas offered the 19-year-old a professional contract in 1986 and Van Hooydonck moved seamlessly into the *peloton*, finishing fifth in his first Paris–Roubaix classic. That was 1987 and he was just 20: the boy had something.

Victory in the 1989 Tour of Flanders classic confirmed the promise of a bright future; a promise further realized with a second victory in Flanders two years later. 'Eddy Bosberg' they called him; Eddy after the great Merckx and Bosberg after the hill in the Tour of Flanders where he made his winning attacks. Heady days which were not as reliable a guide to the future as they seemed.

When Van Hooydonck says he is a good rider but not a great one, he hits the nail on the head.

He thinks now he won too much as an amateur because those victories gave an exaggerated sense of his potential. In those days, Edwig rode away from his rivals and, alone in front, maintained his lead to the finish. Now he does not ride well in groups, simply because he never had to. He suffered too from the expectation that he would become the star Merckx had foreseen.

Van Hooydonck wasn't going to be a star. Physically, he did not have the robust constitution which underpins great careers. He could win only when he was at the peak of his form. 'For a Tour of Flanders or a Paris–Roubaix I would always rate him in the five most likely to win,' says Kelly. 'His form is always good for the spring classics. But, afterwards, you don't see him that much. His form is never as good.'

Furthermore Edwig Van Hooydonck didn't seem interested in stardom. A rival in the *peloton* remembers reading an article in which Edwig rated cycling as his *sixth* favourite pastime. Van Hooydonck talks of the sport as his job and says his amateur days were the happiest. Then he was relaxed and didn't feel he had to win. It didn't matter how the race went, he and his father enjoyed the day and loved the homeward journey.

With the pros, it is different. There is constant pressure to win; endless questions if you do, harsh judgements when you don't. He doesn't like talking to relative strangers about himself and looks upon the journalist as others look upon a visit to the dentist. 'It's not the journalist's fault, I think, it is me,' he says. 'I hate publicity. I just prefer to ride.'

Christel sees him being interviewed on television or hears him on the radio and thinks this is not her husband. The reserved and taciturn man is not her friendly and good-humoured Edwig. She prefers the private man to the public persona. 'He is a very cool guy,' says WordPerfect team-mate Frederic Moncassin, 'a bit gruff on the surface but in fact very nice. Quiet and polite.'

Van Hooydonck is also a very good professional. Whatever the team asks, he does and he causes no trouble. He has ridden for Dutch *directeur* Jan Raas throughout his career and likes the familiarity of Raas' set-up. 'I know everybody in the team; the riders, the mechanics, the *soigneurs* and Raas is a good boss.' His Dutch team-mates are surprised by his mild-mannered ways, which they think unusual for a Fleming. He sees in them the self-assurance and confidence that he lacks and puts it down to the difference between being Dutch and Belgian.

Each year the team likes him to ride the Tour de France and he prepares as well as he can. But having put everything into the spring classics, he struggles in summer. Van Hooydonck would never think of trying to avoid the Tour, because it is too important for the team. Of course if the team left it out of his programme, he would accept that too.

In this race his story is told according to the Book of Hardship. There were many bad days, some very bad days. From the beginning, he found the race uncommonly hard. After the team time trial on the fifth day, he felt so exhausted he knew something was wrong. On the following day he got into a breakaway group of 14 and it established a lead of two minutes. But the slight increase in speed which took the group clear robbed Van Hooydonck of whatever strength he had. That bothered him, being in the group and not being strong enough to contribute to the pacemaking.

On the eighth day he lost contact with the *peloton* and his team-mate Bob Mulders dropped back to help him finish inside the time limit. They were almost 17 minutes down but they made it. Normally one of the strongest in the team, Van Hooydonck was upset that he needed a team-mate's help.

That he wasn't himself was clear from the following day's stage to Verdun. Forty kilometres from the finish he was no longer able to stay with the 170-rider pack. This time he was on his own and very much aware of the danger of finishing outside the time limit. Hilaire Van der Schueren, WordPerfect's assistant *directeur sportif*, drove the team car right behind and never stopped shouting.

'He was encouraging me all the time, too much I think. Wah, wah, wah, wah . . . and I just wanted to go home. I told myself I am going to stop now, this is too hard, my legs were bad but I continued riding, thinking that maybe I could make it inside the limit. You don't do this for your team, you do it for yourself.'

'He said he wanted to stop,' says Van der Schueren; 'he was very, very, very tired. I told him he couldn't and when he kept saying he would stop, I didn't answer. You see for a top rider like him it is important to finish, especially for his morale. If he abandons and goes home, what is he going to do there? He didn't like it when I said he must finish; but a guy like him, he should never quit.'

Through the final 30 kilometres Van Hooydonck set about beating the time limit. 'It is bad because you go as fast as you can and, in your mind, it *is* fast. But the others are going faster.' Even though the effort hurt him, the gap between Van Hooydonck and the *peloton* widened all the way to Verdun. He finished over 21 minutes behind stage winner Lance Armstrong and just 40 seconds inside the time limit. Although still in the race, he felt no sense of achievement. 'You think tomorrow it is going to start again.'

Verdun might have been the worst but there were many tough days. He hated the second Alpine stage to Isola 2000, finishing 32 minutes down and just four minutes inside the limit. By then it was accepted that he wasn't well, and team medical tests, conducted in Metz two days before the Alps, confirmed it. Even so, Van Hooydonck decided to continue. 'There are a lot of good riders,' he says, 'who live in nice houses and earn good salaries and who have never finished the Tour de France. Johan Capiot of TVM, for example.'

The 13th stage to Montpellier was his last wretched day. He lost the *peloton* and rode the final part of the race with the Colombian Nelson Rodriguez and the Dane Per Pedersen. Again, he wanted to stop but he had been through too much. All three were washed up and he wondered whether the other two would make it to the finish. Pedersen abandoned two days later and Rodriguez suffered all the way, but especially in Paris where he found the pace of the pack too much and rode the Avenue des Champs Elysées on his own, over five minutes behind.

By then Edwig Van Hooydonck was feeling a little stronger. But it was never fun. He couldn't look at the classification sheets because he couldn't bear to see his name at the bottom. His WordPerfect team-mates didn't speak of the *lanterne rouge,* and he appreciated that. If he could have done something to climb above Peter Farazijn, he would have tried. But the 22-minute gap was too much. Next season, he said to himself, begins on the morning after this race ends.

The last sprint has been raced, the mood is joyous. It is always thus. Hundreds of thousands of people have come again to celebrate the end. Five or six hundred people are massed on Rue Balzac which slopes down onto the Champs Elysées. It is an extraordinary sight as they stand like terrace fans at a football match, catching but a sliver of action every 10 minutes. For this they wait half a day. But the applause is never-ending and the goodwill is boundless: the people wish to thank the racers for again acting out this twentieth-century epic, and the riders are moved by the welcome.

The Italian Davide Cassani throws his boy onto the bars of his bike and pedals away from Place de la Concorde towards the Champs Elysées. Now, my little son, you can tell your pals you cycled down the most beautiful avenue in Europe. Pippa Yates meets Sean and he tells her he cannot wait to get home to Nice. An emotional Stephen Roche makes his last lap of the Champs Elysées, he is happy to be leaving but the goodbye makes him sad.

Edwig Van Hooydonck cannot wait to turn his back on this Tour. He sits in the Place de la Concorde as deflated as at any moment during the race. Minutes earlier his team-mate Moncassin sprinted shoulder to shoulder with Djamolidin Abdujaparov. As they did, Abdujaparov twice jerked to his left and Moncassin, thrown off balance, hesitated and lost a very prestigious victory. It would have saved WordPerfect's race but that was not meant to happen.

Van Hooydonck thinks it is just their luck. The team that most needs a break is the team that rarely gets it.

Moncassin is angry. 'It's a pain in the arse. He pushed me twice. The first time I had to slow down and start again, the second time just before the line. I was in a good position just behind him, I went to go past him and I can tell you that I have not made an effort like this since the start of the Tour. This time I thought I made it.'

The vacant stares of his silent team-mates tell that he didn't. They don't blame Moncassin, for he has sprinted well but the team needed this win. Jan Raas stands amongst his riders, unable to lift himself above the gloom. For the unspoken law of sport makes him, as *directeur sportif*, responsible for the team's failure.

Seven of WordPerfect's nine riders made it to Paris, but four, Jelle Nijdam, Dieter Runkel, Bob Mulders and Van Hooydonck filled places in the last eight. They are better riders than this and can only explain the performance in terms of something being wrong: maybe they rode too many races in the early season? Only Frans Maassen performed as he can.

WordPerfect were the big losers on the Tour. 'When I consider how my small team did,' said Vincent Lavenu, *directeur sportif* of Chazal, 'I say not bad at all. We finished higher than WordPerfect, a big team backed by a multinational company.'

As the last-placed, Van Hooydonck attracted most attention: moths drawn to the *lanterne rouge*. Edwig could have climbed off on the road to Chalons-sur-Marne, or on the day to Verdun, or later in the Alps, or in the heat of the race to Montpellier: he chose not to.

He kept pedalling because he wanted to finish. For even a rider like Van Hooydonck, ranked 38th in the world, knows there is merit in finishing the Tour de France. Five times he has ridden the Tour and only once did he fail to reach Paris. That was the year he left the race to attend his father's funeral.

12

THE WIFE'S TALE
Love and Need
BRIGITTE ROMINGER

2

3

1. Brigitte Rominger
2. Rominger leads Indurain and Jaskula on the climb to St Lary Soulon. At the summit, Brigitte Rominger waits in the crowd
3. Rominger spent the Tour in Indurain's shadow but, before the end, he would see the light

There are days on the Tour de France when the sun burns and riders hope for overhanging trees around the next turn. And the hottest days often come with the highest mountains, where there is precious little cover.

Wednesday, 21 July, is one of those days; five Pyrenean passes under a scorching sun. For Tony Rominger it is the last throw of the dice. Unless he can beat Miguel Indurain by two or three minutes today, the race is over. Rominger doesn't believe it possible but he owes it to himself to try. He needs two sixes.

At Pla d'Adet, where this 230-kilometre stage finishes, his wife Brigitte waits. Dressed in white jeans and blue top, she sits with her back to an aluminium barrier. There is a television alongside but the glare of the sun makes it difficult to watch and Brigitte follows the race through Daniel Mangeas' commentary over the public address. At the foot of the final 10-kilometre climb to the finish, 27 riders form the leading group. On hitting the first slopes her husband's *équipiers*, Fernando Escartin, Jon Unzaga and Javier Mauleon, accelerate to positions at the front of the pack. And they keep accelerating.

They ride hard to weaken the legs of those in the group, especially the rivals of their team leader. Unzaga is very strong and his tempo shatters the chain of followers. Many drop off the back and settle for a pace more to their liking. Those who stick with Unzaga hurt themselves doing so. Rominger recognizes this and, two kilometres into the climb, he feels it is time to attack – you hit when your rivals are down. He sprints past his team-mate without so much as a glance and, for every one else in the group, it is time to do or die.

Rominger maintains his effort until he has to slow momentarily to catch breath. His acceleration has distanced every rider but the one he most wants to lose. Miguel Indurain is still at his shoulder, as he has been through every mountain stage. There is no escape. Rominger doesn't get angry or demoralized because he now anticipates Indurain's moves. He has grown to know his rival over the last week. He can feel the Spaniard's strength and if there had been a weakness, he would have sensed it before now.

And, anyway, there is still the other race. The Race To Be Second.

Brigitte Rominger moves uneasily around the finish area. Through Tony, she has a visitor's pass which gives her access to the cordoned-off area behind the finish line. But she feels she doesn't belong. This is her sixth day on the Tour and the first time she has come to the finish. It seemed like a good idea. Tony had a chance of winning the stage and that would be nice to see. But now Brigitte is unsure. The journalists are here with their notebooks and pens, the *soigneurs* with their towels and drinks, the radio men with their microphones. And she is here as a wife, a mere wife.

It is so hot. She looks around but there is no place to shelter from the sun. Now drawn to the television, she watches as Tony leads Indurain and is dismayed to see they have been joined by a third racer, Zenon Jaskula of Poland. His presence lessens Tony's chances of winning the stage. As a former international competitor, Brigitte knows cycling and understands too well what the pictures say. Tony cannot shake himself free of Indurain. Not yesterday, not today, not in this race. There are no doubts now about who will win the Tour.

As for her Tour, it hasn't been much fun. Since joining the race on the stage to Marseilles she has felt out of place. It's the French, they think she shouldn't be here. She reacts to this by trying to slip unnoticed through the days. But they are long days away from Rachel, her daughter. And Tony, she sees him so little.

Her days begin with a breakfast which she takes alone and at a time when Tony's Clas team is not in the restaurant. His team-mates cannot have their wives in the hotel and she feels it fairer and more discreet to stay in the background. After breakfast she returns to her room, packs her suitcases and waits until Marcelino Torrontegui is ready to leave. Torrontegui is Tony's *soigneur* and friend and she travels with him on the Tour.

From one hotel they drive directly to the next, arriving in the early afternoon. Brigitte checks in around midday, four or five hours before Tony will arrive. This allows time for a run and time to watch TV's live coverage of the race. When that is over she rings her mother in Switzerland: she is taking care of Rachel. Then she prepares some muesli with fresh fruit for Tony, pouring the milk well before he arrives. That's how he likes it.

Tony arrives and she is always pleased to see him. He showers, takes his muesli and they talk. But soon there are journalists calling, then there is massage and after that dinner with his team-mates. Brigitte and her husband get to spend an hour, maybe an hour and a half in each other's company and that is never enough. All the waiting for this. The Tour is no fun, she thinks, no fun at all.

So when on this afternoon in the Pyrenees, Torrontegui says, 'Come on, come to the finish today,' she can't think of any reason not to.

Five kilometres from the summit Tony leads from Indurain, Jaskula settles in behind the two. From the television Brigitte can barely distinguish the riders' shapes through the sun's glare. But she senses what is about to happen; Jaskula, who makes no contribution to the pacemaking, will sprint at the end and win. Tony, who does all the pacemaking, will be beaten by an opportunist.

A chance conversation that morning between Tony and the Belgian rider Johan Bruyneel makes it certain that Brigitte's hunch will become reality.

Tony knew Bruyneel had been to Pla d'Adet on a training ride and he asked what the finish was like. Bruyneel said it finished at the top of a short but very steep rise, not realizing that when he and his Once team-mates had ridden up this climb, they misjudged where the finish line would be positioned. 'It's really hard at the end,' he said, 'a wall.'

With 600 metres to go Tony prepares himself for the wall, easing his gear lever downwards until he feels the pedals turn with minimum effort. Soon Jaskula bolts from the back, quickly overtaking the two in front. Expecting a steep rise around the final bend, Rominger thinks he can catch Jaskula. But, there is no wall and Jaskula cruises across the finish line for a decisive victory. Rominger is second but feels cheated.

Brigitte is simply disappointed. Tony has been the strongest but he hasn't won. It sometimes happens.

Once the race ends the crush and stampede begin. Jaskula, Indurain and Tony roll to a stop and are surrounded by an inner ring of minders and a wider circle of journalists. Immediate reactions, spontaneous and fragmented by breathlessness, are always the most coveted. Then the riders are taken to the victory podium; Jaskula as stage winner, Indurain for a new yellow jersey and Tony as leader of the mountains race.

Brigitte watches from a distance. She wants to greet Tony, just to make eye contact, to say 'Well done' but even though he is never more than 50 yards away, she cannot get near enough. After the podium, he will do Swiss television, then he must provide a urine sample at the medical control caravan. Maybe she can get into the area behind the podium and catch him before he goes to television. A steward, standing at an entrance bars the way. Her pass does not allow her beyond this point. 'No, no, no, you cannot come in here,' he says.

Some journalists recognize her. 'Come on, let her through,' they say to the steward. He refuses. Brigitte hates this fuss, doesn't want to be identified as Mrs Rominger and doesn't want favours.

This is the Tour de France, she thinks, it's different from the Vuelta a España. In Spain the organizers make sure she has access to the quiet places, they want her to feel welcome and the people are warm and friendly. They say, 'Your husband is important, therefore you are.' At the Tour de France they are not listening when she asks and without actually saying anything, they convey a sense that she should not be here.

She is aware of this as she stands amongst a group of journalists, crushed into a small area, all waiting for the same man. For them, Tony is tomorrow's story and they need him urgently. For her, he is a husband struggling to get away from the office after a hard day. She wants to offer some comfort but she has to wait and the more she waits, the more frustrated she feels.

No matter what, she vows, she will not come to the finish again.

Brigitte comes to the Tour because Tony wants her to come. He doesn't care that having a woman around challenges the sport's traditions nor is he bothered that Brigitte's presence sets him apart from almost every rider in the race. 'Rominger,' said the French journalist Pierre Ballester in a *L'Equipe* piece four days before the start of the race, 'is an independent, a mystery, a marginal, a neutral spirit, a Swiss.'

That description may shed more light on the staunch conformity of the Tour and its followers than it does on Tony Rominger but it is one heard often on the race. You can imagine Rominger laughing at the notion of his mysteriousness. 'Me a mystery,' he would say, 'do I look a mystery?'

But there is independence, a strange kind of independence. Through his cycling career he has tried to work out what is best for him and he has single-mindedly pursued it. He rides in the *peloton* but without courting the respect or affection of the group. If it comes because of his performances, he will be pleased. He is a professional cyclist, it is a job and it is important to him that he does it well.

It is this strong, independent man who needs Brigitte on the Tour.

They met in 1984 coming home from a race. He a 23-year-old amateur, full of ambition but inexperienced and unsuccessful and she a 16-year-old international who had represented Switzerland at the World Championships a year earlier. Brigitte says it was love from the first day. Young, athletic, vivacious; she fell for his seriousness and sincerity. He, too, was smitten. Brigitte was his first girl-friend and he couldn't see beyond her.

At the time her career promised as much as his but that changed. It was an evolution brought about by his spectacular progress and two crushing setbacks to her career. Lack of funds led to the Swiss not sending a women's cycling team to the Olympic Road Race at Los Angeles and Brigitte was one of those to miss out. In the same year she crashed in a race in Germany and lost conscious-ness, lapsing into a coma and not coming round for 16 hours. All this happened the year she met Tony and her career would never be the same.

They began to live together in 1985 and three years later they married. He found it tough when they were apart and, where possible, she travelled with him to races. Through the early years she enjoyed it, he wasn't a famous rider and she liked the people who followed bike racing. Rachel was born in 1989 and soon she was Brigitte's regular companion at races. That worked well because the hours she waited for Tony were shared with Rachel.

But now Rachel is four and four-year-olds find it hard to cope with the migratory habits of Tour de France followers. For this Tour the parents agreed it would be unfair to bring Rachel and it was decided Brigitte would visit on the first rest day and that she and Rachel would come to Paris for the end of the race. Otherwise Brigitte would follow her husband's Tour on television. Once the deci-sion was made, she felt happy about it.

This reflects a change in her attitude. Once it was exciting to go to Tony's races, but it is no longer so. Success brought trappings she never foresaw. Brigitte remembers the 1992 Vuelta a España and how Tony encouraged her to join the race for the last four days. Enthused by the possi-bility of seeing her husband win his first major Tour, Brigitte and the three-year-old Rachel left for Spain. Their arrival on the race was news. She and Rachel were photographed for the newspapers, pictured on television and soon were recognized wherever they went.

People asked to have photographs taken while they stood between her and Rachel, they wanted to shake the child's hand. As they passed Brigitte could hear them say, 'Oh look, Rominger's wife and the baby.' But it was the requests for autographs which most fazed her. 'From me, an auto-graph,' she replied, 'oh my God, you want my autograph. But I am not riding the race.'

At first it was amusing. Within two days Brigitte's response had changed and Rachel grew tired of grown-ups speaking to her in a strange language. And fame, Brigitte discovered, has two sides. 'Because I was being friendly to everybody, it was said in the Swiss newspapers that I liked the attention and they asked why could I not stay at home?'

Furthermore the constant desire of the well-intentioned to touch both Rachel and herself became too much. Brigitte sought space backstage.

Staying away might have been better for her but not for Tony. The compromise was for Brigitte to be there when he needed her but for her to avoid the limelight. It meant more time inside the hotel room, carefully timed visits to the restaurant and fewer appearances at the start and finish of stages. Two months ago she and Rachel went to the Vuelta for the final week but maintained a far more discreet presence than 12 months earlier.

On this year's Tour de France, they planned for just the rest day in Grenoble and the family reunion in Paris. But she knows Tony and knows how she responds to him. What happened in the Hotel Alfa, just north of Grenoble, was what she anticipated. They spoke for a long time as, on this rest day, he did have time. When, next morning, she was leaving, he asked her to stay.

'Oh come on, stay here, don't go home.'

'You know I have no clothes with me, I have to go home.'

'In two days, the Tour will be very close to Nice, Torrontegui can pick you up there and you can come on the rest of the race.'

'Ten days on the Tour de France?'

'Why not?'

'I have to think about this. What would I do with Rachel?'

Brigitte left for home in Monte Carlo in two minds. Tony needed her but she had Rachel and not much enthusiasm for 10 days on the Tour. She thought about this as she drove south, thinking too of her husband who rode east towards the Glandon and Galibier passes. She made it to Monte Carlo before live television began and drove straight to the health club at the Hotel Loews where she would watch the race.

Hardly had the first images appeared when Brigitte felt herself drawn into that world of intense empathy. It happens every time she watches him in an important race; nothing else in the room registers, her friends know to leave her alone as she rides the race with her husband. On the long ascent of the Galibier, Tony rode at the front and Brigitte was proud of him. His pace was too strong for all but Indurain and the Colombian Alvaro Mejia.

She was pleased because she knows he prefers to lead rather than be led, understands that when he makes the pace, he chooses the speed which best suits him. 'Tony is not one to go too fast. He knows what he can do. He would have had his heart monitor on and been guided by that. I watch him and I know he is looking at his monitor, keeping his heart beat at a medium level, knowing he can keep that up for two hours.'

Indurain was content to follow, Mejia looked comfortable but was unable to contribute to the pacemaking. Rominger won the sprint decisively, his first stage win in the Tour de France. She was elated. She saw him do the post-race interviews, then raise his arms on the podium, knew he would have to go to doping control, allowed two hours for that and getting back to the hotel. And then her mobile phone rang.

'Well,' he wanted to know, 'are you joining the race in two days?'

'Of course,' she replied.

'How do you explain this?' she asks. 'He can win without me. It's not because I'm there that he wins. But he needs me, especially in the last week. If I say, "No, I cannot go," I don't feel good about that. I am at home thinking I should be there. But when I go to the race, I don't enjoy being there. After seeing him in Grenoble and then watching him beat Indurain, I decided to do what was important for him, what he wanted me to do. So I go.

'I don't know how to explain it. He likes to have his family with him because after the race he goes to his room, has a massage, goes to eat and then he just stays in his room. His week is like this. When I am not on the race he rings me at least four times each day; in the morning before he goes to the start, immediately when he gets to the hotel after the race and then before and after he eats in the evening. In a long Tour he likes to have someone he can talk with. He is the kind of guy who doesn't speak about his problems to other people but he wants to talk to me about everything. It is good for him to have me there.

'But we don't get a lot of time together. If he's in a room on his own, I will go to his room and sit on the bed. We talk about Rachel and family things. If he's sharing with a team-mate, I don't go to his room because it's not fair on the other rider. When he was a new pro, all of this created a problem for other people. But now they understand that he needs this and because he does his job well they say, "Okay, you can have your wife." And I like to be with him.'

Stephen Roche says Rominger is one of the most intelligent riders. Roche likes Rominger's matter-of-fact and uncomplicated nature. 'Tony has this idea,' says Roche 'that you stay in the sport long enough to earn enough money and then you retire. For him that will be two or three more years, no more.' That may reflect pragmatism but it is hardly the stuff of mystery.

Other riders could easily be intimidated by Rominger's apparent assurance. He speaks German, Danish, English, French, Italian and Spanish and can write in the first four of those languages. The suggestion of sophistication is furthered by the appartment in Monte Carlo and Tony's preference for spending most of the European winter in California. But the impression is misleading.

The apparent sophistication masks a shy, almost small-town Swiss boy. In the early years Brigitte was his guide through the cycling world. He remembers his first encounter with Sean Kelly in the mid-80s, at the time he was an amateur and Kelly was his hero. It was Brigitte who knew Kelly. She lived not far from Besançon and was friendly with Jean de Gribaldy, Kelly's old *directeur sportif.* One evening she and Tony turned up at a hotel where Kelly was staying.

'Brigitte said she would introduce me to Kelly. I was so happy to meet him, he shook my hand and I really didn't want to wash the hand for some time. For me, Kelly was something else.'

It was unsurprising that Rominger should have admired Kelly, because they shared the same narrow and relentless focus. Men who knew what training had to be done and did it. Nothing got in the way. Brigitte sees her husband, the cyclist, and it is his unflinching dedication which continues to impress her. 'If Tony says he is going for a six-hour training ride, he never returns in less than that time.'

That was always his way. When he and Brigitte were amateur racers their lifestyles were different. His life revolved around the bike while she built a social life onto her sporting life. For him, training and preparation for races was everything. Discos were out, nine o'clock was bedtime and, at the time, he was just an aspiring amateur.

'Before I met Tony, I wasn't at all like this. But, within six months to a year, I became like him. You just do it, I don't know why. You don't want to go out, you become relaxed about staying at home, the discotheque is too loud, the smoke is bad. All my friends tell me I've changed but I just met the right man and I am no longer interested in the other things. What he is doing is too important. Everything else is second.'

Rominger's reputation for independence is not misplaced. He does things his way. Before this Tour he spent 24 days preparing at altitude (2500m) in Colorado. Brigitte and Rachel were, of course, with him as were his doctor Michele Ferrari and his *soigneur* Marcelino Torrontegui. 'Altitude training,' says Nicolas Terrados, doctor with the Once team, 'does not suit every rider. One of the reasons is that the rider must train as much at altitude as he would at sea level and that is very difficult because you feel very tired. It suits a guy like Rominger because he is a very tough trainer and he would really follow the schedule.'

After Colorado, Rominger returned to Europe where he rode the Tour of Switzerland. Dr Ferrari explained that after three and a half weeks training at altitude, his body would need time to recover. In the Swiss tour he had to take it easy. 'How easy?' asked the rider. 'Never more than 170 beats a minute,' replied the doctor. Rominger rigged up his monitor each day and never let his heart rate exceed 170.

'I didn't like doing it but my training programme meant I couldn't do it any other way.'

It is this approach and Rominger's refusal to conceal it which portrays the rider as a 'marginal'. Honesty on other questions adds some substance to the image. 'I don't believe Miguel Indurain is unbeatable. In terms of morale, I am not as affected by him as others seem to be. There is one area where Indurain, as strong as he is, has yet to prove himself and that is tactically. I am not the strongest in the *peloton* but I am certainly one of the more intelligent.'

His rivals see this and their first reaction may not be to applaud his candour.

Within the milieu of his team, he contributes to the collective spirit without abandoning his own world. When Clas has seven or nine riders in a race, he gets the single room. To each stage race he brings a video recorder which Torrontegui tunes into the television in his room. He has a supply of his own movies, recorded during idle hours at home in Monte Carlo and, in the evening, he escapes from the race and flies with James Bond to Hong Kong, Hawaii or Rio de Janeiro.

This self-sufficiency encourages the reputation for independence, an independence which sets Rominger apart from his peers. But Tony Rominger's strength does not exist in isolation. It needs the support of those closest to him: Torrontegui, his *soigneur*; Alejandro Torralbo, his mechanic; Dr Ferrari, who helps to organize his training and Marc Beaver, his commercial manager and friend. Rominger can be independent of others provided he can depend upon these.

And then there is Brigitte.

'It is always the same for me in the long Tour,' he says. 'After two weeks on the Vuelta or Tour de France, I begin to feel physically tired and I am also tired of the conversation at the table with my team-mates and all the interviews with the journalists. The race, the race, the race . . . "How are your legs, what about Indurain, who will win tomorrow?" When Brigitte comes and we talk, all that changes. We speak about home and our families and the things which interest us. Suddenly, I don't feel I am on a bicycle race any more.'

Women, and especially the wives of competitors, have never been welcomed to the Tour de France. Part of the antipathy stems from the practical difficulties of accommodating them. Where do they stay? With whom should they travel? A second and more pressing concern is the potential for wives to upset the harmony of the team. A rider whose wife is on the Tour easily attracts the antagonism of a team-mate whose partner is at home.

These difficulties are reinforced by a tradition which asserted that true dedication could not exist unless the rider suspended his interest in women during the racing season. To help the rider, the Tour de France organizers proscribed women and that situation has changed only in the last 20 years. In his book *The Head and the Legs*, Tour founder Henri Desgrange considered the question of chastity and the rider's needs.

Robin Magowan, in his book *The Tour de France*, explained Desgrange's position. 'To excel, a rider had to eat, live, and breathe cycling. Desgrange did not care how this emotional commitment was attained, but once it was, he assured his readers, "from that moment on the rider was saved; he would have no more need of a woman than of his first pair of socks". Because women represented the only true self-denial, she became the test of man's willpower.

'Desgrange was not against sex: natural needs were natural needs, provided it stopped there. "Oh, in the winter, with the tracks closed and the sun gone, go have yourself a ball with one, two, three, four, as many as you want. Make up for lost time anyway you can, so long as you don't act like my smoker friend who told me the other day, 'I'll give it all up on March 11th.' You know as well as I do that that's not something one cuts from one day to the next."'

Fifty-three years after the passing of Desgrange, Brigitte Rominger finds that his influence survives. Just as Greg LeMond's wife Kathy discovered a few years before. Kathy travelled with the 1986 Tour and when that race developed into a bitter struggle between her husband and Bernard Hinault, it was said and written in France that LeMond was not helped by the presence of his family.

'On the Tour de France,' says Brigitte, 'they say no, no, no women. They don't know you and they are not interested in you and I don't like to say, "Excuse me but I am . . ." That is not me.'

Aware of the traditional attitudes, Brigitte is careful of how she behaves while on the Tour. 'I stay in the room most of the time, nobody sees me, I try to eat in a different room from the team and I make sure they don't see me a lot. For the team, there is never a problem with me. When I go to the race I sleep in my room, Tony sleeps in his room and when we are together with the other riders we don't kiss and we never make anyone else crazy.'

They planned to go crazy on the night the Tour ended. The last time Tony rode the Tour, 1990, they went to the Lido after eating. This time it would be the Moulin Rouge, everyone said it was better. But first a meal with family and friends. Brigitte's mother and her husband had come from Switzerland, Marc Beaver was there and also Wily Erzberger, a Swiss journalist.

The restaurant was in the Eiffel Tour, chosen because it was recommended in the Michelin guide. And the food was good. Then it was time for the Moulin Rouge. But Tony, with 4000 kilometres of racing in his legs, stumbled at the thought of this final Tour de France stage. He couldn't face it. Brigitte's mother said she was going anyway and nothing was going to stop her. Wily said he, too, was determined to see this night through.

And Brigitte? She said, like Tony, she was dog-tired. The others went to the Moulin Rouge. They went home early.

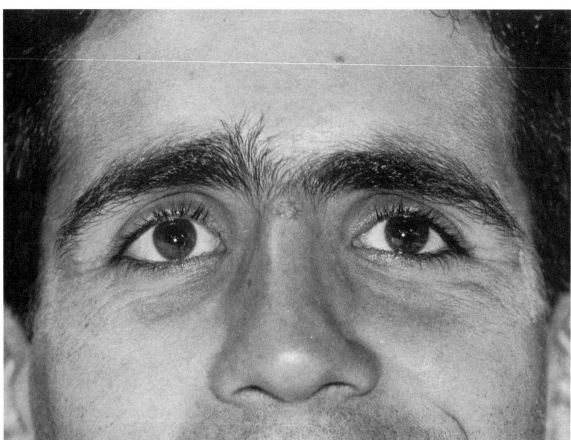

13

THE CHAMPION'S TALE
Mastering Suspense
MIGUEL INDURAIN

1. Miguel Indurain
2. Against the clock, it is a question of time: how much will Miguel gain on his rivals!
3. You can, says Indurain, fight with the press if you wish but it is easier to play along

At an important moment in Oscar Wilde's play *The Importance of Being Earnest*, Gwendolen waits upon the outcome of Jack's search for proof of his ancestry. Jack wants Gwendolen's hand but her mother, Lady Bracknell, is sceptical about the suitability of the alliance. As Gwendolen waits, she turns to her mother and says, 'This suspense is terrible, I hope it will last.'

Anyone who has travelled the three weeks of the Tour de France would understand. The pilgrimage is enlivened by uncertainty, the followers enthralled by suspense. Stephen Roche's duel with Pedro Delgado in the 1987 race kept us riveted by the side of the road because it was impossible to know what would happen next. The '89 clash of Greg LeMond and Laurent Fignon was even better. Then we followed the twisting plot until we figured out the end. That's it, we said, Fignon has it. But we were wrong, wonderfully wrong.

Miguel Indurain, you can bet, turns up at airports in ample time. Appointments are appointments and good time-keeping is a quality. He keeps very good time in the Tour de France, leaving nothing to chance or to the last week. In his first Tour victory, the 1991 race, he finished three minutes and 36 seconds ahead of second-placed Gianni Bugno. A year later he won with four minutes and 35 seconds to spare over Claudio Chiappucci. In both victories, Indurain won the time trials and lost little or nothing to his rivals in the mountains. He was clearly the best. That year he became the first Spaniard to win the Tour for a second time. History without histrionics.

Suspense is not Indurain's style. Which is all very well for the champion and his supporters but he demoralizes his opponents. As for us who like the story of the Tour to read like a thriller, we might as well not turn up. But we do because class is class and its attraction eternal. Miguel Indurain is doing to his contemporaries what Hinault, Merckx and Anquetil did to theirs and it is worth seeing.

However, the mood at Le Puy du Fou on the day before the Tour began was a mixture of excitement and apprehension. There was a very obvious fear that Indurain would control the race, and this led to a frantic search for genuine rivals. Alex Zülle and Tony Rominger were new challengers and their presence generated the hope that Indurain might not dominate as he did the previous year. There was also the theory, half-baked and not quite believed, that the Spanish champion had not been at his best in the Giro d'Italia a month earlier.

This view of things receded from the moment Indurain descended the ramp to begin his prologue at Le Puy du Fou. He won the 6.8-kilometre test decisively, just as he had done at San Sebastian 12 months earlier. Then he could and did say that he needed to be on his best form at the beginning because the mountains came on the second day. This time there was no reason for his excellence except the desire to stamp his name on the race. Those who saw his power marvelled at it but couldn't ignore the obvious question. Were we going to have a race at all? The suspense was far from terrible.

For the first three road stages, the sprinters were a welcome distraction. Towards the end of each day their teams swarmed to the front of the *peloton* and coalesced. Breakaways didn't have a chance as the way was prepared for Cipollini, Nelissen and Abdujaparov. They slugged it out and, momentarily, Indurain's shadow disappeared into the background.

The team time trial from Dinard to Avranches on the fifth day was a second test for Indurain. It was important because for once his result depended upon the performance of others, on this occasion his team-mates. Without the strong roadmen so suited to this test, Banesto was not expected to do well and Indurain's rivals saw it as an opportunity to gain time. They did, but not enough. Banesto placed seventh of the 20 teams, losing one minute 22 seconds to the riders of the GB-MG team and just 59 seconds to the Once team of Zülle and Erik Breukink. Losses which were not enough to worry Indurain.

On day 10, there was a 65-kilometre individual time trial at Lac de Madine. Over a relatively flat course, this test was made for Indurain and he did pretty much what everyone expected. He beat Bugno by two minutes and 11 seconds and other rivals by much more. Rominger was two minutes 42 seconds down in fourth place, Zülle was beaten by three minutes, Chiappucci by over five. Through the mountain stages which would follow, Indurain only had to stay with his principal rivals. Once again, he was in a position from which defeat was unimaginable.

Two moments emphasized his supremacy. The first is of the champion unclasping his aerodynamic hat and flinging it to the side of the road during his time trial ride. Accustomed to his poise, this seemed close to a crisis. What caused it? 'Well,' said Miguel afterwards, 'it's very simple. The rain was flowing down onto my visor and I couldn't see the road. And if you don't see the road, it is as well to do something about it.' We were clutching at straws, but not catching any.

The second picture is of Indurain at Rominger's shoulder on the climb of the Galibier. Although the pace was punishing, Indurain's expression was full of tranquillity, a calmness one flicker removed from a smile. This is not to say that Indurain smiled on that never-ending mountain but neither did he openly show the pain so obvious in the expressions of others.

His performance on the Galibier, which was the first mountain stage, ended the contest for the yellow jersey. Rominger had ridden exceptionally well but had not distanced Indurain. Furthermore there was no other rider in the race capable of pushing the leader as the Swiss had. 'I am aiming for a place on the podium,' said Rominger that evening, tacitly accepting that the race for first place was, in fact, no race at all.

Those who make it to the top in sport are given to saying that however difficult the struggle to get there, the real challenge is to stay at the summit. This is only partially true, or it is a truth which conceals another truth. Champions who win again and again develop an aura which ranges from formidable to invincible. And because they are perceived to be superior, they become more difficult to beat. How can a champion be beaten if his rivals consider him unbeatable?

Bernard Hinault played on the perception of his prowess and did whatever he could to further it. Hinault knew it was easier if the others accepted he was the best. On this Tour, Hinault noticed many of the challengers defer to Indurain, as they had to him, and he railed against their submissiveness. According to Hinault, they talked themselves into second place and allowed Indurain a soft ride.

Take Claudio Chiappucci! Twice second and once third in the last three Tours, Chiappucci was one of Indurain's greatest rivals in this race. On the day before it began he was interviewed by *L'Equipe* and asked about the champion's ability as a time triallist. Claudio was generous in his admiration. 'I am very impressed by him. I have never seen a rider like him. One with that force, with that physique. It is extraordinary. And what is more astonishing is that this physique also allows him to be amongst the best in the mountains. He must have an extraordinarily strong character.

'It is almost supernatural to be as good as he is in two disciplines which are so different. And it is because of this that Indurain is such a great champion.'

While Chiappucci's honesty might be laudable, his suggestion that Indurain might not be beatable betrayed his own lack of belief. Whoever beat Indurain, it would not be Claudio. He was beaten before the race began. Gianni Bugno, another in the short list of serious rivals, was beaten after the Lac de Madine time trial.

Bugno had been impressive through the first nine days. He rode very strongly and appeared unusually calm. He performed well in the time trial to take second place but the two minutes 11 seconds loss to Indurain demoralized him. 'Once and for all,' he said, 'it has to be admitted that you cannot compete against this guy in the time trial. He is still much too strong and when one admits this principle, there is less disappointment.

'The only thing that I regret is that he is the same age as me. If things were better arranged, the good Lord would have allowed me to come along at the same time as his brother.' Prudencio Indurain, four years younger than Miguel, is an *équipier* in the Banesto team and some way below his brother's level.

A week before the end of the race Guy Roger of *L'Equipe* asked Chiappucci about Indurain. Did he consider him rival or friend?

'Most of the time, I try not to think too much about him,' said Claudio. 'It's bad for the morale. It is hard to sleep peacefully with a man like him in the race. Sometimes I tell myself he's a bit of a Superman, or a Martian, or some force from another planet. But not terrestrial. Not like you and I. I took a long time to admit this. Today, no one can refute it. It is impossible to beat Indurain. The reality is hard to accept, but for all of us, for me in any case, it is the starting point.

'When I am at my lowest point, crushed, as I was after the Madine time trial, I tell myself "There must be a weakness in his 188 centimetres and his 80 kilos. Go Claudio, try again. You must try again." And I try.

'I remember the first time I saw him, close-up, in action. I was wearing the yellow jersey, he was working for Delgado. It was the 1990 Tour and I had attacked in the Tourmalet, about a dozen were left in front, including him. And when we were alone, me, LeMond and him, I said "this great big carcass cannot climb Luz-Ardiden better than me." But at each corner, he was still there. At the top he went on and won. That was it, the first real episode between him and I. Since then there have been many.

'The second serious battle was the following year, again in the Tour, this time the stage to Val Louron. It was the first time we spoke. When LeMond had been eliminated, Miguel said just three words. "Will you ride?" And we blasted along. But there, Miguel was still terrestrial, you understand? One rival like another. A year later at the 1992 Tour, you could not see the same rider, he crushed us in the Luxembourg time trial, like you'd crush a mosquito. It was a Ferrari against a Fiat Uno. You could do what you wanted, at the finish you were five minutes behind.

'Miguel is not an ordinary rider. As for our relationship, it has never been bad. But in the *peloton* each has his own worries, his own preoccupations. Sometimes we end up riding side by side, he asks news of my family. He knows that Rita, my wife, is expecting a baby and, jokingly, I have told him that for once a Chiappucci is going to arrive before an Indurain.'

While Claudio's thoughts on Indurain convey a sense of the champion's strength, they provide a greater insight into the mind of the challenger. The challenger who didn't believe winning was possible, just as Bugno's admission that Indurain 'is just too strong' reflects his lack of faith. Essentially, Chiappucci and Bugno doubt they have the ability to beat Indurain but can only handle this by conferring invincibility upon their rival.

The effect of this on the mood of the 1993 Tour was immense. Indurain's superiority was never seriously questioned. Riders with less talent and fewer results than Chiappucci and Bugno felt they had no right to look further than the Race To Be Second. Indurain's performance in winning his third consecutive Tour was magnificent but the race did not excite in the way that great Tours do.

On the second to last mountain stage, Indurain did not feel strong. When Rominger attacked near the bottom of the final climb to Pla d'Adet, the Spaniard was fully stretched to counter his rival's attack and then had to dig into his reserves of strength and courage to remain in Rominger's slipstream. Even though it was a stage he wanted to win, Indurain did not have the strength to contest the sprint and he finished third behind Zenon Jaskula and Rominger.

At Pla d'Adet, Indurain waited with many other riders and journalists for a cable car to take him down to the town of St Lary in the valley. Inside the car, everyone was packed tightly. A Spanish journalist near Indurain said, 'We are like sardines in a tin, and you are the freshest of all.'

Often on this Tour opinions and strategies were based not on Indurain's strength, but on the perception of his strength.

Tony Rominger was the exception. From the beginning of the Tour, his luck was out. Crashes over the first three days cost his team two riders, Arsenio Gonzalez and Abrecham Olano, and greatly diminished Clas' chances of doing well in the team time trial. In the circumstances the team rode courageously to finish 12th, just two minutes and 16 seconds down on GB-MG. However, they were further penalized when one minute was added to the time of each rider because one of its riders, Jon Unzaga, momentarily pushed a flagging team-mate, Jorg Muller. This is an offence often committed but seldom penalized.

Rominger fell to 100th place overall, hardly the right position for a man with ambitions of winning the Tour. Because of his lowly placing, Rominger set off early in the day on the long individual time trial at Lac de Madine and experienced terrible weather conditions. Into the gale-force wind and driving rain, he rode extremely well and would have done better than fourth had he not punctured with a kilometre to go. Miguel Indurain started his time trial two hours later and experienced much better weather conditions.

Brigitte Rominger followed the time trial on television and wondered why her husband should have all the bad luck. Yet when she spoke with Tony on the telephone he was calm and uncomplaining. These things happen, he said. There was time for him to show what he could do.

It is the morning after the rest day, two days after the long time trial. Today is the Tour's first mountain race and Miguel Indurain knows it will be decisive. If he survives today, he will be more than halfway to his third Tour victory. At the foot of the Col du Telegraphe, 65 kilometres from the finish, Rominger accelerates and only Andy Hampsten, Indurain, Oliveiro Rincon, Stephen Roche and Zenon Jaskula react. Rominger likes to ride at the front, sitting back in the saddle for long stretches and then accelerating suddenly, as if deciding there was a race to the next corner.

Indurain watches from third position, following Rominger's accelerations without getting out of the saddle and conveying an impression of ease which is more imaginary than real. He stays in the saddle better to preserve his strength. 'I am heavy and I don't have the same cards as Chiappucci, Bugno or Rominger who climb the mountains with 10 or 12 kilos less than me. Each time I'm there, I fear my body is going to betray me,' he says.

His fear protects more than it betrays and Indurain stays in control. He passes Hampsten to stalk Rominger. As they climb the Telegraphe, the sun is on the riders' backs and the shadow of the yellow jersey creeps up on Rominger. A shadow which will remain.

They make the short descent of the Telegraphe and begin the climb of the Galibier. Jaskula now leads, Indurain at his shoulder, as ever in the controller's position. Hampsten rides in third place and Rominger recuperates in fourth, Alvaro Mejia is fifth. Jaskula's pace is not as severe as Rominger's and Indurain is comfortable. Every so often the Spaniard moves past Jaskula to share the pacemaking and show his yellow jersey at the head of the race. Rominger knows this is too easy for Indurain, too reassuring. He rides to the front and increases the tempo.

Close to the top, Hampsten and Jaskula can no longer bear Rominger's pace and they let the leader, Indurain and Mejia go. Because the end of the climb is near, Indurain counters Rominger with little accelerations of his own. He knows now he will not lose on this stage. Seven or eight hundred metres from the summit, Indurain glides past his rival and his impressive physique fills the sliver of roadway which divides the thousands of spectators. Rominger has given everything on the Galibier but cannot escape.

Indurain, Rominger and Mejia ride the descent together, clear of Hampsten and Jaskula. All that remains to be decided is the stage victory. Rominger wants it, Mejia hopes and Indurain's intentions are unclear. Inside the last kilometre he accelerates to the front, followed by Rominger then Mejia. This is an indication to Rominger that he is not seriously contesting the sprint, and when the Swiss rider sprints past Indurain there is no attempt to counter. Surging into a sharp corner just before the finish line, Rominger poaches the advantage which remains his all the way to the line. Mejia is second and Indurain is a contented third, for his lead of the race has been strengthened.

'He did what is pretty normal,' said Rominger later, 'he acknowledged that I had done most of the pacemaking by not trying to win the stage. He had the yellow jersey and was increasing his lead.' That interpretation was shared by many.

There was one dissenting voice. Indurain's. 'It isn't true. I knew from the map of the finish that there were a few tight corners and I decided not to risk sprinting. In a big Tour, the general classification is the most important thing and I don't go for sprints if it is dangerous.'

At the Banesto table on any Tour evening, it is not easy to pick out the champion. For you don't find him at the centre holding court, nor is he at the top presiding over the evening. Miguel Indurain takes up the quietest place and chats amiably with whoever is nearest. He likes to think of the team as family, refusing always to pick out one over another. 'There was great responsibility on the team but they handled it well,' he said the day before the Tour ended.

'I am proud of them, I thank them and I will not cite one before another even if some of them appeared more often in front of the television. I give one mention for them all.'

Indurain is the man he was brought up to be. His parents Miguel and Isabel raised five children on a farm near Villava in the Spanish province of Navarra. 'All I wanted was bread on the table and peace in the home,' says Miguel senior. 'I never asked anything else of the Virgin of Rosario, the patron of Villava.'

'My father and his brother married two sisters,' says Prudencio Indurain, 'and they each had five children. When we were small we lived with our cousins, all in the same house. In the evening there was a minimum of 14 at the table.' It is easy to relate that environment to the Indurain one sees at the Banesto table.

'Each time he comes home, having been in another country, it is not the bike he speaks of,' says his father, 'but the tractor which does not raise any dust as it ploughs. He tells of how the barley and maize is stacked and how it is dried differently from ours, he speaks of the colour of the land and the kind of fertilizers being used. He never speaks of the bike, never.'

But it is his profession and he has made a good fist of it. Having ridden for his local club, Villava C.C., Indurain joined the bigger Reynolds club which was managed by Eusebio Unzue who lived in the village of Orcoyen, a 10-minute tractor drive from Villava. Unzue was good for Indurain and it is not a coincidence that he is now assistant *directeur sportif* at Banesto. But when Reynolds decided to fund a professional team it chose Jose Miguel Echavarri to direct it.

Echavarri's influence on Indurain's career has been profound, not just in making him a champion but in making him a particular kind of champion. A former professional racer, Echavarri rode the 1969 season with Jacques Anquetil and was deeply impressed by the style of the French champion. 'I always dreamed of making Miguel a champion,' Echavarri says, 'but above all I wanted to make him a man. Like Anquetil, who was a fabulous man, whose philosophy was "Live and let live". You have to think of yourself but you should never humiliate others. It pleases me very much when people compare Miguel and Anquetil.'

Echavarri appeals to Indurain's intelligence and innate decency. Before the team time trial on the fifth day, many Banesto riders were apprehensive. They needed a good time but Miguel's power could burn off half of the team and put them in danger of finishing outside of the time limit. Teammate Gerard Rue was concerned that the other French rider in the team, Jean François Bernard, might be eliminated. Others were simply concerned about their ability to go with Miguel's pace. Much time was spent considering who should ride in the leader's slipstream, for that was the shortest straw of all.

'The lads are afraid to ride behind Miguel,' says Rue. 'His turns at the front are too long and too hard and they finish totally exhausted. The risk is that you lose your place early in the test, in which case elimination is certain.'

Bernard, Rué, Delgado and Prudencio Indurain talked about it and agreed with Prudencio's suggestion that he follow Miguel's wheel. 'I know him better than the others and if he was going a little too fast, it would be easier for me to ask him to slow down.'

Jose Miguel Echavarri then offered the important suggestion. 'I took Miguel aside and I said to him that when a king comes to see his people, it is not the people who must rise to the level of the king but the king who must come down to the level of the people.'

Echavarri's approach has ever been thoughtful. He recognized Indurain's potential at an early point and understood that much of the force came from his long and powerful legs. 'But every time Miguel pushed himself, it seemed that he strained a tendon or something. It was clear he needed time and I wanted him to have it.'

This strategy was helped by the presence of Delgado, who was then the team's undisputed leader. Here was a popular man, to whom Indurain could dedicate himself while his own body developed. The benefits for Indurain were twofold: he got the time he needed and, through riding as Delgado's *équipier,* he learned to empathize with the role of team riders. When his leadership turn came in 1991, he was well prepared

It might have come in the Tour of 1990 but Delgado was riding well and Echavarri wanted his young protégé to have as much time as possible. He rode spectacularly well in his *équipier's* role in that Tour, winning the mountain stage to Luz-Ardiden and performing heroically for Delgado on the day to Alpe d'Huez. Having got into a breakaway, Indurain was asked by his *directeur sportif* to wait on the Glandon pass for his team leader. He did, and paced Delgado to the foot of Alpe d'Huez. 'By then even a horse like Indurain was winded,' wrote Samuel Abt in his book *Champion.*

But the point of that Tour could not be missed; Indurain finished 10th overall, 12 minutes 47 seconds behind race winner Greg LeMond. But almost 12 minutes was conceded on the Alpe d'Huez stage. Had he ridden for himself, Indurain would have been close to victory. He never complained, always understanding that his opportunity would come. It was that Tour which convinced Echavarri of his rider's potential.

'It was the day after he waited for Perico [Delgado] on the Glandon pass and paced him to Alpe d'Huez. His legs were awfully tired and there was a time trial at Villard-de-Lans. I didn't know what to expect of him but he finished third. That day I said to myself, "There you are. Miguel is ready." And he was.'

Echavarri, too, was ready, for, as Indurain soared, his *directeur* helped to create the right environment. His Banesto team is by no means the strongest in the *peloton* but it has been good in the major Tours. The *directeur's* own contribution is notable for he manages to remain faithful to his champion's natural modesty while saying that his rider really is something else. This, Echavarri managed to do with stunning success on the evening of the long time trial.

The modesty came first. 'Miguel is no Charles V, nor is he the Pope, nor the King of Spain. He is a man, like any other, a man who works more than the others for what he wants. Because of this he is called super-this and super-that. In truth he is just giving a super lesson in professionalism to everyone.'

Later on the same evening, it was explained to Echavarri that Prudencio Indurain remained in the race only because his brother punctured eight kilometres from the end. Had Miguel not lost the 20 or 25 seconds caused by the flat tyre, the deficit between him and his brother, who finished last in the race against the clock, would have been greater than the official limit for the day. 'Ah,' said Echavarri, 'from the summit, one sees everything.'

He sits before a press room full of journalists on the evening before the race ends. It is the victory press conference in all but name, for it is certain that the final stage to the Champs Elysées will not change anything. As Indurain surveys his audience, his look is strangely distant, a look which tempted the Belgian reporter Harry Van den Bremt to liken him to a sphinx. There is something mysterious in an expression which is at once pleasant and closed.

Yet there could not be a more straightforward interviewee. For well over a half an hour, Indurain responded honestly to every question. Often his answers were low-key and sparingly expressed, but that is his nature. Maybe this is the conseqence of growing up in a home where it was customary for 14 to eat together? But in their studied diplomacy and natural good sense, the answers did reveal the intelligence which Echavarri claims for Indurain.

It is said you lack panache?

'I have my style and I am not that concerned with what is said. I only know that this third victory in the Tour de France has cost me a lot of energy.'

Your style hides your suffering?

'It is perhaps my way of pedalling. But I am not trying to hide anything. In the Tour I have good days and I have bad days.'

You're too nice to be the boss of the *peloton*?

'I try to stay calm, to give the maximum, to be the best I possibly can, to be professional. When I win, that's fine, but when I lose, it is not a big deal.'

Laurent Fignon says you were never attacked in this Tour?

'That is not my problem. The road is free. I don't stop people from attacking. And Fignon, when he dominated his second Tour (1984), I don't know if he was attacked. This doesn't worry me too much.'

Three victories in the Tour, you have the chance of equalling Anquetil, Merckx and Hinault by winning five?

'As I have always said, I don't ride for records.'

You don't care about them?

'I didn't say that. I hope to remain at the level I am at now for as long as I can. And if that is the case . . .'

You escaped bad luck in this Tour?

'By the grace of God. Up to now, everything has gone well for me. I haven't been injured, I haven't had an accident, but I may not always be this fortunate. In Marseilles, a dog crossed the road two metres in front of me. It was another rider [Jim Van de Laer of Belgium] who was brought down.'

In the Giro this year, you were once in trouble, on the second last day. Here Rominger has beaten you in a time trial, on the second last day. A coincidence?

'I am not invincible. I have never pretended to be. Because I have won all the time trials in the Tour since 1991, people think I can never lose one. They wish me to be Merckx or Hinault.'

Is that not the case?

'You overestimate me. I cannot ride like Merckx or Hinault, who attacked whenever they wished. I have not the same qualities, I am less aggressive than them. I am obliged to calculate. As I have said, I am not invincible.'

The irony of the 1993 Tour de France is that Miguel Indurain was right all along. Presumed invincible at the beginning, he won the race as everyone expected he would. Those rivals who considered him unbeatable made his race to Paris less hazardous. But when the figures were totalled at the end, it was clear that only Tony Rominger's bad luck denied us a race full of suspense. The Swiss rider's time trial victory on the second to last day was Indurain's first such loss in his last five Tours.

Brigitte Rominger followed her husband's performance avidly. 'The win in the time trial was the best, it was really nice because people can see Indurain is not like the machine he was made out to be and doesn't come from another planet. I'm quite sure Tony can catch this guy.

'And it's not possible that Indurain will always have luck, luck, luck. He has had this for four or five years now so . . . and maybe Tony will have it in the next Tour. For me Indurain is really good, probably the best you know. But I know also Tony can catch him.'

Mr Rominger is a little more circumspect, preferring to focus on his preparation for the next serious confrontation. He thinks of staying healthy, of honestly completing his training programme and of being properly motivated. If he gets these things right, he can only be beaten by a rider who is equally well prepared but more talented. 'I know Indurain is a person, a human, you can beat him, that's not the problem.

'You have to be strong, you have to be confident. You can never know how strong and confident the other guy is. But that's never interested me, for me what's important is how I am.'

But Indurain, he scares you a little?

Tony Rominger shakes his head in bemused disagreement. 'Ah no, no I don't think he does.'

At the end of the 1993 race, there was the beginning of the 1994 race. Without saying as much, Rominger was promising suspense.

EPILOGUE

On the day after the Tour de France ended, the 136 survivors were already at home or on their way. Soon they would rediscover there was life beyond the race. One of the 44 who did not make it to Paris, Jean-Paul Van Poppel soon forgot the race. Leontine, his wife, was expecting their third child.

Danny Van Poppel arrived on the day after the Tour ended, making the point that people don't just go on, they reproduce and their lives evolve.

Van Poppel would not have minded a move away from the Festina team and he negotiated seriously with TVM. The deal collapsed because they could not come up with the money Festina paid him in 1993 and were contracted to pay him in 1994. He stayed with Festina but was very disappointed they could not find a place for his friend and *équipier,* Gert Jakobs. They trained through the winter together, Jakobs' enthusiasm infecting his friend so much that at the very beginning of the 1994 season Van Poppel won the first stage race of his life. Without a team Jakobs was determined to ride on as an independent. He has the spirit to do that.

Lance Armstrong has the spirit of a champion. He left the Tour after 11 stages. He and his team thought he had had enough. At 21 the American has time on his side. But Lance is in a hurry and soon after his return to Lake Como in Italy, he commenced training for the world championship at Oslo in Norway. Shortly before that race Lance spoke to Linda, his mother, about making the trip to Norway. Linda thought this would cost a lot of money, her son said not to worry and Mom thought, 'This boy is planning something.' Linda arrived in Oslo a week before the race and the feeling grew. Lance's plan was to become world champion in Norway. He did. Spectacularly. Linda appeared in many of the post-race photos and people thought how 'Lance's wife looked so happy'. Linda and Lance would have been pleased about that.

After the Tour ended, Bernard Hinault picked up the thread of his life as a Breton entrepreneur. Serious business, he says, as he aims to achieve the success in the boardroom that was once his on the road. Stephen Roche didn't ride that many races before abandoning his bike to the basement garage of his home near Paris. He did, however, race in the San Sebastian classic and rode very well in helping Claudio Chiappucci to victory. It was a gift from Roche to his friend.

Stephen is now retired from bicycle-racing, if not from sport. He has taken to car rallying and seems determined to make a name for himself in that sport. You see him at the bigger bicycle races in France, working for a PR company. He swears there is no yearning for the old thrills. It is easier to follow the breakaways on four wheels, he says. But you know this has not been an easy break and Roche's return to 'civilian' life is not as comfortable as he makes out.

Harry Van den Bremt has spent his working life following the breakaways on four wheels and has no regrets. Journalism is, he says, a beautiful profession. After the Tour you could show up at a press room after an important race in Belgium, France or Holland and find Harry there.

Sean Yates tried to plan an end-of-season campaign but he was more excited about the imminent arrival of Liam. He returned to England two days before Pippa gave birth to the baby. Everything went well. Yates has begun the new season promisingly, placing fifth in cycling's most punishing one-day race, the Paris–Roubaix classic.

The struggle of managing a small team continues for Vincent Lavenu. By the end of the Tour he better understood what he needed and whom he didn't need. Most of all, he wanted a couple of strong riders who would produce good time trial performances and achieve higher placings on general classification. Lavenu also realized the team would be better off without Patrice Esnault and the sponsors MBK. Both were more trouble than they were worth and were replaced. The emergence of another small French team, Catavan, crowds the space occupied by Chazal. For Lavenu, the future is daunting. But it has always been so.

Claudio Chiappucci sails on. After escaping from the Tour with a stage win, he then went to Spain and did what he repeatedly told his team-mates he would do – he won the San Sebastian classic. Chiappucci's simple explanation for his collapse on the first Alpine stage to Serre Chevalier was that his form was slow to come. He would prove this to everyone by winning in San Sebastian soon after the Tour ended. And *El Diablo* was as good as his word.

On the afternoon the Tour ended Neil Stephens raced and won in the north of Spain. That augured well for his end-of-season campaign but, a week later, the Australian crashed and broke his collarbone at the Tour of Holland. A season which began with a hernia operation in March, and suffered through illness on the Tour de France, ended with a spill in Holland. Neil returned to Canberra to get away from it all but, as he trained, he began to experience severe pain in his groin area.

Australian doctors explored and then explained: the thread used to stitch the internal wound caused by the hernia operation was not soluble, as it should have been, and it was now causing inflammation. He was opened again to remove the stitches, and again to clean the infected area. What a year! Stephens began the new season by breaking his collarbone again in February but he was now hardened and has refused to allow this to be a setback. Three weeks after the latest break he was back racing and contributed to a fine Once performance in the Vuelta a España.

Neil Stephens is just one of Nicolas Terrados' patients, and when the Tour ended, the doctor was in need of a break. He remains an important part of the Once team, travelling with it to the bigger stage races and providing supervised medical attention in a sport where too much is left to the unqualified and the unscrupulous.

Edwig Van Hooydonck made it to Paris, last but not least. As he promised, he went for a quiet meal with his wife Christel and tried to forget the race. Even though Brigitte Rominger had travelled with the Tour through the last 10 days, she felt reunited with her husband Tony only on the evening the race ended. Rachel was there as well and they were happy to be getting away from the race. Not that Brigitte doesn't like the Tour. By October she was planning her return. The second baby would arrive in late April or early May 1994, that would rule out the Vuelta a España. But, by early July, the baby would be eight weeks old and she would be able to join Tony for the last week of the Tour. By then, she expected he would be fighting it out with Miguel Indurain. And winning. As for Indurain, he is prepared for that. He tried to win the world championship in Norway a month after the Tour but, for once, had to settle for second. His form through the early months of 1994 wasn't as good as it had been in previous years. Rominger's was better than ever. What, Indurain was asked in March, should Rominger be doing to increase his chances of winning the Tour de France. 'He should,' replied Indurain, 'train very hard, prepare himself physically and mentally so that he arrives to the Tour in the best possible condition. But I am sure he is doing this anyway.'

Indurain offered the advice with the confidence of one who didn't expect to lose.